SPSS® DEMYSTIFIED

Without question, statistics is one of the most challenging courses for students in the social and behavioral sciences. Enrolling in their first statistics course, students are often apprehensive or extremely anxious toward the subject matter. And while SPSS is one of the more easy-to-use statistical software programs available, for anxious students who realize they not only have to learn statistics but also new software, the task can seem insurmountable. Keenly aware of students' anxiety with statistics (and the fact that this anxiety can affect performance), Ronald D. Yockey has written *SPSS® Demystified: A Simple Guide and Reference*, now in its third edition. Through a comprehensive, step-by-step approach, this text is consistently and specifically designed to both alleviate anxiety toward the subject matter and build a successful experience analyzing data in SPSS.

Key features of the text:

- Step-by-step instruction and screenshots
- Designed to be hands-on with the user performing the analyses alongside on their computer as they read through each chapter
- Call-out boxes provided, highlighting important information as appropriate
- SPSS output explained, with written results provided using the popular, widely recognized APA format
- End-of-chapter exercises included, allowing for additional practice

Features and updates to this edition include: material updated to IBM SPSS 24 (available Fall 2016), including screenshots and data sets / end-of-chapter exercises.

Ronald D. Yockey, an award winning professor of Quantitative Methods, has been teaching statistics at the undergraduate and graduate levels for nearly 20 years. While enjoying both teaching and research, Professor Yockey's greatest professional thrill is in seeing others discover that statistics is a subject that can not only be understandable, but can also be fun!

SPSS® DEMYSTIFIED

A Simple Guide and Reference

Third Edition

Ronald D. Yockey

Routledge
Taylor & Francis Group
NEW YORK AND LONDON

Third edition published 2018
by Routledge
711 Third Avenue, New York, NY 10017

and by Routledge
2 Park Square, Milton Park, Abingdon, Oxon, OX14 4RN

Routledge is an imprint of the Taylor & Francis Group, an informa business

First edition published by Pearson 2008
Second edition published by Pearson 2011

Library of Congress Cataloging-in-Publication Data
Names: Yockey, Ronald D., author.
Title: SPSS demystified : a simple guide and reference / Ronald D. Yockey.
Description: Third edition. | New York, NY : Routledge, 2017. | Includes bibliographical references and index.
Identifiers: LCCN 2017005719 | ISBN 9781138286276 (hardback) | ISBN 9781138286283 (pbk.) | ISBN 9781315268545 (ebook)
Subjects: LCSH: SPSS for Windows. | Social sciences—Statistical methods—Computer programs. | Social sciences—Statistical methods—Data processing.
Classification: LCC HA32 .Y63 2017 | DDC 005.5/5—dc23
LC record available at https://lccn.loc.gov/2017005719

ISBN: 978-1-138-28627-6 (hbk)
ISBN: 978-1-138-28628-3 (pbk)
ISBN: 978-1-315-26854-5 (ebk)

Typeset in Times
by Apex CoVantage, LLC

Visit the companion website: www.routledge.com/cw/yockey

MIX
Paper from
responsible sources
FSC® C013056

Printed and bound in Great Britain by
TJ International Ltd, Padstow, Cornwall

For JMJ, my wife Michele, and my children, Christian, Samuel, Timothy, William, Stephen, Catherine, and Anthony. Each and every one of you are my joy and inspiration. And for those who have continued to press on in their work, *especially* when things look the most difficult.

Contents

Preface

Without question, statistics is one of the most dreaded courses for students in the social and behavioral sciences. Enrolling in their first statistics course, students are often apprehensive, fearful, or extremely anxious toward the subject matter. And while IBM SPSS Statistics Software ("SPSS") is one of the more easy-to-use statistical software programs available, for anxious students who realize they not only have to learn statistics, but also new software, the task can seem insurmountable.

Keenly aware of students' anxiety with statistics (and the fact that this anxiety can affect performance), I've incorporated a number of features into this text with the goal of helping to both alleviate anxiety toward the subject matter and build a successful experience analyzing data in SPSS. Several of these features are described below.

Features of the Text

First and foremost, the book is designed to be hands-on, with the reader performing the analyses alongside on their computer as they move through each chapter. To help the reader stay on track, a step-by-step approach is utilized, beginning with creating the variables in SPSS and ending with writing the results in the format of the American Psychological Association. Screenshots of each step in SPSS are included, and call-out boxes are used to highlight important information in the results. These features are designed to create a user-friendly and successful experience in SPSS, with the goal of reducing anxiety toward the subject matter. Each of these features (and others included in the book) are detailed in Table 1.

In addition to the features described in Table 1, exercises are included at the end of each chapter, with the solutions to the exercises provided in Appendix B. Students are encouraged to work through the exercises to gain the experience required to become more proficient in statistics and with SPSS.

Coverage and Organization of the Text

The text is designed for students in introductory statistics and research methods courses, as well as for those in intermediate statistics and graduate courses in quantitative methods. Procedures in the text that are often covered in introductory statistics or research methods courses include descriptive statistics, t tests, one-way between ANOVA, one-way within ANOVA, two-way between ANOVA, chi-square, correlation, and regression. For intermediate statistics and graduate courses, more in-depth coverage of the two-way between subjects ANOVA is presented in Chapter 9, and chapters on multiple regression, one-between–one-within ANOVA, and reliability are also included. As individual classes will differ in their coverage of the material, each chapter provides stand-alone coverage of a given procedure so that instructors can choose the chapters that best meet their course objectives and their students' needs.

Regarding the organization of the text, the book is divided into two sections. The first section introduces the SPSS software program (Chapter 1), covers descriptive statistics (Chapter 2), discusses how to use SPSS to produce a variety of graphs (Chapter 3), and concludes with a chapter

Table 1   Features of the Text

Feature	Description
Four-step process of data analysis	In each chapter,[a] the process of data analysis is divided into four easy-to-follow steps, including:
	Step 1: Create the variables. Variables are created, including entering value labels as necessary.
	Step 2: Enter the data. The correct structuring of the data file is illustrated.
	Step 3: Analyze the data. How to run the correct analysis using the appropriate drop-down menus in SPSS is illustrated.
	Step 4: Interpret the results. Each table of output is discussed, one table at a time, with sample write-up of the results in APA format provided for Chapters 4–16.
Screenshots	Several screenshots are included in each chapter, helping the reader stay on-track as they progress through each chapter.
Call-out boxes	Call-out boxes are used to highlight important information and to alert the reader to areas of potential confusion in SPSS (e.g., what to enter in the Test Value box for the one-sample *t* test).
Research question and null and alternative hypotheses	A research question and the null and alternative hypotheses are presented for each procedure to help better connect the data to the research question and hypotheses of interest (applies to Chapters 5–16).
Effect sizes	How to calculate, report, and interpret effect sizes is presented. (Reporting of effect sizes is recommended by the APA and is required by several journals for manuscript submission; applies to Chapters 5–14 and 16.)
Assumptions	The assumptions of each inferential procedure are provided, along with the impact of violating the assumption on the accuracy of the procedure, allowing the reader to determine whether their data meet the requirements for a statistical procedure of interest (applies to Chapters 5–16).

[a]Chapter 3 does not include Steps 1 and 2.

on estimating the internal consistency reliability of a scale using coefficient alpha (Chapter 4). The second section covers inferential statistics, including: *t* tests (Chapters 5–7), analysis of variance procedures (Chapters 8–11), correlation (Chapter 12), simple and multiple regression (Chapters 13–14), and chi-square procedures (Chapters 15–16). Also, data transformations and other topics related to database management are covered in Appendix A.

For those who are new to SPSS and have chosen this text for help with a specific procedure, after reading the introductory chapter you should be able to turn to the chapter of interest and follow the instructions to enter and analyze your data.

Formatting Used in the Book

As far as the formatting of the text is concerned, variables and important terminology are presented in lowercase **boldface** type. When referring to specific windows, dialog boxes, or options to select within a dialog box, *italics* are used. Italics will also be used for information to be entered into SPSS (with the exception of variables).

SPSS Version 24 (and Previous Versions)

While this book is written using SPSS version 24, those using most previous versions shouldn't experience difficulty following the instructions to analyze their data successfully. For the procedures we'll be covering in the text, all recent versions (SPSS 23, 22, 21, and 20, as well as earlier versions) are all highly similar. In terms of the tables of *output*, the classic style of output is utilized in this text, as I believe it's easier to read and interpret in a textbook format than the default style used in version 24. However, this change results only in relatively minor differences in the formatting of the tables, such as the use of gridlines and shading, with all the numbers and results being identical. If interested, you can easily change to the classic style on your computer. To utilize classic style in your output, go to *Edit*, *Options*, and select the *Pivot Tables* tab. Under *TableLook*, select <*Classic Default*> and then click *OK*. Any *new* analyses that are run will then be formatted in the classic style used in this text. These style differences only refer to the tables of *output*; the Data Editor window and all other screenshots and menu commands in the text are identical to the IBM SPSS version 24 defaults.

Acknowledgments

I would like to offer my appreciation to all those who have helped in the development of the first three editions of this text, including the reviewers, editors, and friends who proofread the text. I would also like to especially thank all my students over the years whose many questions and feedback have provided extremely valuable information in learning "what works" in teaching both statistics and SPSS. Thanks to Hannah Shakespeare, Senior Commissioning Editor with Routledge for both her consistent support and very prompt and helpful feedback in the development of the third edition of the text.

While I've strived to write a book that "demystifies" the process of analyzing data in SPSS, ultimately you're the judge of whether I've succeeded in this endeavor. I sincerely hope that this book helps you to successfully analyze and understand your data. Please feel free to contact me (ryockey@csufresno.edu) to provide any feedback you might have about the text (please put *SPSS Demystified* in the subject line of your message).

Now that you know about the approach we'll be taking in the text as well as the topics we'll be covering, it's time to get started. The best way that I know how to do that is to dive in!

Ronald D. Yockey

Introduction to SPSS, Descriptive Statistics, Graphical Procedures of Data, and Reliability Using Coefficient Alpha

In this first unit, Chapter 1 introduces the SPSS software program, including creating variables, entering and analyzing data, saving files, and printing the results. In Chapter 2, using SPSS to calculate a number of different descriptive statistics is illustrated, including frequencies, measures of central tendency, and measures of variability. Chapter 3 illustrates how to produce a number of different graphs in SPSS, including a bar chart, histogram, scatterplot, and a boxplot. Finally, Chapter 4 illustrates how to use SPSS to estimate the internal consistency reliability of a scale using coefficient alpha.

1

Introduction to SPSS

In this chapter, the SPSS software program is introduced, including starting SPSS, creating variables, entering data, performing a basic analysis using the drop-down menus, saving files, and printing the results. Let's begin by starting SPSS.

Starting SPSS

To start SPSS, first you'll need to find where it's located on your computer. Depending on the configuration of your computer, SPSS should be located in one or more of the following places:

1. As an icon[1] (Σ) on your desktop (the desktop is the main area of workspace on your computer screen).
2. Within the *Programs* menu.
3. On the Quick Launch Toolbar (if applicable, the Quick Launch Toolbar is located to the right of the *Start* button at the bottom of your computer screen).

Starting SPSS from each of these locations is described next. (As you read the instructions below, choose only *one* of the following methods to open SPSS, so that multiple copies of the program are not open on your computer.)

Starting SPSS from the icon on your screen

1. Locate the SPSS icon (Σ) on your desktop.
2. Double-click[2] the SPSS icon. SPSS should open shortly thereafter.

Starting SPSS from the Programs *menu*

1. Click the *Start* button (Start).
2. Click *Programs* (or *All Programs*).
3. Select *IBM SPSS Statistics*.
4. Select *IBM SPSS Statistics 24* (or the current version you are using, if not 24). See Figure 1.1 for details.

Starting SPSS from the Quick Launch Toolbar

1. Depending on the configuration of your computer, you may have an SPSS icon (Σ) to the right of the *Start* button. If you see an SPSS icon located to the right of the *Start* button on your computer, you can single-click it to start the SPSS program. (In Figure 1.1, SPSS is the second icon to the right of the *Start* button.)

If you haven't done so already, open SPSS using one of the methods described above.

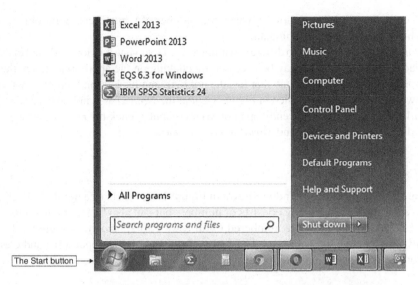

Figure 1.1   Opening SPSS from the *Programs* menu. (*Note*: While your screen will not be identical to the one above, SPSS should be located within the *Programs* menu on your computer.)

The *Data Editor* Window

When SPSS opens, the *Data Editor* window is presented on the screen (the *Data Editor* window is shown in Figure 1.2). The *Data Editor* window is used to create variables and enter data in SPSS. At the very top of the window the SPSS file name is displayed (the name *Untitled* indicates

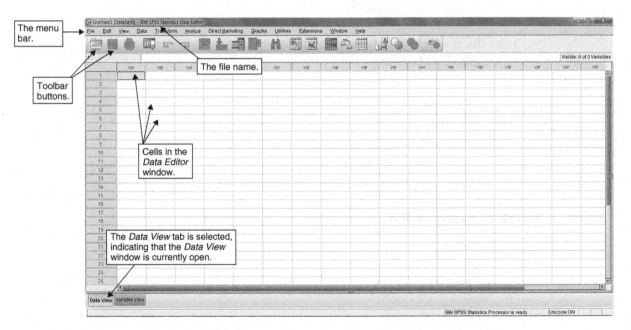

Figure 1.2   The *Data Editor* window in SPSS (with the *Data View* tab selected).[3]

that the file hasn't been given a name yet). Located below the filename is the menu bar, which contains several different menu options (*File, Edit, View,* etc.) that are used to complete a variety of tasks in SPSS (such as saving files, printing results, etc.). Directly below the menu bar are a number of toolbar buttons that provide quick access to several different options in SPSS. The main area of the *Data Editor* window consists of a number of white rectangular objects (known as cells) which are used for entering data.

The *Data Editor* consists of two different windows, the *Data View* window and the *Variable View* window. Each of these windows may be accessed by clicking on the appropriate tab at the bottom left-hand corner of the screen. The tab that has the gold-colored background indicates which of the two windows is currently open (notice in Figure 1.2 that the *Data View* window is currently open). If the *Data View* window is not currently open on your computer, click the *Data View* tab to open it.

We'll discuss the *Data View* and *Variable View* windows next.

The *Data View* Window

The main area of the *Data View* window shown in Figure 1.3 consists of a number of cells, which are used to enter **data** (data usually consists of numbers but can also be letters or symbols).[4] The rows of the *Data View* window are numbered (with rows 1 to 25 shown in Figure 1.3), and the columns all initially have the name *var*. The first cell (the cell in the upper left-hand corner) has a gold-colored background, indicating that it is **active** or ready to receive input.

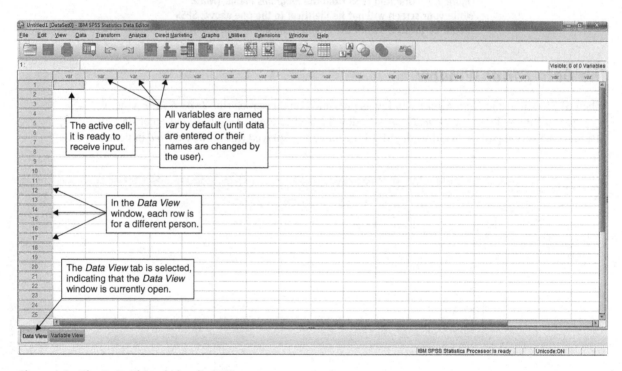

Figure 1.3   **The *Data View* window in SPSS.**

Data View window—The window in SPSS that is used for entering data.

The *Variable View* Window

The *Variable View* window is used for creating variables in SPSS and adding information to a data file. The *Variable View* window is accessed by clicking the *Variable View* tab at the bottom of the screen. Since the *Data View* window is currently open, we'll need to click on the *Variable View* tab to open the *Variable View* window.

1.   Open the *Variable View* window by clicking on the *Variable View* tab. The *Variable View* window is presented in Figure 1.4.

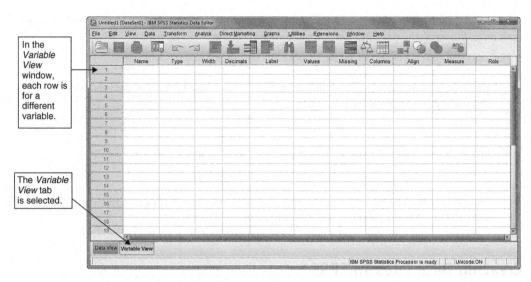

Figure 1.4   **The *Variable View* window in SPSS.**

As was the case with the *Data View* window, each of the rows of the *Variable, and Measures View* window is numbered, and the main area of the window consists of a number of cells. Unlike the *Data View* window, however, each of the columns in the *Variable View* window has a different name and function. The different columns of the *Variable View* window are described in Figure 1.5.

Name of column	Function
Name	*Name* is used for naming a variable. Variable names can be up to 256 characters in length. Each variable must begin with a letter, and no two variables can have the same name. No spaces are allowed in variable names.
Type	*Type* indicates the type of data that are stored in a variable. A number of different types exist, including numeric, comma, dot, scientific notation, etc. In this text, we will be working with numeric data.
Width	*Width* indicates the number of characters that are displayed in the *Data View* window. The default* is 8.
Decimals	*Decimals* indicates the number of decimals that are displayed in the *Data View* window. The default is 2.
Label	*Label* is used for describing a variable. Up to 256 characters are allowed. The information entered in the *Label* column will appear in the output.
Values	*Values* is used for coding categorical variables (categorical variables are discussed in the next section). This feature will be used throughout this text.
Missing	*Missing* indicates the values that are read as missing data (missing data means that certain values are not available or are "missing" for a variable). The default value for missing data is a period, "."
Columns	*Columns* indicates the width of the columns that are displayed in the *Data View* window. The default width is 8 characters.
Align	*Align* positions the data either to the left, to the right, or in the center of the cells in the *Data View* window. The default alignment is to the right.
Measure	*Measure* describes the measurement level of the variable. The available options are nominal, ordinal, and scale. In nearly all instances in this text, categorical variables will be classified as nominal and continuous (or quantitative) variables will be classified as scale.
Role	*Role* is a relatively newer feature in SPSS that allows for preclassifying variables for use in certain dialog boxes. Role categories include *Input, Target, Both, None, Partition*, and *Split*. The default value for Role is *Input*, which will be used throughout the text.

Figure 1.5   **The name and function of the different columns of the *Variable View* window.**

* Default values are the settings in SPSS that are in place when the SPSS program starts.

Of the *Variable View* window column attributes, we will use the *Name, Values,* and *Measures* options in this text (the default values for the other columns will be used).

> *Variable View* window—The window in SPSS that is used for creating variables and adding information to a data file.

With the key features of the *Data Editor* introduced, let's create a data file in SPSS.

> Remember: In the *Data Editor*, the *Variable View* window is for creating *variables* and the *Data View* window is for entering *data*.

Creating Data Files in SPSS

An SPSS **data file** is a computer file that contains information (data) on one or more variables. A **variable** is an attribute or characteristic that takes on two or more values.

> Data file—A computer file that contains information on one or more variables.
> Variable—An attribute or characteristic that takes on two or more values.

To create a data file in SPSS, we'll use the data set shown in Figure 1.6. Figure 1.6 contains data for five people on the variables **gender**, **age**, **employment**, and **iq** (variables will be shown in boldface type throughout the text). Notice that each row in Figure 1.6 contains the values for a different person on the variables of interest. In the first row, for example, the values for the first person are displayed: Person 1 is male, 23 years old, employed, and has an IQ score of 115. The values for the remaining four people are presented in rows 2–5.

Person	Gender	Age	Employment (Employment status)	IQ (IQ score)
Person 1	Male	23	Employed	115
Person 2	Male	19	Not employed	90
Person 3	Female	32	Employed	120
Person 4	Female	28	Not employed	90
Person 5	Male	18	Employed	116

Figure 1.6   **The sample data set to be entered into SPSS. (*Note*: The *Person* column is included for illustration but will not be entered into SPSS.)**

Notice in Figure 1.6 that the variables **age** and **iq** are in numeric form (i.e., they have numbers for values), while **gender** and **employment** are in character form (i.e., they have words for values). An important point to remember (for the vast majority of the procedures covered in this text) is that *to perform analyses on a variable in SPSS, it must be in numeric form.* Therefore, before entering the data into SPSS, we'll need to change the variables that are currently in character form (**gender** and **employment**) to numeric form. This process is illustrated next.

Assigning Numbers to the Categories of **Gender** and **Employment**

We'll begin by assigning numbers to the different categories of **gender**. As far as the rules for assigning numbers are concerned, any number can be assigned to the different categories of a variable as long as each category is assigned a different number (you may recognize this as an example of a nominal scale of measurement). To illustrate this process, we'll assign males a 1 and females a 2. Therefore, for every male in the data set we'll enter a 1, and for every female we'll enter a 2.

For **employment**, we'll assign employed a 1 and not employed a 2.

The data set (with the numeric values entered for the variables **gender** and **employment**) is presented in Figure 1.7.

	Gender	Age	Employment (Employment status)	IQ (IQ score)
Person 1	1	23	1	115
Person 2	1	19	2	90
Person 3	2	32	1	120
Person 4	2	28	2	90
Person 5	1	18	1	116

Figure 1.7 **The revised data with numeric values entered for gender and employment. (*Note*: For gender, 1 = "male," 2 = "female"; for employment, 1 = "employed," 2 = "not employed.")**

Variables such as **gender** and **employment** are known as categorical variables. **Categorical variables** take on a limited number of values; categorical variables that take on only two values (such as **gender** and **employment**) are known as **dichotomous variables**. The variables **age** and **iq** are **continuous variables**. Continuous variables take on a large number of different values.

> Categorical variable—A variable that has a limited number of values.
> Dichotomous variable—A categorical variable that has only two values.
> Continuous variable—A variable that has a large number of different values.

Data Entry and Analysis

With all the variables now in numeric form, we can enter and analyze the data in SPSS. Throughout this text, the process of data entry and analysis will be divided into the following four steps: (1) create the variables, (2) enter the data, (3) analyze the data, and (4) interpret the results. In this chapter, each of these steps will be illustrated using the sample data set provided in Figure 1.7.

Step 1: Create the Variables

We'll start by creating the variables **gender**, **age**, **employment**, and **iq**. To create variables in SPSS, follow the instructions below.

Creating variables in SPSS

1. Make sure the *Variable View* window is open. If it isn't open, click the *Variable View* tab at the bottom left-hand corner of the screen.
2. The first cell in the upper left-hand corner of the *Variable View* window should be active. If the first cell is not active, click on it.
3. In the first row of the *Variable View* window, enter the name **gender** and press the *Enter* key. Notice that all the cells to the right are automatically filled in with the default values (the default value for *Label* is an empty cell).
4. In row 2, enter the name **age** and press the *Enter* key.
5. In row 3, enter the name **employment** and press the *Enter* key.
6. In row 4, enter the name **iq** and press the *Enter* key. The four variables are now created in SPSS.
7. Finally, under *Measure* (the second-to-last column in the *Variable View* window), classify the categorical variables **gender** and **employment** as nominal and the continuous variables **age** and **iq** as scale. See Figure 1.8 for details.

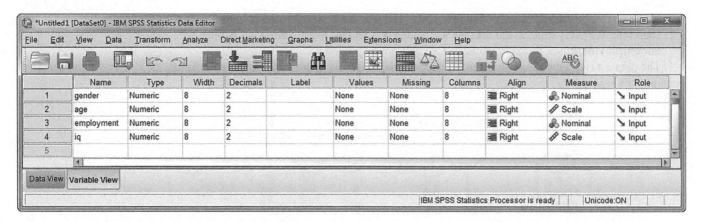

Figure 1.8   The *Variable View* window with the variables gender, age, employment, and iq entered.

Value Labels

Recall that we assigned numbers (i.e., 1, 2) to the different categories of **gender** and **employment** because they needed to be changed to numeric form to be analyzed in SPSS. You may also recall that the numbers we assigned were arbitrary (any two numbers could have been chosen), as they served only to differentiate between the categories of the variable. To help us keep track of our numeric assignments more easily, we'll enter the categories that the different numbers represent into SPSS (e.g., that 1 is for males and 2 is for females), a process known as creating value labels. We'll create value labels for the categorical variables **gender** and **employment**.

Let's start by creating value labels for **gender**.

*Creating value labels for **gender***

1. Make sure the *Variable View* window is open. In the first row of the *Variable View* window (the row for **gender**), click the cell in the *Values* column (where the word *None* is displayed). After clicking on the cell labeled *None*, an ellipsis ( ) should appear in the right-hand corner of the cell.[5]
2. Click the ellipsis button ( ). See Figure 1.9 for details.
3. The *Value Labels* dialog box opens (see Figure 1.10).
4. First, we'll code into SPSS that males were assigned a 1. Enter a *1* to the right of *Value* and *male* to the right of *Label*. See Figure 1.11 for details.
5. Click *Add*. To the right of the *Add* button, *1.00 = "male"* should now be displayed. See Figure 1.12 for details.

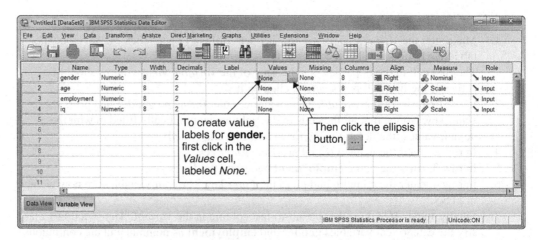

Figure 1.9   Selecting the *Values* cell for gender.

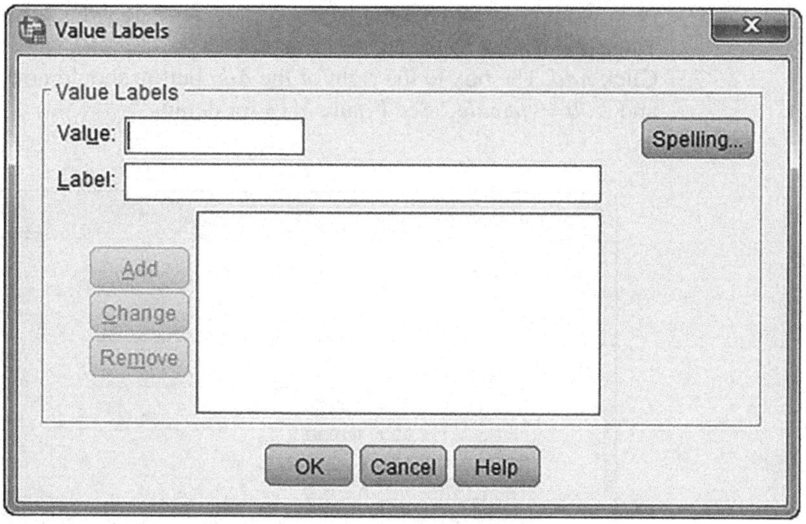

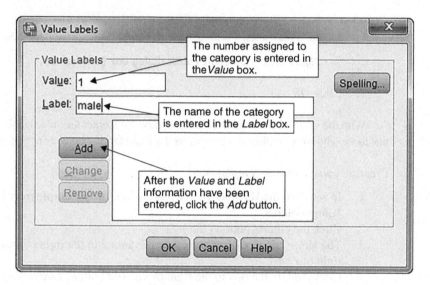

Figure 1.10 The *Value Labels* dialog box.

Figure 1.11 The *Value Labels* dialog box (continued).

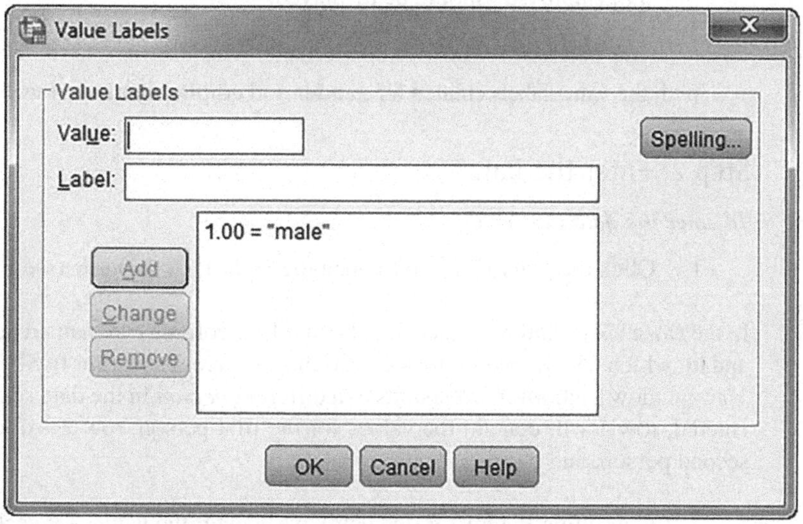

Figure 1.12 The *Value Labels* dialog box (continued).

6. Next we'll code into SPSS that females were assigned a 2. Enter a *2* to the right of *Value* and *female* to the right of *Label*.
7. Click *Add*. The box to the right of the *Add* button should now display *1.00 = "male"* and *2.00 = "female."* See Figure 1.13 for details.

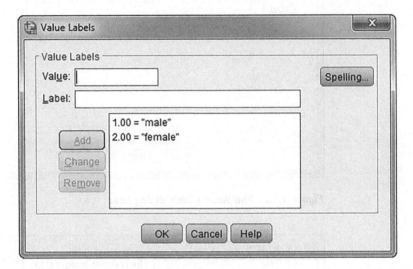

Figure 1.13   The *Value Labels* dialog box (continued).

8. Click *OK*.

With the value labels for **gender** entered, next we'll enter the value labels for **employment**. Recall that those who were employed were assigned a 1 and those who were not employed were assigned a 2.

*Creating value labels for **employment***

1. In row 3 of the *Variable View* window (the row for **employment**), click the cell in the *Values* column.
2. Click the ellipsis button ( ).
3. The *Value Labels* dialog box opens. Enter a *1* to the right of *Value* and *employed* to the right of *Label*.
4. Click *Add*. In the box to the right of the *Add* button, *1.00 = "employed"* is displayed.
5. Enter a *2* to the right of *Value* and *not employed* to the right of *Label*.
6. Click *Add*. In the box to the right of the *Add* button, both *1.00 = "employed"* and *2.00 = "not employed"* should be displayed.
7. Click *OK*.

With the value labels created for **gender** and **employment**, next we'll enter the data into SPSS.

Step 2: Enter the Data

To enter the data into SPSS

1. Click the *Data View* tab to open the *Data View* window (see Figure 1.14).

In the *Data View* window, notice that the first four columns are named **gender**, **age**, **employment**, and **iq**, which correspond to the four variables we created earlier in SPSS. Recall that in the *Data View* window each *row* corresponds to a different *person* in the data set, so that when the data are entered, row 1 will contain the values for the first person, row 2 will contain the values for the second person, and so on.

2. Consulting Figure 1.7 (the data), we'll enter the values for each person on the four variables of interest. To enter the values for the first participant, click the first cell in row 1

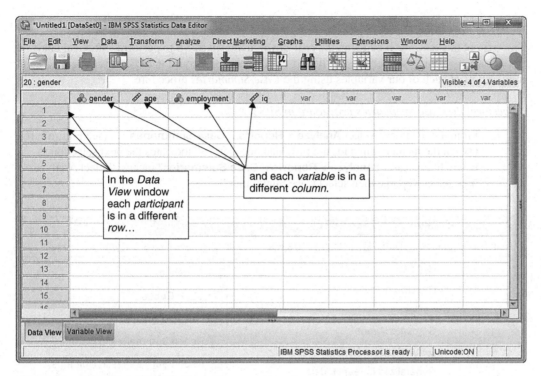

Figure 1.14 SPSS *Data View* window with the variables gender, age, employment, and iq in the first four columns.

of the *Data View* window. Enter the values *1, 23, 1*, and *115* for the variables **gender**, **age**, **employment**, and **iq**, respectively. (An efficient method of data entry is to press the right-arrow key (→) on the keyboard after entering each value for a variable. For example, for the first person you would enter a *1* for **gender** and then press the right-arrow key, enter a *23* for **age** followed by the right-arrow key, and so on.)

3. To enter the values for the second participant, click the first cell in the second row of the *Data View* window. Enter the values *1, 19, 2*, and *90*, for the variables **gender**, **age**, **employment**, and **iq**, respectively.

4. Enter the data for the remaining three participants. The completed data file is shown in Figure 1.15.

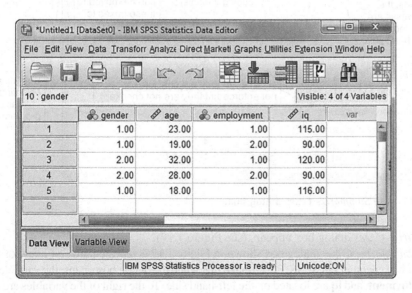

Figure 1.15 The completed data file in SPSS.

Now that the data are entered, we'll perform a basic analysis in SPSS.

Step 3: Analyze the Data

Throughout this text, we'll be using the pull-down menus in SPSS to perform statistical analyses of our data. For our first analysis, we'll start with a basic procedure in SPSS—producing a summary report of each of our variables using the *Case Summaries* procedure.

To perform the Case Summaries procedure in SPSS

1. From the menu bar, select **Analyze > Reports > Case Summaries** . . . (see Figure 1.16). (When the menu commands are provided, the sign ">" indicates the next selection to make. In this case, **"Analyze > Reports > Case Summaries"** means "Select Analyze, then select Reports, then select Case Summaries.")

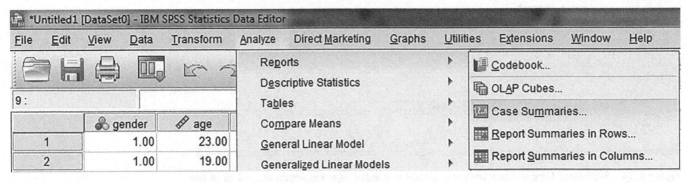

Figure 1.16   **Menu commands for the *Case Summaries* procedure in SPSS.**

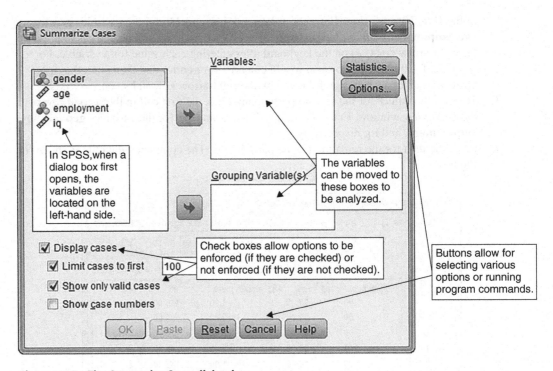

Figure 1.17   **The *Summarize Cases* dialog box.**

A *Summarize Cases* dialog box appears (see Figure 1.17).

The *Summarize Cases* dialog box shown in Figure 1.17 is representative of many of the dialog boxes you will encounter in SPSS. First, notice that when the dialog box opens, the variables **gender**, **age, employment**, and **iq** are located on the left-hand side. To the right of the variables are two right-arrow buttons ( ) which are used for moving the variables on the left to the boxes on the right to be analyzed. There are also a number of buttons (*Statistics, Options, OK, Paste, Reset,* etc.) which perform different operations in SPSS, and check boxes which allow certain options to be turned on or off. The boxes that are checked when the dialog box opens are known as the default settings.

Let's perform the *Case Summaries* procedure on each of the variables by moving them to the *Variables* box.

2. To move the variables to the *Variables* box, select **gender** and press and hold down the *Shift* key. With the *Shift* key continued to be held down, select the last variable **iq**. All four variables should be selected. Click the upper-right arrow button (➡) to move the four variables to the *Variables* box.[6] See Figure 1.18 for details.

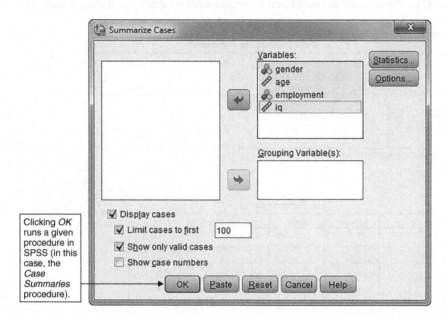

Figure 1.18   **The *Summarize Cases* dialog box (continued).**

3. Click *OK*.

SPSS opens a new window containing the output—called the *Viewer* window—that presents the results of the *Case Summaries* procedure. We'll discuss the output next.

Step 4: Interpret the Results

The output of the *Case Summaries* procedure is presented in Figure 1.19.

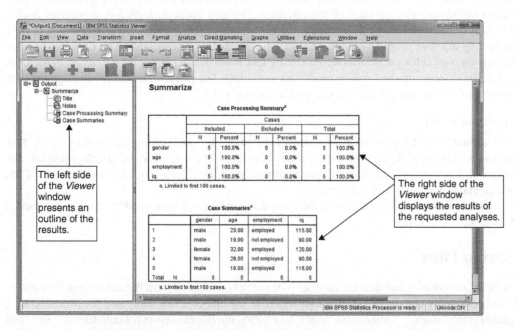

Figure 1.19   **The SPSS *Viewer* window with the results of the *Case Summaries* procedure shown.**

Viewer (Output) Window

In SPSS, the *Viewer* window is divided into two different sections, with the left side of the window containing an *outline* of the requested analyses, and the right side of the window displaying the *results* of the analyses. We'll focus our attention throughout this text on the results shown in the right side of the *Viewer* window which, in this case, consist of the *Case Processing Summary* and *Case Summaries* tables. These tables will be discussed next.

The *Case Processing Summary* and *Case Summaries* tables are displayed in Figure 1.20.

Summarize

Case Processing Summary[a]

	Cases					
	Included		Excluded		Total	
	N	Percent	N	Percent	N	Percent
gender	5	100.0%	0	.0%	5	100.0%
age	5	100.0%	0	.0%	5	100.0%
employment	5	100.0%	0	.0%	5	100.0%
iq	5	100.0%	0	.0%	5	100.0%

a. Limited to first 100 cases.

> Notice that the labels (male/female, employed/not employed) are displayed for **gender** and **employment** (instead of 1 and 2), which is one of the benefits of creating value labels in SPSS.

Case Summaries[a]

	gender	age	employment	iq
1	male	23.00	employed	115.00
2	male	19.00	not employed	90.00
3	female	32.00	employed	120.00
4	female	28.00	not employed	90.00
5	male	18.00	employed	116.00
Total　N	5	5	5	5

a. Limited to first 100 cases.

Figure 1.20　**The output of the *Case Summaries* procedure in SPSS.**

Summarize

At the top of the output is the title, *Summarize*, which indicates the procedure we selected in SPSS (the *Case Summaries* procedure).

Case Processing Summary

The first table of results, *Case Processing Summary*, displays the number of participants (i.e., cases) in the data file for each of the variables. The first column, *Included*, reports an *N* of 5 for each of the variables (*N* corresponds to the number of participants or cases in the data file), indicating that five people were included in the analysis for each variable. The *Excluded* column reports an *N* of 0 for each variable, indicating that none of the participants were *excluded* from the analyses (everyone had values on all four variables). The last column, *Total*, displays the total number of participants in the data set, which is equal to 5.

Case Summaries

The second table, *Case Summaries*, displays the values for each of the participants on the four variables of interest. Notice that the value labels we created for **gender** and **employment** are displayed in the table instead of the numeric values (i.e., 1 and 2) we originally entered into SPSS, which makes it easier to read the results.

This concludes the discussion of the *Case Summaries* procedure in SPSS. Next we'll discuss how to save SPSS files.

Saving Files

In SPSS, output files and data files are saved separately using different file extensions. File extensions commonly consist of three or four letters at the end of a file name and are preceded by a period (e.g., ".*docx*," ".*html*," and ".*mp3*"). In SPSS, the file extension for data files is ".*sav*" and the file extension for output files is ".*spv*."

We'll practice saving both data files and output files in SPSS. Let's start by saving an output file. To save the output file, first make sure the *Viewer* (output) window is active. (If the *Viewer* window is active, you should see it on your screen with a dark blue bar at the top of its window.) If the *Viewer* window is not active, click on it.

To save the output file

1. With the *Viewer* window active, select **File > Save As** . . . (see Figure 1.21).
2. The *Save Output As* dialog box opens (see Figure 1.22).

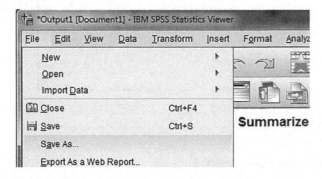

Figure 1.21   Menu commands for saving a file.

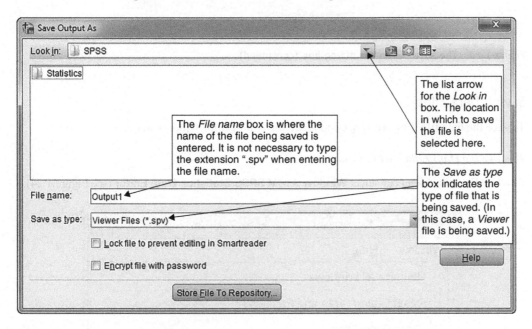

Figure 1.22   The *Save Output As* dialog box.

Toward the bottom of the *Save Output As* dialog box are the *File name* and *Save as type* boxes (see Figure 1.22). In the *File name* box, the default name *Output1* appears, and in the *Save as type* box, *Viewer Files (*.spv)* is shown, confirming that we're saving the results of the *Viewer* window (the output). Notice that *Output1* is selected (highlighted), indicating that the file name is in edit mode and will be replaced by what is entered on the keyboard.

Let's name the file *Introduction output.*

3. Type the name *Introduction output.* (You should now see *Introduction output* in the *File name* text box.)

Next, we'll select a location for the file to be saved. Let's save the file to the desktop. To save the file to the desktop,

4. Click the list arrow ( ) to the right of the *Look in* box (located near the top of the dialog box). A list of folders and/or drives should appear.

5. Select *Desktop* (see Figure 1.23). (*Note:* If you prefer to save the file elsewhere, select the location of your choice.)
6. Click *Save.* You should see the name *Introduction output.spv* (with or without the file extension) in the upper left-hand corner of the *Viewer* window, indicating that the file has been saved.

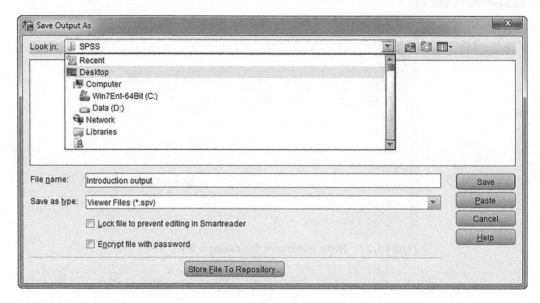

Figure 1.23 The *Save Output As* dialog box (continued).

Saving Data Files

To save the data file, first we'll need to make the *Data Editor* window active.

To make the Data Editor window active

1. From the menu bar select **Window > IBM SPSS Statistics Data Editor** (see Figure 1.24).

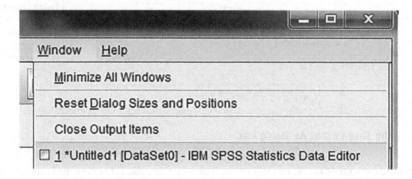

Figure 1.24 Menu commands for making the *Data Editor* window active.

To save the data file

1. With the *Data Editor* window active, select **File > Save As . . .** (see Figure 1.25).
2. The *Save Data As* dialog box opens.
3. In the *File name* box, type the name *Introduction data.*
4. Click on the list arrow (▼) to the right of the *Look in* box to select the location where you would like the file to be saved.
5. Click *Save.* You should see the name *Introduction data.sav* (with or without the file extension) in the upper left-hand corner of the *Data Editor* window, indicating that the file has been saved.

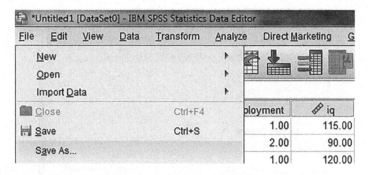

Figure 1.25   The *Save As* command from the *File* menu.

Printing Files

Next, how to print an output file in SPSS will be illustrated. To print the output, we'll first need to make the *Viewer* window active.

To make the Viewer window active

1. From the menu bar, select **Window > Introduction output.spv–IBM SPSS Statistics Viewer**.

To print the output

1. With the *Viewer* window active, select **File > Print . . .** (see Figure 1.26).

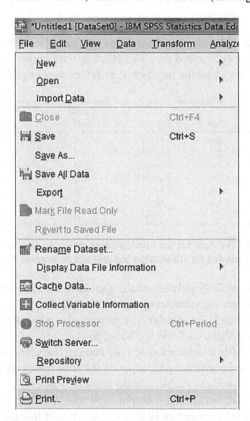

Figure 1.26   **Menu commands for printing the output in SPSS.**

2. The *Print* dialog box opens (see Figure 1.27 on page 18 for details). (The *Print* dialog box shown on your screen may look different from the one presented in Figure 1.27.)
3. Click *OK*.

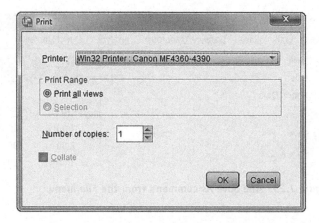

Figure 1.27 **The *Print* dialog box in SPSS.**

Assuming you have access to a printer, the *Case Processing Summary* and *Case Summaries* tables should print (along with the title *Summarize*). You can also print a single table by selecting it and then selecting *Print* from the *File* menu. (The data file can also be printed by making the *Data Editor* window active [with the *Data View* tab selected] and selecting *Print* from the *File* menu.)

This concludes the introduction to SPSS.

Exercises

1. Shown in Figure 1.28 are data on seven nursing home residents, including their age, gender, well-being (measured on a 1 to 10 scale with higher scores indicating greater levels of well-being), and the number of activities they engage in each week.

Person	Age	Gender	Well-being	Number of Activities
1	86	Male	4	2
2	72	Female	7	6
3	59	Female	6	5
4	86	Female	8	7
5	92	Female	4	1
6	68	Male	2	3
7	73	Male	8	5

Figure 1.28 **The data for the nursing home residents. (*Note:* The person variable is included for illustration but will not be entered into SPSS.)**

Enter the data in SPSS and perform the appropriate analyses to answer each of the questions below. Name the variables **age, gender, wellbeing,** and **activities,** respectively.
a. Create value labels for **gender**, assigning males a Value of *1* and the Label *male,* and females a Value of *2* and the Label *female.*
b. Save the data file to a location of your choice. Name the file *Nursing home data.*
c. Run the *Case Summaries* procedure on the data and print your results.
d. In the *Case Summaries* table, are the numeric values (i.e., 1 and 2) or the value labels (i.e., male and female) output in SPSS? Why?
2. A researcher wanted to compare two different types of therapy on children's self-esteem and anger management skills. The therapies investigated were nondirective play therapy (i.e., child directs the play) and directive play therapy (e.g., therapist leads the child through structured play activities). A total of 12 children were included in the study with 6 children (3 boys and 3 girls) receiving each type of therapy. After six weeks of therapy, the childrens' self-esteem (measured on a 10 to 50 scale) and

anger management skills (measured on a 5 to 25 scale) were assessed. The data are presented in the file *Chapter 1_Exercise 2.sav* in the Chapter 1 folder on the web at www.routledge.com/cw/yockey (the variables are named **therapy**, **gender**, **selfesteem**, and **angermanage**). Open the file and perform the appropriate analyses in SPSS to answer the questions below.

    a.   Create value labels for **therapy** and **gender**. For **therapy**, 1 = "nondirective" and 2 = "directive." For gender, 1 = "male" and 2 = "female."

    b.   Run the *Case Summaries* procedure on the data and print your results.

3.   The data file *Chapter 1_Exercise 3.sav* in the Chapter 1 folder on the web at www. routledge.com/cw/yockey contains the values for 10 students on the following three variables: **gender**, number of classes enrolled in (**numberclasses**), and the number of hours worked per week (**hoursworked**). Open the file in SPSS and perform the appropriate analyses to answer the questions below.

    a.   Create value labels for **gender**. For **gender**, 1 = "male" and 2 = "female."

    b.   Run the *Case Summaries* procedure on the data and print your results.

Notes

1. An icon is a picture on your computer. Σ and _Start_ are examples of icons.
2. To ensure clarity throughout the text, to "double-click" the mouse means to press the left button twice in rapid succession; to "click" the mouse means to press the left button once (also referred to as a single click); and to "right-click" the mouse means to press the right button once.
3. Reprint Courtesy of International Business Machines Corporation, © International Business Machines Corporation.
4. The word "data" is plural, referring to two or more values. Datum is singular, referring to one value.
5. If you click on the far right-hand side of the *Values* cell (where the ellipsis button is located after clicking the cell), the *Value Labels* dialog box will open immediately (i.e., it will only take one step to open the box instead of two).
6. If you prefer to move the variables over individually, select **gender** and click the upper-right arrow button, then select **age** and click the upper-right arrow button, and continue with this process until all variables are moved into the *Variables* box.

2

Descriptive Statistics: Frequencies, Measures of Central Tendency, and Measures of Variability

In this chapter, we'll use SPSS to calculate a number of descriptive statistics, including frequencies, measures of central tendency, and measures of variability. Each of these statistical measures is discussed below.

Frequencies refer to the number of observations in each category of a variable. If, for example, for a variable **gender** there were four males and six females in the data set, the frequency reported in SPSS for males would be four and for females would be six. Frequencies are typically obtained on categorical variables.

Measures of central tendency are used to describe the center (or central location) of a set of scores and consist of the mean, median, and the mode. The **mean** is the arithmetic average (the sum of the scores divided by the total number of scores), the **median** is the middle score (assuming the scores were ordered from lowest to highest), and the **mode** is the most frequently occurring score (or scores) in the data set.

Measures of variability are used to describe the amount of spread or variability in a set of scores. The **standard deviation** and **variance** are two of the most commonly used measures of variability. The standard deviation is a measure of how far, on average, scores vary from the mean, and the variance is equal to the standard deviation squared. Other examples of measures of variability include the range (the difference between the highest and the lowest scores) and the interquartile range (the difference between the scores at the 25th and 75th percentiles of a distribution).

How to calculate frequencies, measures of central tendency, and measures of variability in SPSS will be illustrated using the sample data set presented in Figure 2.1.

Participant	Gender	Mathexam	College	Satquant
1	1	24	1	570
2	1	18	2	450
3	2	34	1	600
4	2	27	2	450
5	1	15	1	580
6	1	26	1	550
7	1	42	2	480
8	2	25	1	520
9	2	31	1	450
10	2	44	2	550

Figure 2.1 The sample data set. (*Note:* The participant variable is included for illustration but will not be entered into SPSS.)

The Data

For each of the participants in Figure 2.1, their **gender**, score on a math entrance exam (**mathexam**), whether they were attending college at home or away (**college**), and their score on the math portion of the SAT (**satquant**) were recorded. **Gender** and **college** are categorical variables, while **mathexam** and **satquant** are continuous variables, with higher scores indicating better performance on both measures (the **mathexam** scores range from 0 to 50 and **satquant** scores range from 200 to 800). For **gender**, males are assigned a "1" and females are assigned a "2"; for **college**, those attending college at home are assigned a "1" and those attending college away are assigned a "2."

With an overview of the data set provided, next we'll enter the data into SPSS.

Data Entry and Analysis in SPSS

Steps 1 and 2 below describe how to enter the data in SPSS. The data file is also available online at www.routledge.com/cw/yockey under the name *descriptive statistics.sav* in the Chapter 2 folder. If you prefer to open the file from the web site, skip to Step 3 below.

Step 1: Create the Variables

1. Start SPSS.
2. Click the *Variable View* tab.

   In SPSS, four variables will be created. The variables will be named **gender**, **mathexam**, **college**, and **satquant**, respectively.

3. Using the process described in Chapter 1, enter the variable names **gender**, **mathexam**, **college**, and **satquant**, respectively, in the first four rows of the *Variable View* window. Under *Measure*, classify **gender** and **college** as nominal and **mathexam** and **satquant** as scale (see Figure 2.2).

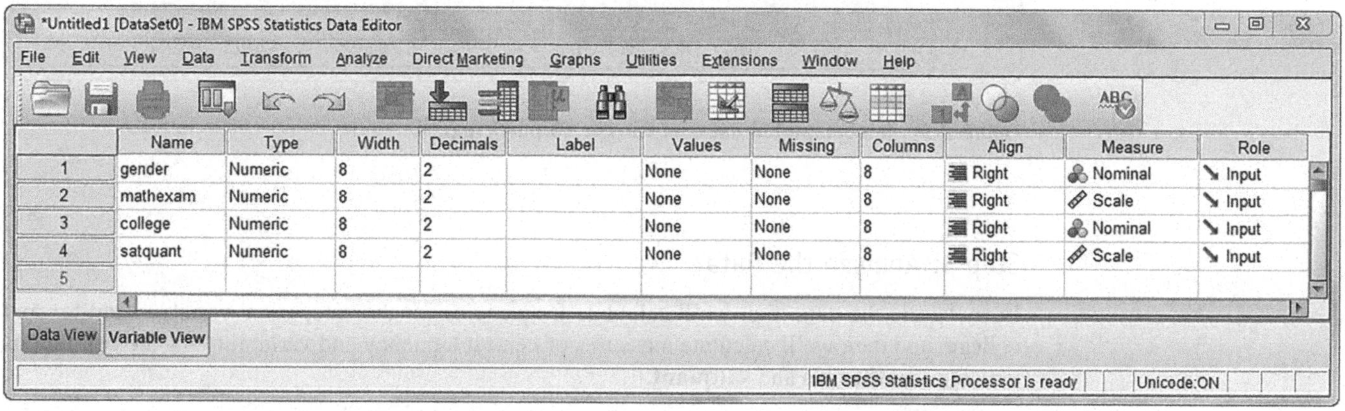

	Name	Type	Width	Decimals	Label	Values	Missing	Columns	Align	Measure	Role
1	gender	Numeric	8	2		None	None	8	Right	Nominal	Input
2	mathexam	Numeric	8	2		None	None	8	Right	Scale	Input
3	college	Numeric	8	2		None	None	8	Right	Nominal	Input
4	satquant	Numeric	8	2		None	None	8	Right	Scale	Input
5											

Figure 2.2 **The *Variable View* window in SPSS with the variables gender, mathexam, college, and satquant entered.**

Prior to entering the data, we'll create value labels in SPSS for the categorical variables **gender** and **college**.

4. Using the process described in Chapter 1, create value labels for **gender** and **college**. For **gender,** 1 = "male" and 2 = "female." **For college,** 1 = "home" and 2 = "away."

Step 2: Enter the Data

Next, we'll enter the data into SPSS.

To enter the data

1. Click on the *Data View* tab. The variables **gender**, **mathexam**, **college**, and **satquant** appear in the first four columns of the *Data View* window.
2. Consulting Figure 2.1, enter the scores for each of the participants on the four variables of interest. For the first participant, enter the scores *1*, *24*, *1*, and *570*, for the variables **gender**, **mathexam**, **college**, and **satquant**, respectively. Using this approach, enter the data for all 10 participants. The completed data set is shown in Figure 2.3.

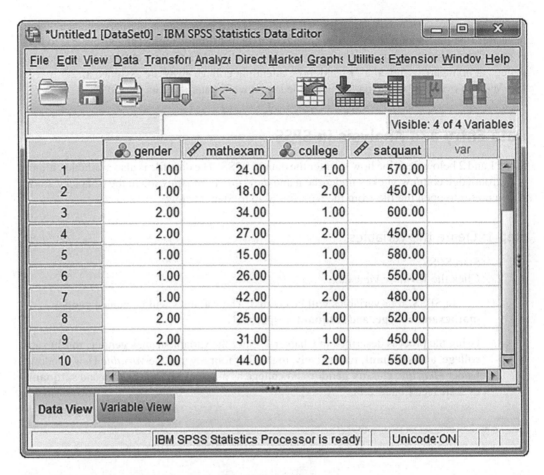

Figure 2.3 **The completed data set for the 10 participants.**

Step 3: Analyze the Data

In analyzing the data, first we'll calculate frequencies for the categorical variables **gender** and **college**, and then we'll calculate measures of central tendency and variability for the continuous variables **mathexam** and **satquant**.

Frequencies

To calculate frequencies for **gender** and **college**, from the menu bar, select

1. **Analyze > Descriptive Statistics > Frequencies . . .** (see Figure 2.4).

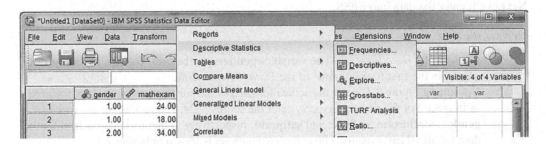

Figure 2.4 **Menu commands for the *Frequencies* procedure.**

A *Frequencies* dialog box opens with the variables **gender**, **mathexam**, **college**, and **satquant** on the left-hand side of the dialog box (see Figure 2.5).

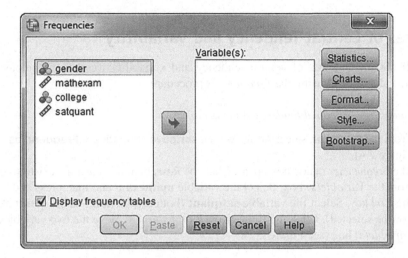

Figure 2.5   **The *Frequencies* dialog box.**

2. Select the variable **gender** and then press and hold down the *Ctrl* key (the *Ctrl* key is located in the bottom left-hand corner of your keyboard; Mac users, select the *Command* key, ⌘). Select the variable **college** (**gender** and **college** should now be selected). Click the right-arrow button (➥) to move the two variables to the *Variable(s)* box.[1] See Figure 2.6 for details.

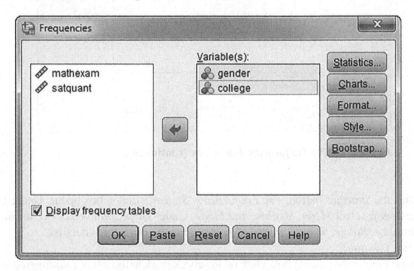

Figure 2.6   **The *Frequencies* dialog box (continued).**

3. Click *OK*.

The *Frequencies* procedure runs and the results are presented in the *Viewer* window. Prior to discussing the results of the *Frequencies* procedure for **gender** and **college**, we'll obtain descriptive statistics for **mathexam** and **satquant**.

(For consistency throughout the text, we'll be running procedures from within the *Data Editor* window. Since the *Viewer* window is currently active, we'll make the *Data Editor* window active prior to running the next procedure.)

To make the Data Editor window active

1. From the menu bar, select **Window > Untitled—IBM SPSS Statistics Data Editor**. The *Data Editor* window should now be active. (If you opened the data from the web site, you'll select **Window > descriptive statistics.sav-IBM SPSS Statistics Data**

Editor from the menu bar. These latter instructions will apply throughout the chapter for those using the online data file.)

Measures of Central Tendency and Variability

Next we'll obtain measures of central tendency and variability for the continuous variables **mathexam** and **satquant** using the *Frequencies* procedure.

To obtain measures of central tendency and variability

1. From the menu bar, select **Analyze > Descriptive Statistics > Frequencies** . . . (see Figure 2.4).[2]
2. The *Frequencies* dialog box opens. Click the *Reset* button to clear the existing variables from the *Variable(s)* box. Select the variable **mathexam** and then press and hold down the *Ctrl* key. Select the variable **satquant** (both **mathexam** and **satquant** should now be selected). Click the right-arrow button (⮕) to move the two variables to the *Variable(s)* box (see Figure 2.7).

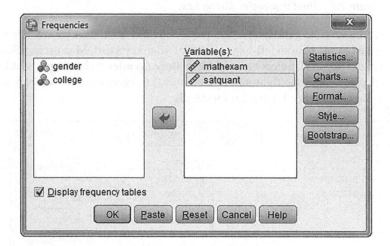

Figure 2.7 **The *Frequencies* dialog box (continued).**

3. Click the *Statistics* button. The *Frequencies: Statistics* dialog box opens. Under *Central Tendency*, select *Mean*, *Median*, and *Mode*. Under *Dispersion* select *Std. deviation*, *Variance*, *Range*, *Minimum*, and *Maximum*. See Figure 2.8 for details.
4. Click *Continue*.
5. In the *Frequencies* dialog box, click on the check mark to the left of *Display frequency tables* to turn this option off. The box should now be empty, indicating that frequency tables will *not* be produced for the variables **mathexam** and **satquant** (frequency tables are typically not produced for continuous variables, as measures of central tendency and variability are more informative). See Figure 2.9 for details.
6. Click *OK*.

The *Frequencies* procedure runs in SPSS and the results are presented in the *Viewer* window. Prior to discussing the results of the *Frequencies* procedure, the *Means* procedure will be illustrated.

Analysis of Groups Using the Means Procedure

The *Means* procedure is useful for obtaining descriptive statistics *separately* for each group of a variable (or variables) of interest. For example, instead of obtaining the mean **satquant** score for all participants, the mean **satquant** scores could be obtained separately for those who attended

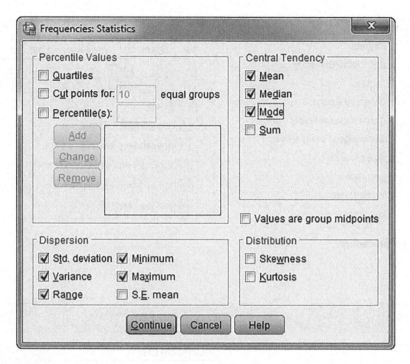

Figure 2.8 The *Frequencies: Statistics* dialog box.

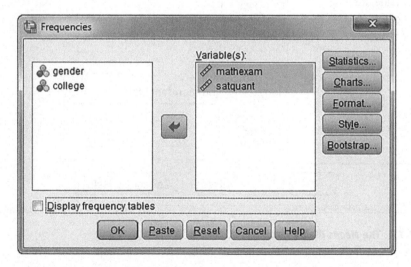

Figure 2.9 The *Frequencies* dialog box (with the *Display frequency tables* check box unchecked).

college at home and those who attended college away. We'll illustrate the *Means* procedure by obtaining the mean and standard deviation on **satquant** separately for the different college groups.

To obtain the Means procedure

1. Make the *Data View* window active (select **Window > Untitled—IBM SPSS Statistics Data Editor**).
2. From the menu bar, select **Analyze > Compare Means > Means** . . . (see Figure 2.10 on page 26 for details).
3. The *Means* dialog box opens (see Figure 2.11 on page 26 for details).

The variable that the mean and standard deviation will be obtained on (**satquant**) goes into the *Dependent List* box and the variable that contains the different groups (**college**) goes into the *Independent List* box.

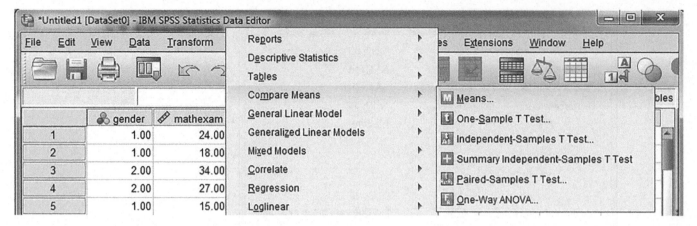

Figure 2.10 Menu commands for the *Means* procedure.

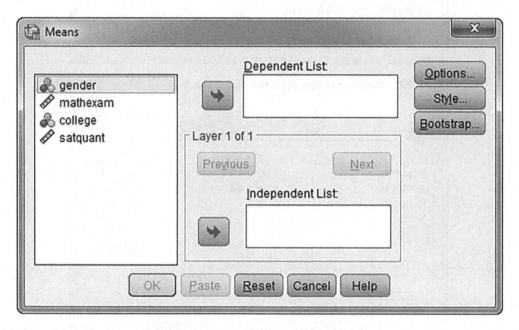

Figure 2.11 The *Means* dialog box.

4. Select **satquant** and click the upper right-arrow button (➡) to move it to the *Dependent List* box.
5. Select **college** and click the lower right-arrow button (➡) to move it to the *Independent List* box (see Figure 2.12).
6. Click *Options*. The *Means: Options* dialog box opens (see Figure 2.13).

On the left-hand side of the dialog box (labeled *Statistics*) are a number of statistics that can be selected, and on the right-hand side (labeled *Cell Statistics*) are the statistics that are calculated by default. Since the *Mean* and *Standard Deviation* are on the right-hand side already, we'll leave the default options in place. (*Number of Cases* could be moved to the *Statistics* box by selecting it and clicking the arrow button, but we'll leave it there since it won't adversely affect our results.)

7. Click *Continue*.
8. Click *OK*.

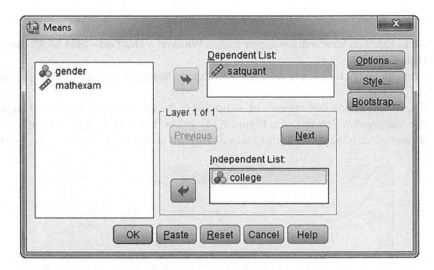

Figure 2.12   **The *Means* dialog box (continued).**

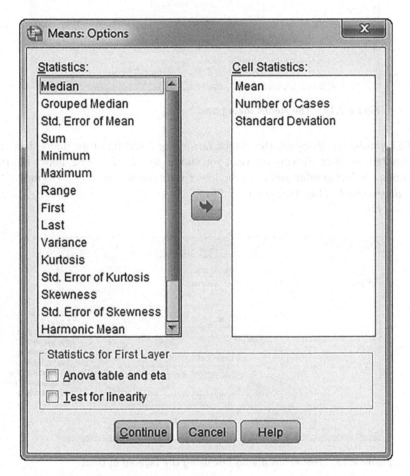

Figure 2.13   **The *Means: Options* dialog box.**

The *Means* procedure runs in SPSS and the results are presented in the *Viewer* window. Prior to discussing the results, we'll perform a final analysis using the *Means* procedure. Instead of obtaining the mean and standard deviation separately for the different groups of a *single* variable (as we did with **college**), we'll obtain means for *two* categorical variables using the layered option. To illustrate this procedure, we'll obtain means on **satquant** for the different **college** groups layered (or further subdivided) by **gender**. This will result in four different mean **satquant** scores: males who attended college at home, females who attended college at home, males who attended college away, and females who attended college away.

To perform the Means procedure using the layered option

1. Make the *Data View* window active (select **Window > Untitled—IBM SPSS Statistics Data Editor**).
2. From the menu bar, select **Analyze > Compare Means > Means** . . . (see Figure 2.10 for details).
3. The *Means* dialog box opens with **satquant** in the *Dependent List* box and **college** in the *Independent List* box (see Figure 2.14). (*Note*: If you did not perform the previous *Means* procedure, you'll need to move **satquant** and **college** to their respective boxes.)

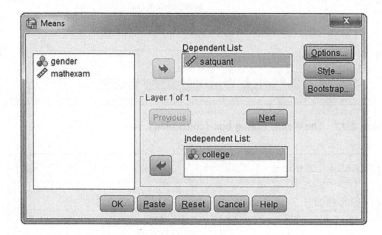

Figure 2.14 The *Means* dialog box.

4. To layer the results by **gender**, in the *Layer 1 of 1* section of the dialog box, click the *Next* button (after clicking on *Next*, you should see '*Layer 2 of 2*' above the *Previous* button). Select **gender** and click the lower-right arrow button (⬇) to move it to the *Independent List* box (see Figure 2.15).
5. Click *OK*.

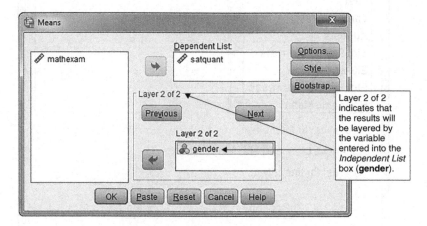

Figure 2.15 The *Means* dialog box using the layered option.

The *Means* procedure runs in SPSS and the results are presented in the *Viewer* window. Next we'll discuss the output for the four analyses we conducted in this chapter. As a review, the four analyses were:

1. Frequencies on the variables **college** and **gender**.
2. Measures of central tendency and variability on **mathexam** and **satquant**.
3. Means and standard deviations on **satquant** for the different **college** groups.
4. Means and standard deviations on **satquant** for the different **college** groups layered by **gender**.

Step 4: Interpret the Output

The output of the four analyses is presented in Figures 2.16–2.19. [If you've conducted the analyses on your own computer as you've read through the chapter, scroll to the top of the output (*Viewer*) window to the first set of results—frequencies for **gender** and **college**.]

Analysis 1: Frequencies Procedure—**Gender** and **College**

The results of the first analysis we conducted—frequencies for **gender** and **college**—are provided in Figure 2.16.

Frequencies

Statistics

		gender	college
N	Valid	10	10
	Missing	0	0

Frequency Table

gender

		Frequency	Percent	Valid Percent	Cumulative Percent
Valid	male	5	50.0	50.0	50.0
	female	5	50.0	50.0	100.0
	Total	10	100.0	100.0	

college

		Frequency	Percent	Valid Percent	Cumulative Percent
Valid	home	6	60.0	60.0	60.0
	away	4	40.0	40.0	100.0
	Total	10	100.0	100.0	

Figure 2.16   **Output of the *Frequencies* procedure for gender and college.**

Frequencies—Statistics

The *Statistics* table displays the sample size for the variables **gender** and **college**. The table indicates that there were 10 valid observations for **gender** and **college** (all 10 people had values on both variables). The value of zero in the *Missing* row indicates that there were no missing values for either of the variables (a missing value for **gender**, for example, would indicate that the **gender** of one of the participants was not recorded).

Frequency Table—Gender

The frequency table for **gender** indicates the frequency, or number of participants, for each category of **gender**. In the table there are five males and five females, with each gender representing 50% of the data set.

Frequency Table—College

The frequency table for **college** indicates the frequency for each category of **college**. The table shows that six students attended college at home and four students attended college away from home, representing 60% and 40% of the data set, respectively.

Analysis 2: Frequencies Procedure—**Mathexam** and **Satquant**

The results of the second analysis we conducted—frequencies for **mathexam** and **satquant**—are presented in Figure 2.17 on page 30.

The *Statistics* table displays the results of the *Frequencies* procedure for the continuous variables **mathexam** and **satquant**. (Recall that we requested measures of central tendency and

Frequencies

Statistics

		mathexam	satquant
N	Valid	10	10
	Missing	0	0
Mean		28.6000	520.0000
Median		26.5000	535.0000
Mode		15.00[a]	450.00
Std. Deviation		9.38320	58.30952
Variance		88.044	3400.000
Range		29.00	150.00
Minimum		15.00	450.00
Maximum		44.00	600.00

[a]. Multiple modes exist. The smallest value is shown

Figure 2.17 Output of the *Frequencies* procedure for **mathexam** and **satquant**.

variability for these variables.) As is shown in Figure 2.17, the mean and standard deviation for **mathexam** is 28.60 and 9.38 (rounding to two decimal places) and for **satquant** is 520.00 and 58.31, respectively. The minimum and maximum values indicate the lowest and highest values in the data set and are helpful for ensuring that all the data are within the possible range of values (a value outside of this range would most likely indicate that a data entry error has been made). The minimum and maximum values of 15.00 and 44.00 for **mathexam** and 450.00 and 600.00 for **satquant** show that there were no out-of-range values for either variable (as indicated earlier, the range of possible scores for **mathexam** is 0 to 50 and for **satquant** is 200 to 800).[3]

Analysis 3: Means Procedure—**Satquant** by **College**

The results of the third analysis we conducted—*Means* of **satquant** for the different college groups—are presented in Figure 2.18.

Means

Case Processing Summary

	Cases					
	Included		Excluded		Total	
	N	Percent	N	Percent	N	Percent
satquant * college	10	100.0%	0	.0%	10	100.0%

Report

satquant

college	Mean	N	Std. Deviation
home	545.0000	6	53.94442
away	482.5000	4	47.16991
Total	520.0000	10	58.30952

Figure 2.18 Output of the *Means* procedure on satquant for the college groups *home* and *away*.

Case Processing Summary

The *Case Processing Summary* table indicates the number of observations included in the analysis (10), the number of observations excluded (0), and the total number of observations in the data set (10). The table indicates that all 10 participants were included in the analysis (all 10 people had values on **satquant** and **college**).

Report

The *Report* table shows the mean, sample size (*N*), and standard deviation for the college groups home, away, and total (home and away combined). Inspecting the means for the two groups shows that the six students who attended college at home had a higher mean **satquant** score (545.00) than the four students who attended college away (482.50). Those who stayed at home for college also had **satquant** scores that were slightly more variable than those who attended college away (the standard deviation for home was 53.94 compared to a standard deviation of 47.17 for away). The mean **satquant** score for the entire sample (*Total*) was 520.00 with a standard deviation of 58.31 (this agrees with the values obtained in our second analysis shown in Figure 2.17).

Analysis 4: Means Procedure—**Satquant** by **College** Layered by **Gender**

The results of the last analysis we conducted—*Means* of **satquant** by **college** layered by **gender**—are presented in Figure 2.19.

Means

Case Processing Summary

	Cases					
	Included		Excluded		Total	
	N	Percent	N	Percent	N	Percent
satquant * college * gender	10	100.0%	0	.0%	10	100.0%

Report

satquant

college	gender	Mean	N	Std. Deviation
home	male	566.6667	3	15.27525
	female	523.3333	3	75.05553
	Total	545.0000	6	53.94442
away	male	465.0000	2	21.21320
	female	500.0000	2	70.71068
	Total	482.5000	4	47.16991
Total	male	526.0000	5	57.70615
	female	514.0000	5	65.03845
	Total	520.0000	10	58.30952

Figure 2.19 **Output of the *Means* procedure on satquant for college layered by gender.**

Case Processing Summary

The *Case Processing Summary* table indicates the number of observations included in the analysis (10), the number of observations excluded (0), and the total number of observations in the data set (10). The table indicates that all 10 participants were included in the analysis (all 10 people had values on **satquant**, **college**, and **gender**).

Report

The *Report* table displays the mean, sample size (*N*), and standard deviation on **satquant** for **college** layered by **gender**. The first section of the table displays the mean and standard deviation for males and females who attend college at home. Notice that males have a higher mean score than females on **satquant** (566.67 vs. 523.33) and that females have a larger standard deviation (75.06 vs. 15.28). The second section of the table displays the mean and standard deviation for males and females who attend college away from home. For this group of students, females have a higher mean than males on **satquant** (500.00 vs. 465.00) and a larger standard deviation (70.71 vs. 21.21). Finally, the last section of the table displays the mean and standard deviation for males and females for home and away combined. When the **college** groups are combined, males have a higher mean **satquant** score than females (526.00 vs. 514.00), while females have a larger standard deviation (65.04 vs. 57.71).

This concludes the discussion of the *Frequencies* and *Means* procedures in SPSS.

Summary of Steps to Conduct the *Frequencies* and *Means* Procedures

I. Data Entry
1. Create the variables in SPSS by entering the variable names in the *Variable View* window.
2. Create value labels for each of the categorical variables. In the *Variable View* window, enter the numeric values and labels as appropriate. Click *OK*.
3. Enter the data for each of the participants in the *Data View* window.

II. Analysis of the Data

Obtaining frequencies using the Frequencies procedure
1. From the menu bar, select **Analyze > Descriptive Statistics > Frequencies** . . .
2. Move the categorical variables to be analyzed to the *Variable(s)* box.
3. Click *OK*.

Obtaining descriptive statistics using the Frequencies procedure
1. From the menu bar, select **Analyze > Descriptive Statistics > Frequencies** . . .
2. Move the continuous variables to be analyzed to the *Variable(s)* box.
3. Click *Statistics*.
4. Select the statistics of interest.
5. Click *Continue*.
6. In the *Frequencies* dialog box, uncheck *Display frequency tables*.
7. Click *OK*.

Obtaining descriptive statistics on one or more categorical variables using the Means procedure
1. From the menu bar, select **Analyze > Compare Means > Means** . . .
2. Move the variable(s) that the descriptive statistics will be obtained on to the *Dependent List* box. Move the categorical variable to the *Independent List* box.
3. If you want to layer the results by a second categorical variable, click the *Layered* button and move the categorical variable to the *Independent List* box. (Disregard this step if you don't want to layer the results by a second variable.)
4. Click *OK*.

Exercises

1. A soccer coach evaluated the impact of two different kicking methods (a toe kick and a heel kick) on the effectiveness of kicking a soccer ball. Four boys and four girls kicked a ball using one of the two methods and the distance (in feet) and accuracy (on a 1–10 scale) of the kicks were recorded. The experience level of each child was also ascertained, with higher values indicating greater experience. Half of the children (two boys and two girls) kicked the ball using a toe kick and the other half kicked the ball using a heel kick. The data are provided in Figure 2.20. For **gender,** 1 = "boys" and 2 = "girls." For **method,** 1 = "toe kick" and 2 = "heel kick."

Gender	Method	Experience	Distance	Accuracy
1	1	5	50	5
1	1	6	45	4
1	2	2	35	6
1	2	9	40	9
2	1	2	42	3
2	1	7	39	6
2	2	4	28	7
2	2	2	32	6

Figure 2.20 Data for the eight children in the soccer ball kicking study.

Enter the data in SPSS and perform the appropriate analyses to answer each of the questions below. Enter value labels as appropriate for **gender** and **method**.

a. Report the frequencies for **gender** and **method**.

b. Report the mean and standard deviation for **experience**, **distance**, and **accuracy** for the entire sample.

c. Report the mean and standard deviation for **experience**, **distance**, and **accuracy** separately for boys and girls. Which group has a higher mean on each of the three variables? Which group has a larger standard deviation?

d. Report the mean and standard deviation for **experience**, **distance**, and **accuracy** separately for the toe kicking and heel kicking methods. Which group has a higher mean on each of the three variables? Which group has a larger standard deviation?

e. Report the mean and standard deviation for **experience**, **distance**, and **accuracy** for **gender** layered by **method**. Which of the four conditions has the lowest mean **experience** and **accuracy** scores? Which has the highest mean kicking **distance**?

2. A student collected data on the perception of water quality in three different cities across the United States. She sampled 10 people (five males and five females) each from major cities in the Midwest, on the West Coast, and on the East Coast. Each person tasted the municipal water from their respective city (the water was provided by the researcher) and rated its taste and clarity on a 1–10 scale (with higher ratings indicating better perceived taste and clarity, respectively). The data file is located in the Chapter 2 folder online at www.routledge.com/cw/yockey and is named *Chapter 2_Exercise 2.sav*. The data file consists of the values of 30 participants on the variables **location**, **gender**, **taste**, and **clarity**. For **location**, 1 = "West Coast," 2 = "Midwest," and 3 = "East Coast." For **gender**, 1 = "male" and 2 = "female." Open the file in SPSS and perform the appropriate analyses to answer the questions below.

a. Report the frequencies for **location** and **gender**.

b. Report the mean and standard deviation for **taste** and **clarity** for the entire sample.

c. Report the mean and standard deviation for **taste** and **clarity** separately for the different locations. Which location has the highest mean on each of the two variables? Which location has the largest standard deviation?

d. Report the mean and standard deviation for **taste** and **clarity** separately for males and females. Which group has the highest mean on each of the two variables? Which group has the largest standard deviation?

e. Report the mean and standard deviation for **taste** and **clarity** for **gender** layered by **location**. Which of the six conditions has the lowest mean **taste**? Which has the lowest mean **clarity**? Which has the highest mean **taste** and **clarity**?

3. A researcher collected data on the reading performance and number of hours of television watched per day of 30 children. The gender and socioeconomic status (SES) of each participant were also collected. The data file is located in the Chapter 2 folder online at www.routledge.com/cw/yockey and is named *Chapter 2_Exercise 3.sav*. The data file contains the variables **gender**, **ses**, **hourstv**, and **readingscores**. For **gender** 1 = "male", and 2 = "female." For **ses**, 1 = "low," 2 = "middle," and 3 = "high." The reading scores are on a 0–50 scale with higher scores indicating better reading performance. Open the data file in SPSS and perform the appropriate analyses to answer the questions below.

a. Report the frequencies for **gender** and **ses**.

b. Report the mean and standard deviation for **hourstv** and **readingscores** for the entire sample.

c. Report the mean and standard deviation for **hourstv** and **readingscores** separately for males and females. Which group has the highest mean on each variable? Which group has the largest standard deviation?

d. Report the mean and standard deviation for **hourstv** and **readingscores** for **gender** layered by **ses**. Which group watches the most television on average? Which group has the highest mean reading scores?

Notes

1. Alternatively, each variable may be moved over individually by selecting **gender** and clicking the right-arrow button (✱), and then selecting **college** and clicking the right-arrow (✱) button.
2. Measures of central tendency and variability may also be obtained using the *Descriptives* procedure in SPSS. To run the *Descriptives* procedure, from the menu bar select **Analyze > Descriptive Statistics > Descriptives . . .** and move the variables to be analyzed to the *Variable(s)* box. In the *Descriptives* procedure, the mean, standard deviation, minimum, and maximum values are selected by default. Additional descriptive statistics may be selected by clicking the *Options* button.
3. An out-of-range value is a data point that is outside the minimum and maximum values for a variable (a value of 50 would be an example of an out-of-range value for **satquant**). While having no out-of-range values does not ensure that there are no data entry errors (there can be errors within the possible range of values as well), it is a simple check against one fairly common type of data entry error. For protection against data entry errors within the range of possible values, enter the data carefully and at a minimum double-check all entered values.

Graphical Procedures

In this chapter we'll create a number of different graphs in SPSS. By creating graphs, you can quickly determine the general shape of a distribution of scores, the overall variability of the data, and can detect outliers, or scores that are unrepresentative of the majority of the values in the data set. We'll use SPSS to create a number of commonly used graphs, including bar charts, histograms, scatterplots, and boxplots.

To create graphs in this chapter, we'll use the data file we created in Chapter 2. A copy of the file is located in the Chapter 3 folder online at www.routledge.com/cw/yockey under the file name *descriptive statistics.sav*. (*Note*: The following commands assume that the *SPSS Demystified* files have been downloaded from the web site to your computer.)

To open the file from your computer

1. Start SPSS.
2. From the menu bar, select **File > Open > Data** . . .
3. The *Open Data* dialog box appears. Click on the list arrow and select the location of the *SPSS Demystified* files on your computer.
4. Double-click the *Chapter 3* folder to open it. You should see the file *descriptive statistics.sav* (the file extension '.*sav*' may not be shown on your computer). Double-click the file to open it. After a few moments, the file should open in the SPSS *Data Editor* window. The data file is shown in Figure 3.1. (*Note*: If you don't see the file on your computer screen, select **Window > descriptive statistics.sav—IBM SPSS Statistics Data Editor** from the menu bar to make the *Data Editor* window active.)

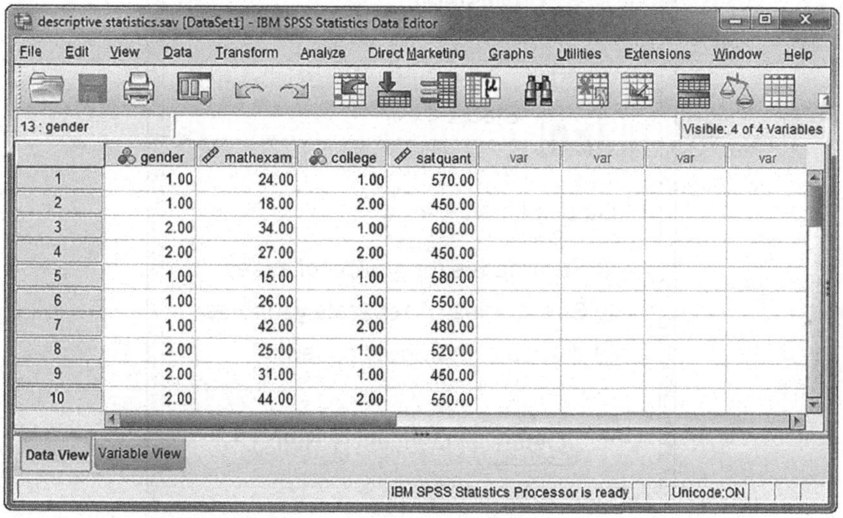

Figure 3.1 The *descriptive statistics.sav* data file.

Bar Charts

The first graph we'll create in SPSS is a bar chart. Bar charts indicate the frequency, or number of observations, for each category of a variable (bar charts are typically produced on categorical variables). We'll create a bar chart for **college**.

To create a bar chart in SPSS

1.   From the menu bar select **Graphs > Legacy Dialogs > Bar** . . . (see Figure 3.2).

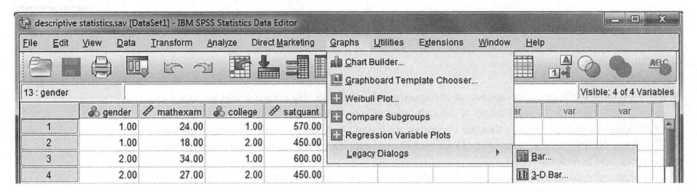

Figure 3.2   **Menu commands for the bar chart procedure.**

2.   The *Bar Charts* dialog box opens. To create a bar chart for **college**, the default option, *Simple,* will be used. Click *Define* (see Figure 3.3).

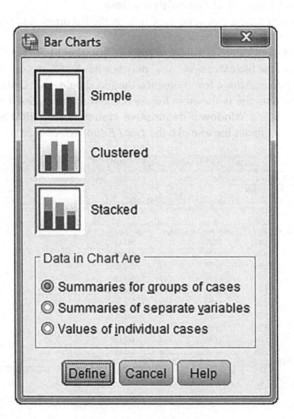

Figure 3.3   **The *Bar Charts* dialog box.**

3. The *Define Simple Bar: Summaries for Groups of Cases* dialog box opens. Select **college** and click the second right-arrow button (⮕) from the top to move it to the *Category Axis* box. See Figure 3.4 for details.
4. Click *OK*.

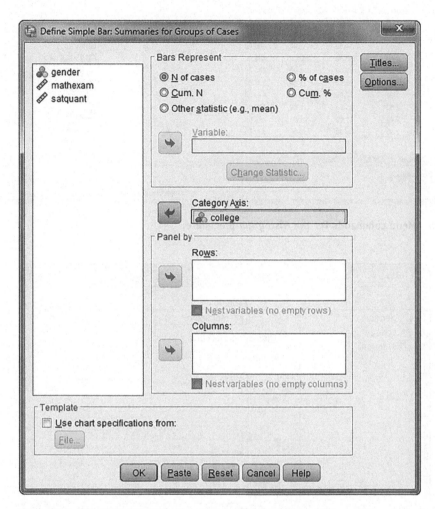

Figure 3.4   The *Define Simple Bar: Summaries for Groups of Cases* dialog box.

A bar chart for **college** is produced in the *Viewer* window (the bar chart will be discussed after all of the graphs have been produced in SPSS).

Histograms

Next, we'll create a histogram in SPSS. Histograms are graphs that indicate the frequency, or number of observations, for intervals of a continuous variable. We'll create a histogram for the variable **mathexam**.

To create a histogram in SPSS

1. Make the *Data Editor* window active by selecting **Window > descriptive statistics. sav – IBM SPSS Statistics Data Editor** from the menu bar.
2. To produce a histogram in SPSS, from the menu bar select **Graphs > Legacy Dialogs > Histogram** (see Figure 3.5 on page 38).
3. The *Histogram* dialog box opens.
4. Select **mathexam** and click the upper right-arrow button (⮕) to move it to the *Variable* box (see Figure 3.6 on page 38 for details).
5. Click *OK*.

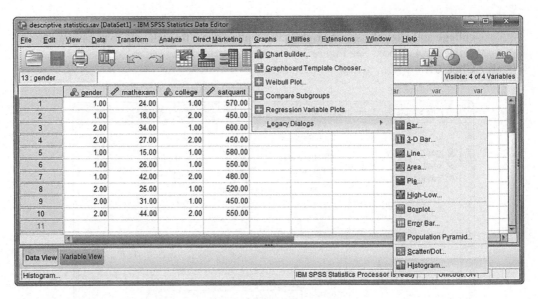

Figure 3.5 Menu commands for the *Histogram* procedure.

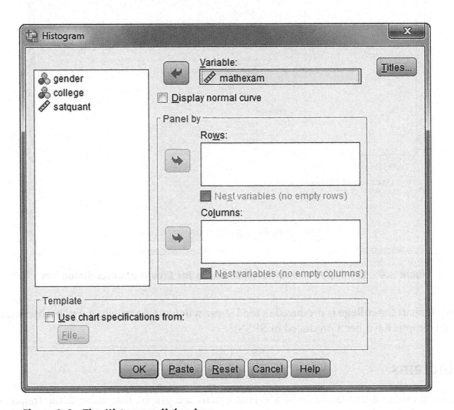

Figure 3.6 The *Histogram* dialog box.

A histogram of **mathexam** is produced in the *Viewer* window (the histogram will be discussed after all of the graphs have been produced in SPSS).

Scatterplots

Next, we'll produce a scatterplot in SPSS. Scatterplots plot the coordinates (a point where the scores on two variables meet) of participants' responses on two variables and are often used when calculating correlation coefficients (correlation is discussed in Chapter 12). We'll create a scatterplot of the variables **mathexam** and **satquant**.

To create a scatterplot in SPSS

1. Make the *Data Editor* window active by selecting **Window > descriptive statistics. sav—IBM SPSS Statistics Data Editor** from the menu bar.
2. To produce a scatterplot, from the menu bar select **Graphs > Legacy Dialogs > Scatter/Dot . . .** (see Figure 3.7).

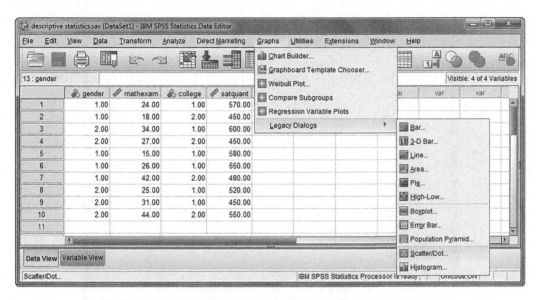

Figure 3.7   **Menu commands for the scatterplot procedure in SPSS.**

3. The *Scatter/Dot* dialog box opens (see Figure 3.8). To produce a scatterplot of **mathexam** and **satquant**, the default option, *Simple Scatter,* will be used. Click *Define*.

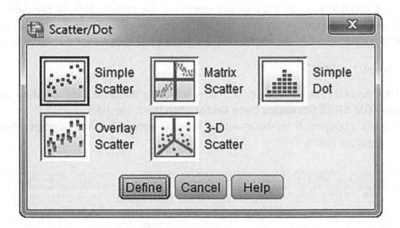

Figure 3.8   The *Scatter/Dot* dialog box.

4. The *Simple Scatterplot* dialog box opens. Select **mathexam** and click the upper right-arrow button (⮕) to move it to the *Y-axis* box. Select **satquant** and click the second right-arrow button (⮕) to move it to the *X-axis* box (see Figure 3.9 on page 40 for details).
5. Click *OK*.

A scatterplot of **mathexam** and **satquant** is produced in the *Viewer* window (the scatterplot will be discussed after all of the graphs have been produced in SPSS).

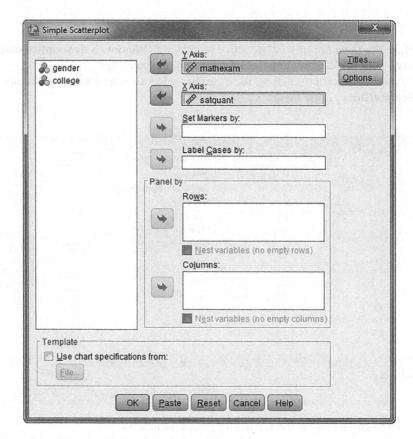

Figure 3.9   **The *Simple Scatterplot* dialog box.**

Boxplots

Next we'll illustrate how to produce a boxplot in SPSS. Boxplots are useful for displaying information about a variable including the center (median), the middle 50% of the data, the overall spread, and whether or not there are any outliers in the data (outliers are points that are unrepresentative of the other values in the data set). We'll produce a boxplot for the variable **mathexam**.

To create a boxplot in SPSS

1.   Make the *Data Editor* window active by selecting **Window > descriptive statistics. sav—IBM SPSS Statistics Data Editor** from the menu bar.
2.   To create a boxplot, from the menu bar select **Graphs > Legacy Dialogs > Boxplot . . .** (see Figure 3.10).

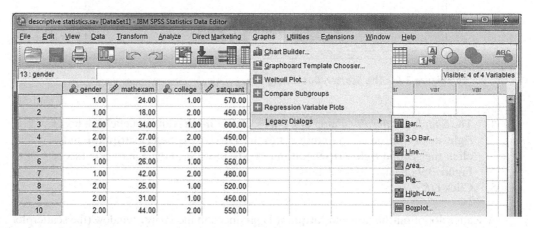

Figure 3.10   **Menu commands for the *Boxplot* procedure.**

3. The *Boxplot* dialog box opens. Leave the default option, *Simple*, selected. In the *Data in Chart Are* section of the dialog box, select *Summaries of separate variables*. (See Figure 3.11.)

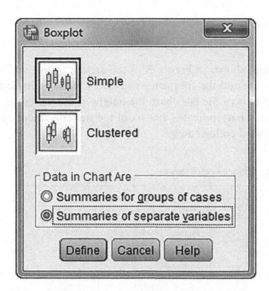

Figure 3.11   The *Boxplot* dialog box.

4. Click *Define*.
5. The *Define Simple Boxplot: Summaries of Separate Variables* dialog box opens. Select the variable, **mathexam**, and click the upper right-arrow button (⬕) to move it to the *Boxes Represent* box (see Figure 3.12).
6. Click *OK*.

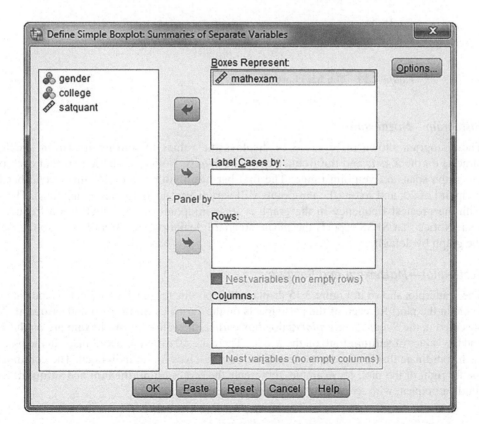

Figure 3.12   The *Define Simple Boxplot: Summaries of Separate Variables* dialog box.

A boxplot for **mathexam** is produced in the *Viewer* window.

Next, the results of the four different graphs we created—the bar chart, histogram, scatterplot, and boxplot—will be described.

Interpret the Results

Bar Chart—*College*

In the bar chart of **college** shown in Figure 3.13 the groups (*home* and *away*) are displayed on the horizontal axis (*X-axis*) and the frequency (labeled *Count*) is displayed on the vertical axis (*Y-axis*). On the vertical axis of the bar chart, the height of the bar corresponds to the frequency for a given group. The bar chart indicates that six of the students attended college at home, while four of the students attended college away.

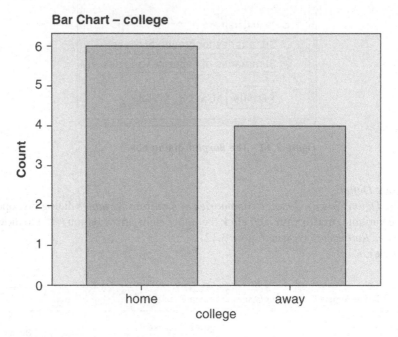

Figure 3.13   **The bar chart of college.**

Histogram—*Mathexam*

The histogram shown in Figure 3.14 displays the values of **mathexam** (from smallest to largest) on the *X-axis* and the frequency on the *Y-axis*. Notice on the *X-axis* that each bar in the graph spans a five-point range: The first bar has a midpoint of 15, the second bar has a midpoint of 20, and so on (the midpoints will vary from one histogram to another). The value with the greatest frequency in the graph is for a midpoint of 25, which has a frequency of four. Notice that SPSS reports the mean, standard deviation, and sample size to the right of the graph by default.

Scatterplot—*Mathexam and Satquant*

The scatterplot shown in Figure 3.15 displays the coordinates (each coordinate is indicated by a circle in the plot) for each of the participants on the variables **mathexam** and **satquant**. As we specified in the *Simple Scatterplot* dialog box earlier, the values of **mathexam** are on the *Y-axis* and the values of **satquant** are on the *X-axis*. There are 10 different coordinates in the plot, with each coordinate displaying the scores on the two variables for an individual. The coordinate on the far right of the plot, for example, represents the scores on **mathexam** and **satquant** for the third participant, with scores of 34 and 600, respectively.

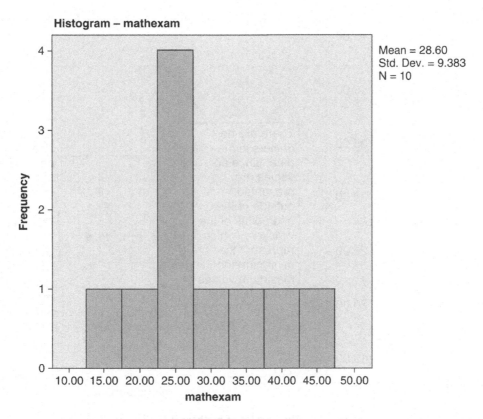

Figure 3.14 **The histogram of mathexam.**

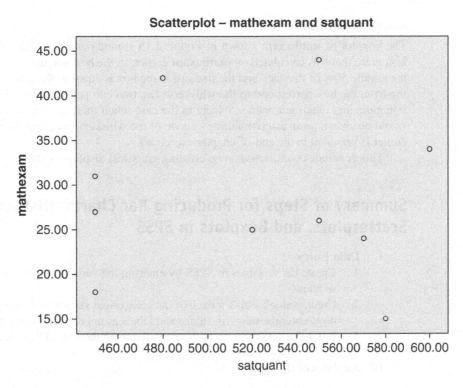

Figure 3.15 **The scatterplot of mathexam and satquant.**

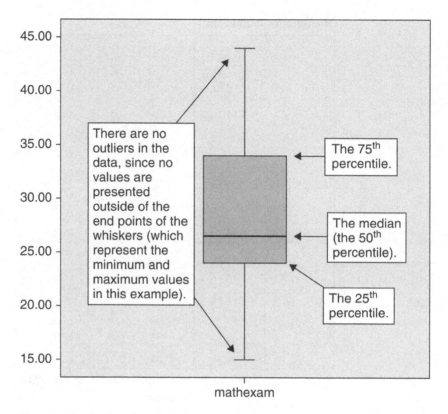

Figure 3.16 **The boxplot of mathexam.**

Boxplot—*Mathexam*

The boxplot of **mathexam** shown in Figure 3.16 summarizes the scores differently from the histogram that was calculated on **mathexam** earlier. In the boxplot, the rectangular box contains the middle 50% of the data, and the line inside the box is equal to the median. The lines extending from the box correspond to the whiskers. The two end points of the whiskers represent the minimum and maximum values, except in the case when there are one or more outliers, which would be shown as an asterisk falling outside of the whiskers (an example of a boxplot with an outlier is provided in the end-of-chapter exercises).

This concludes our discussion on creating graphical displays of data.

Summary of Steps for Producing Bar Charts, Histograms, Scatterplots, and Boxplots in SPSS

I. Data Entry

1. Create the variables in SPSS by entering the variable names in the *Variable View* window.
2. Create value labels for each of the categorical variables. In the *Variable View* window, enter the numeric values and labels as appropriate. Click *OK*.
3. Enter the data for each of the participants in the *Data View* window.

II. Analysis of the Data

Obtaining a Bar Chart
1. From the menu bar, select **Graphs > Legacy Dialogs > Bar . . .**
2. In the *Bar Charts* dialog box, leave the default option *Simple* selected. Click *Define*.

3. In the *Define Simple Bar: Summaries for Groups of Cases* dialog box, move the variable of interest to *Category Axis* box.
4. Click *OK*.

Obtaining a Histogram
1. From the menu bar, select **Graphs > Legacy Dialogs > Histogram . . .**
2. In the *Histogram* dialog box, move the variable of interest to the *Variable* box.
3. Click *OK*.

Obtaining a Scatterplot
1. From the menu bar, select **Graphs > Legacy Dialogs > Scatter/Dot . . .**
2. In the *Scatter/Dot* dialog box, leave the default option *Simple Scatter* selected. Click *Define*.
3. In the *Simple Scatterplot* dialog box, move one variable to the *Y-axis* box and the other variable to the *X-axis* box.
4. Click *OK*.

Obtaining a Boxplot
1. From the menu bar, select **Graphs > Legacy Dialogs > Boxplot . . .**
2. In the *Boxplot* dialog box, leave the default option *Simple* selected. Under *Data in Chart Are*, select *Summaries of Separate Variables*. Click *Define*.
3. In the *Define Simple Boxplot: Summaries of Separate Variables* dialog box, move the variable of interest to the *Boxes Represent* box.
4. Click *OK*.

Exercises

1. Data were collected from 10 sophomores at a local university, including their **gender** (1 = "male," 2 = "female"), the number of hours they studied per day (**hoursstudied**), the number of cups of coffee they drank per day (**cupscoffee**), and their grade point average (**gpa**). The data are in the file *Chapter 3_Exercise 1.sav* in the Chapter 3 folder online at www.routledge.com/cw/yockey. Open the file and perform the appropriate analyses in SPSS to answer the questions below.
   a. Create a bar chart for **gender** and print your results. How many males and females are in the data set?
   b. Create a histogram for **hoursstudied** and print your results. What is the mean number of hours studied per day?
   c. Create a scatterplot using the variables **gpa** and **hoursstudied** and print your results (put **gpa** on the *Y-axis*).
   d. Create a boxplot of **cupscoffee** and print your results. Are there any outliers in the plot?
2. The data file *Chapter 3_Exercise 2.sav* contains data on 15 people including whether or not they had allergies (**allergy**; 1 = "yes," 2 = "no"), the number of (sick) visits made to a doctor over the last year (**doctorvisits**), and the number of days missed from work during that same time period (**daysmissed**). Open the file and perform the appropriate analyses in SPSS to answer the questions below (the file is located in the Chapter 3 folder at www.routledge.com/cw/yockey).
   a. Create a bar chart for **allergy** and print your results. How many people have allergies? How many people do not have allergies?
   b. Create a histogram of **daysmissed** and print your results. What is the mean number of days missed per year?
   c. Create a boxplot of **doctorvisits**. Are there any outliers in the plot?
3. Data were collected from seven children including the number of times per week (on average) they ate fast food (**fastfood**) and the degree to which they like **corn, carrots,**

and **cabbage** (expressed on a 1–10 scale with higher scores indicating more favorable ratings). The data are in the file *Chapter 3_Exercise 3.sav* in the Chapter 3 folder online at www.routledge.com/cw/yockey. Open the file and perform the appropriate analyses in SPSS to answer the questions below.

a. Create a histogram of **fastfood** and print your results.
b. Create a histogram of **corn** and print your results. What is the mean rating for **corn**?
c. Create a scatterplot for **fastfood** and **carrots** and print your results (put **carrots** on the *Y-axis*).
d. Create a boxplot for **cabbage**. Are there any outliers in the plot?

Reliability (as Measured by Coefficient Alpha)

R eliability refers to the consistency or repeatability of scores on some measure of interest. For example, consider a 10-item measure of assertiveness given twice over a two-week period to a group of participants. If the participants' responses to the items are the same or are very similar across the two administrations, then the measure would possess a high degree of reliability. If the responses are fairly different across the two administrations, then the scale would possess a fairly low degree of reliability.

While there are several different methods of estimating reliability, most fall into one of two types: reliability based on multiple administrations of a measure and reliability based on a single administration of a measure.[1] Assessing reliability over multiple administrations of a measure consists of administering a scale on two different occasions and measuring the consistency of participants' responses to the items over the two administrations. For this type of reliability, **test-retest** reliability (administering the same measure twice) and **alternate form** reliability (administering two very similar versions of a measure once each) are two commonly used methods.

Reliability over a single administration of a measure consists of administering a scale once and measuring the consistency of the participants' responses across the items of the measure. Two different types of reliability for a single administration of a measure are **split-half** reliability and **coefficient alpha** (also known as Cronbach's alpha). With split-half reliability, the measure is split in half and the consistency of the participants' responses on the two halves is estimated. Coefficient alpha, on the other hand, is not calculated on a single split of a measure but is instead mathematically equivalent to the mean of all possible splits that could have been taken of the measure. When using either split-half reliability or coefficient alpha as an estimate of the reliability of a measure, it is important that all of the items on the scale measure the same characteristic; otherwise the internal consistency will most likely be reduced. In this chapter, we'll focus on coefficient alpha, which is one of the most commonly used methods of estimating the reliability of a measure.

Values of coefficient alpha typically range from 0 to 1 with higher values indicating greater internal consistency among a set of items.[2] Shown in Figure 4.1 is an approximate guideline of the adequacy of a range of different values of coefficient alpha.

An example in which coefficient alpha may be used is presented next.

Coefficient Alpha	Adequacy
.90 and above	Excellent
.80 – .89	Good
.70 – .79	Fair
.60 – .69	Marginal
.59 and below	Poor

Figure 4.1 **Adequacy of internal consistency reliability estimates for different values of coefficient alpha.**

Example

As part of a research project, a student wanted to estimate the internal consistency reliability of a five-item measure of meaning in life, which is presented in Figure 4.2.

The range of responses for each item on the meaning in life scale shown in Figure 4.2 is from 1–5, where 1 = strongly disagree and 5 = strongly agree. A total score on the scale may be calculated by adding together the responses on the five items, with total scores ranging from 5–25 for each participant. Higher scores on the scale correspond to higher levels of meaning in life. Twenty-five college students responded to the five-item measure.

Items on the Meaning in Life Scale	Strongly Disagree	Disagree	Neither Disagree nor Agree	Agree	Strongly Agree
1. I feel good about the direction of my life.	1	2	3	4	5
2. My life has meaning.	1	2	3	4	5
3. In general, I feel like I'm on track in my life.	1	2	3	4	5
4. I never feel lost in my life.	1	2	3	4	5
5. I'm currently working toward fulfilling my goals in life.	1	2	3	4	5

Figure 4.2 **Items on the meaning in life scale. For each item, the response options are 1 (strongly disagree), 2 (disagree), 3 (neither disagree nor agree), 4 (agree), and 5 (strongly agree). Each participant was instructed to choose only one response option for each question.**

If the items on the meaning in life scale have a high degree of internal consistency (i.e., if the scale is reliable), then the participants should respond in a fairly consistent manner to each of the items on the scale. For example, for the items presented in Figure 4.2, people who have a high degree of meaning in life should agree or strongly agree with the items, while people with a low degree of meaning in life should disagree or strongly disagree with the items. This type of consistent response pattern for the participants will result in a high value of coefficient alpha since the participants are responding in a consistent manner on the scale (e.g., one person agrees with all the items, another person disagrees with the items, etc.). The exception to this rule is when one or more negative items are included on the scale, which is discussed next.

Negative Items and Reverse Coding

The meaning in life scale shown in Figure 4.2 is written so that a person with a high degree of meaning in life would tend to agree or strongly agree with each item on the scale (assuming the scale is reliable). Some measures, however, are designed with a mixture of items, where a person high on the characteristic of interest would agree with some items and *disagree* with others. Those items that a person high on the characteristic of interest would disagree with are known as *negative* items. (An example of a negative item would be if item 2 in Figure 4.2 was rewritten as "My life has *little* meaning." A person with a high degree of meaning in life would most likely disagree or strongly disagree with this item.) If a scale contains one or more negative items, each of these items needs to be reverse coded prior to estimating the internal consistency of the scale. Reverse coding is a process where the responses to the negative items are literally reversed, so that a 1 becomes a 5, a 2 becomes a 4, and so on. Reverse coding of items is illustrated in Appendix A.

Objective and Data Requirements of Coefficient Alpha

Coefficient Alpha

Objective	Data Requirements	Example
To estimate the internal consistency of responses on a measure.	Scores on at least two items (variables) are required (although more than two items are recommended). All items should measure the same trait or characteristic.	Meaning in life scale, consisting of five items (variables). The internal consistency of the participants' responses on the five items will be determined.

The Data

The responses of the 20 participants to each of the five items of the meaning in life scale are presented in Figure 4.3. Each row in the table contains the responses for a participant, and the columns represent the different items on the scale. **Meaning1** corresponds to the responses on the first item on the scale, **meaning2** corresponds to the responses on the second item, and so on.

Participant	meaning1	meaning2	meaning3	meaning4	meaning5
1	5	5	4	5	4
2	2	3	2	1	3
3	1	2	2	1	2
4	5	5	5	4	5
5	3	4	4	2	3
6	5	5	2	4	3
7	5	4	4	3	4
8	4	4	4	4	4
9	5	4	4	4	3
10	4	5	5	4	3
11	5	5	5	5	5
12	3	2	2	3	3
13	1	1	1	2	1
14	5	5	5	5	5
15	5	4	4	4	5
16	4	4	3	4	3
17	4	4	4	4	3
18	5	5	5	5	5
19	5	4	5	5	4
20	4	5	5	5	4

Figure 4.3 **The responses of the participants on the five items of the meaning in life scale. (*Note*: The participant variable is included for illustration but will not be entered into SPSS.)**

Data Entry and Analysis in SPSS

Steps 1 and 2 below describe how to enter the data in SPSS. The data file is also available online at www.routledge.com/cw/yockey under the name *meaning.sav* in the Chapter 4 folder. If you prefer to open the file from the web site, skip to Step 3.

Step 1: Create the Variables

1. Start SPSS.
2. Click the *Variable View* tab.

   In SPSS, five variables will be created, one for each item of the meaning in life scale. The variables will be named **meaning1**, **meaning2**, **meaning3**, **meaning4**, and **meaning5**, respectively.

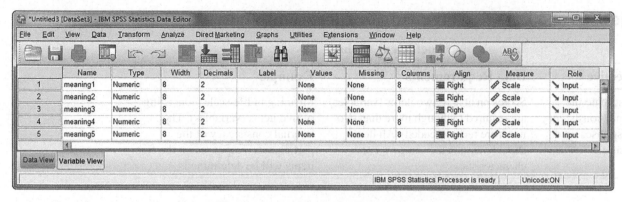

Figure 4.4 The *Variable View* window with the variables meaning1–meaning5 entered.

3. Enter the variable names **meaning1**, **meaning2**, **meaning3**, **meaning4**, and **meaning5**, respectively, in the first five rows of the *Variable View* window. Under *Measure*, classify all five variables as scale (see Figure 4.4).

Step 2: Enter the Data

1. Click the *Data View* tab. The variables **meaning1**, **meaning2**, **meaning3**, **meaning4**, and **meaning5**, respectively, appear in the first five columns of the *Data View* window.
2. Consulting Figure 4.3, enter the scores for each of the participants on the five variables of interest. For the first participant, enter the scores *5, 5, 4, 5* and *4*, for the variables **meaning1**, **meaning2**, **meaning3**, **meaning4**, and **meaning5**, respectively. Using this approach, enter the data for all 20 participants. The completed data file is shown in Figure 4.5.

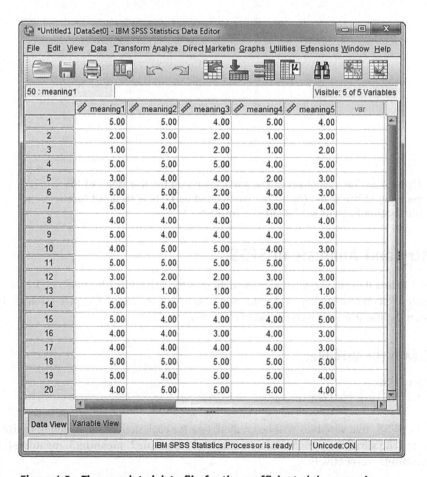

Figure 4.5 The completed data file for the coefficient alpha example.

Step 3: Analyze the Data

1. From the menu bar, select **Analyze > Scale > Reliability Analysis** . . . (see Figure 4.6).

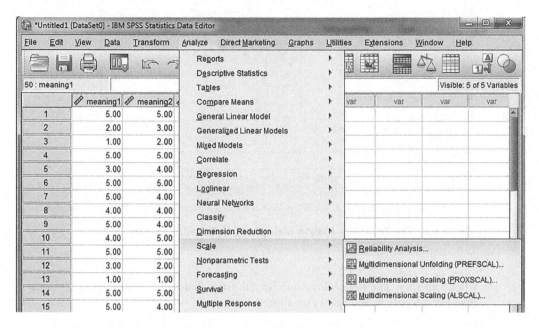

Figure 4.6   **Menu commands for the *Reliability Analysis* procedure.**

2. A *Reliability Analysis* dialog box appears with the variables **meaning1–meaning5** in the left-hand side of the dialog box (see Figure 4.7).

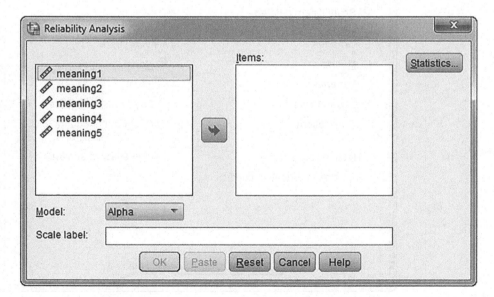

Figure 4.7   **The *Reliability Analysis* dialog box.**

3. Select the variable **meaning1** and press and hold down the *Shift* key. With the *Shift* key continued to be held down, select the variable **meaning5**. All five variables should be selected. Click the right-arrow button (⮕) to move the variables to the *Items* box (see Figure 4.8 on page 52 for details).

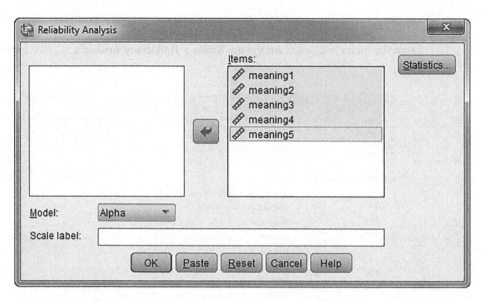

Figure 4.8 The *Reliability Analysis* dialog box (continued).

4. Click *Statistics*. The *Reliability Analysis: Statistics* dialog box opens. Under *Descriptives for* select *Item* and *Scale* (see Figure 4.9).

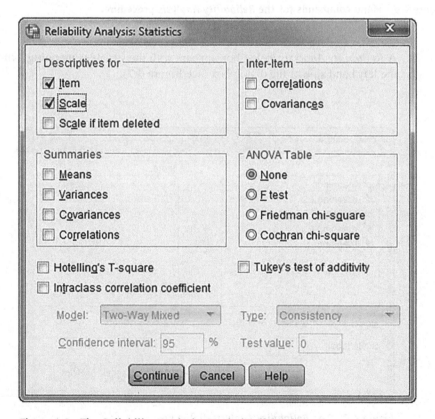

Figure 4.9 The *Reliability Analysis: Statistics* dialog box.

5. Click *Continue*.
6. Click *OK*.

The reliability procedure runs in SPSS and the results are presented in the *Viewer* window.

Step 4: Interpret the Results

The output of the reliability analysis is displayed in Figure 4.10.

Case Processing Summary

The first table, *Case Processing Summary*, shows the number of cases (participants) used in calculating the reliability of the scale. An *N* of 20 is presented in the table, indicating that all 20 participants were included in the analysis (they had complete data on all five variables).

Reliability
Scale: ALL VARIABLES

Case Processing Summary

		N	%
Cases	Valid	20	100.0
	Excluded[a]	0	.0
	Total	20	100.0

a. Listwise deletion based on all variables in the procedure.

Reliability Statistics

Cronbach's Alpha	N of Items
.943	5

The value of coefficient alpha for the 5–item meaning in life scale.

Item Statistics

	Mean	Std. Deviation	N
meaning1	4.0000	1.33771	20
meaning2	4.0000	1.16980	20
meaning3	3.7500	1.29269	20
meaning4	3.7000	1.30182	20
meaning5	3.6000	1.09545	20

Scale Statistics

Mean	Variance	Std. Deviation	N of Items
19.0500	31.418	5.60521	5

Figure 4.10 **Output for the reliability procedure.**

Reliability Statistics

The second table, *Reliability Statistics*, displays the value of coefficient alpha (also called Cronbach's alpha) for the five-item scale. The value of coefficient alpha is .94 (rounded to two decimal places), which indicates a very high degree of internal consistency among the items on the scale.

Item Statistics

The next table, *Item Statistics*, displays the mean, standard deviation, and sample size for each of the items on the scale. Examining the means of the five items shown in the *Item Statistics* table, notice that the participants had the highest mean rating on items 1 (**meaning1**) and 2 (**meaning2**), with an average response of 4.00, which corresponds to a response of "agree" on the scale. The remaining three items had mean responses between 3.60 and 3.75. Item 1 was the most variable, with a standard deviation of approximately 1.34 (the standard deviations were fairly similar across all five items). Overall, the participants' responses on the five items indicated that they found their lives to be fairly meaningful, with a mean response on each of the items either equal to or in the direction of "agree" on the scale (i.e., a value of 4.00).

Scale Statistics

The last table, *Scale Statistics*, provides the mean, variance, standard deviation, and number of items for the total scale (the total scale is equal to the sum of the five items). With a possible range of 5 to 25 on the scale, the mean of the five-item scale is 19.05 with a standard deviation of 5.61. Therefore, the participants rate fairly highly on personal meaning, since the mean scale rating of 19.05 is approaching the high end of the scale. The mean of the scale is an alternative way of assessing where the participants fall on the characteristic of interest, and it is equal to the sum of the means of the five items (4.00 + 4.00 + 3.75 + 3.70 + 3.60 = 19.05).

Expression of the Results

Beginning with this chapter, a brief write-up of the results of each procedure will be presented. In writing the results of a reliability analysis, the value of coefficient alpha and the mean and standard deviation of the entire scale will be presented (the mean and standard deviation of the individual items may also be presented in a table if desired). A sample write-up of the results is presented below.

Written Results

A study was conducted to estimate the internal consistency of the five-item meaning in life scale. Coefficient alpha for the scale was .94, indicating a high degree of internal consistency among the items on the scale. The means of the individual items ranged from 3.65 to 4.00, with a mean on the total scale of 19.05 (*SD* = 5.61). Overall, the participants' responses on the scale indicated that they possessed a fairly high degree of meaning in their lives. The mean and standard deviation of the items of the meaning in life scale are provided in Figure 4.11.[3]

Item	M	SD
1	4.00	1.34
2	4.00	1.17
3	3.75	1.29
4	3.70	1.30
5	3.60	1.10

Figure 4.11 **The mean and standard deviation of the items of the meaning in life scale.**

Summary of Steps for Conducting a Reliability Analysis in SPSS

I. **Data Entry and Analysis**
 1. Create as many variables in SPSS as there are items on the scale.
 2. Enter the participants' responses to each of the items on the scale.
 3. Select **Analyze > Scale > Reliability Analysis . . .**
 4. Move each of the items on the scale to the *Items* box.
 5. Click *Statistics*. Under *Descriptives for* select *Item* and *Scale*. Click *Continue*.
 6. Click *OK*.

II. **Interpretation of the Results**
 1. Note the value of coefficient (Cronbach's) alpha in the *Reliability Statistics* table.
 2. Inspect the *Item Statistics* table and the *Scale Statistics* table to determine the mean response on the items and total scale, respectively.
 3. Write the results indicating the value of coefficient alpha and the mean and standard deviation of the total scale (the mean and standard deviation of each of the items may also be presented in a table if desired).

Exercises

1. A researcher administered a seven-item measure of resident satisfaction to 20 nursing home residents, whose responses are provided in Figure 4.12. For each item on the measure, a 1 corresponds to a response of strongly disagree and a 7 corresponds to a response of strongly agree. Higher scores on the scale indicate greater levels of resident satisfaction with the nursing home.

item1	item2	item3	item4	item5	item6	item7
4	3	5	4	4	3	4
1	2	1	1	5	1	2
4	5	2	3	1	1	1
4	3	2	1	1	4	2
6	5	4	2	2	3	1
4	2	6	6	4	2	3
4	2	1	1	5	4	5
4	3	3	2	5	4	6
4	1	1	2	4	4	2
5	4	6	4	5	7	7
5	6	4	2	2	4	7
2	4	6	5	7	7	5
2	4	6	5	4	4	7
1	1	4	2	2	4	2
2	3	4	4	5	4	2
4	6	2	3	5	5	4
2	4	3	4	2	3	4
2	4	5	6	4	4	5
2	4	6	6	5	4	5
6	4	5	5	6	4	5

Figure 4.12   **The seven items of the resident satisfaction scale.**

Enter the data in SPSS and perform the appropriate analyses to answer the questions below. Name the variables **item1–item7**, respectively.
a. What is the reliability (Cronbach's alpha) of the scale?
b. How would you characterize the reliability?
c. Provide a written summary of your reliability analysis. Be sure to include the overall reliability of the scale and the mean and standard deviation of the total scale in your written results.

2. The responses of 30 people on a 10-item measure of resilience are provided in the file *Chapter 4_Exercise 2.sav* in the Chapter 4 folder online at www.routledge.com/cw/yockey (the variables are named **resilience1** to **resilience10**, respectively). The range of possible responses on each of the items is from 1 (strongly disagree) to 7 (strongly agree), with higher scores indicating greater resilience. Open the file in SPSS and perform the appropriate analyses to answer the questions below.
a. What is the reliability (Cronbach's alpha) of the scale?
b. How would you characterize the reliability?
c. Provide a written summary of your reliability analysis. Be sure to include the overall reliability of the scale and the mean and standard deviation of the total scale in your written results.

3. A student used two different scales for a research project, with one scale measuring self-confidence and the other scale measuring manual dexterity. He calculated coefficient alpha on the combined scales and found an overall reliability coefficient of .41. Why might the reliability be so low?

Notes

1. Interrater reliability is one type of reliability that does not fall into either of these categories. Interrater reliability measures the consistency of raters or judges who are assessing some characteristic of interest.
2. While coefficient alpha can be negative, this typically indicates that an error has been made in the calculation, such as including one or more negative items that have not been reverse coded in the estimate (negative items will be discussed shortly).
3. *M* and *SD* are abbreviations for the mean and standard deviation, respectively, using the format of the American Psychological Association (APA).

Inferential Statistics

Unit II is the heart of the text and consists of many commonly used inferential procedures. The following chapters are included in the second unit: the one-sample *t* test (Chapter 5), the independent-samples *t* test (Chapter 6), the dependent-samples *t* test (Chapter 7), the one-way between subjects ANOVA (Chapter 8), the two-way between subjects ANOVA (Chapter 9), the one-way within subjects ANOVA (Chapter 10), the one-between–one-within subjects ANOVA (Chapter 11), correlation (Chapter 12), simple regression (Chapter 13), multiple regression (Chapter 14), the chi-square goodness of fit test (Chapter 15), and the chi-square test of independence (Chapter 16).

Before starting Chapter 5 (the one-sample *t* test), it would be beneficial to review some terminology relevant to hypothesis testing. If you are new to statistics, consulting a chapter on hypothesis testing from an introductory statistics textbook may also be helpful.

Samples and Populations

In statistics, we frequently talk about samples and populations. A **population** consists of an entire collection of events of interest and a **sample** is a smaller part (or subset) of the population. Suppose, for example, that we wanted to conduct research on cell phone usage in the United States and randomly selected 200 cell phone users from various U.S. cities. All people who own a cell phone in the United States would make up the population, and the 200 people selected for the study would make up the sample. In practice, we almost always work with samples, as populations are either too costly or difficult to obtain.

Inferential Statistics

Inferential statistics are statistical procedures that use samples to make generalizations about populations. For example, consider trying to forecast the winner in a presidential election. Using inferential statistics, with a relatively small sample (e.g., 2000 people), statements about the population of *all* U.S. voters can be made with a fairly high degree of accuracy (assuming the sample is representative of the population from which it comes). Inferential statistics are extremely useful because they allow us to draw conclusions about populations based on limited information (i.e., samples).

Hypothesis Testing

When we use a sample to make an inference about a population, we engage in a process known as **hypothesis testing**. In hypothesis testing, it is customary to state two hypotheses, a **null hypothesis** and an **alternative hypothesis**. The **null hypothesis** typically states that a treatment did *not* have an effect, while the **alternative hypothesis** states that the treatment had an effect. Suppose, for example, that a new therapy is being evaluated to determine if it helps people who are suffering from depression. The null hypothesis would state that the therapy did *not* have an effect on depression (i.e., it did not change the way people felt), while the alternative hypothesis would state that the therapy had an effect on depression (i.e., it changed the way people felt). In hypothesis testing, we evaluate the null hypothesis with the purpose of either rejecting it or not rejecting it. If, based on the results found in our study, the null hypothesis seems reasonable, we do *not* reject it. If, however, the null hypothesis seems unreasonable, we reject it (and side with the alternative hypothesis).

One-Tailed and Two-Tailed Tests

Hypotheses are evaluated using either a **two-tailed** test or a **one-tailed** test. A two-tailed test is used when a treatment is evaluated to see whether it has an impact in either direction (to see if scores are higher *or* lower), while a one-tailed test is used when the intent is to investigate only a single direction (*only* higher or *only* lower). Consider an example where two different therapies are investigated to see which one is more effective at helping people with anxiety (we'll refer to the therapies as therapy A and therapy B). A two-tailed test would allow for the possibility of *either* therapy being more effective (i.e., either A < B or B < A), while a one-tailed test would specify beforehand a single direction to be investigated (e.g., A < B). The advantage of a one-tailed test is that it has a greater chance of finding the effect (assuming it exists in the hypothesized direction); the disadvantage of a one-tailed test is that if the effect is located in the opposite direction of what was anticipated, it cannot be declared. In practice, two-tailed tests are more common in research, and for this reason they will be emphasized in this text.

Type I and Type II Errors

Recall that in hypothesis testing samples are used to make inferences about populations. Because samples are incomplete "pictures" of populations, it is possible to make a mistake in the hypothesis testing process. There are two different types of mistakes that can be made—a Type I error and a Type II error. A **Type I error** occurs if the null hypothesis is rejected when it is true (if it is true, it should not have been rejected). A **Type II error** occurs if the null hypothesis is *not* rejected when it is false (if it is false, it should have been rejected). Both are errors in hypothesis testing since the conclusion made from the hypothesis test is contrary to the true situation.

Power

While Type I and Type II errors are mistakes in hypothesis testing, power is concerned with making a correct decision. **Power** is equal to the probability of rejecting the null hypothesis when it is false (if the null hypothesis is false and it is rejected, a correct decision has been made). Power ranges from 0 to 1, with higher values indicating greater power. Power of .80, for example, means that there is an 80% chance of rejecting the null hypothesis prior to conducting the study. (Put another way, if a study was conducted many times, power of .80 means that 80% of the time the null hypothesis would be rejected—a correct decision—and 20% of the time it would not be rejected—a Type II error.)

Sampling Error

Sampling error is a very important concept in inferential statistics and it's one that, if understood, will make following the logic of hypothesis testing easier. Consider a problem where two different strategies for remembering words are compared. Suppose that there is no difference between the two strategies so that whichever strategy is used, the number of words recalled is the same *in the population*. Imagine that I took a sample of 10 people and gave them the first strategy, and then I took a sample of another 10 people and gave them the second strategy, and then compared the number of words recalled for the two groups. While the strategies result in the same number of words recalled *in the population*, it is extremely unlikely that the number of words recalled for the two groups will be the same *in the samples*. This is because samples are subsets of the population, and since only part of the population is taken, it will not be represented perfectly. Generally speaking, the smaller the sample, the larger the discrepancy between the sample and the population. The discrepancy between the sample and the population is known as **sampling error**. It is a normal part of statistics and it's important to keep it in mind in the following chapters. When different samples are drawn from the same population, the *samples* will typically not be the same (e.g., they will not have the same mean).

p-Values

Continuing with the word strategy example, if samples are not typically the same when drawn from a population, how can we determine whether there is really a meaningful difference between the samples (i.e., one strategy is really better than the other in the population), or if the difference is just due to sampling error (i.e., the strategies are the same in the population)? This decision is made based on the *p*-value obtained from the output in SPSS. A ***p*-value** indicates the exact probability of obtaining the specific results (or results even more extreme) if the null hypothesis is true. For example, in the learning strategy problem described previously, let's assume there was a difference of two words recalled between the strategies with a *p*-value of .03. The *p*-value of .03 would indicate that there is only a 3% chance of getting a difference of two words (or more) between the groups *if the null hypothesis was true*. In hypothesis testing, the *p*-value for a test is compared to a predetermined value, known as alpha (represented by the symbol α), and based on that comparison, a decision is made about the null hypothesis. In this text, we will use an alpha level of .05 (the most commonly used value in the social and behavioral sciences) and evaluate the *p*-value against that level.

The process of evaluating the *p*-value is as follows:

If the *p*-value is *less than or equal to .05* (alpha), the null hypothesis is *rejected* (a difference between the strategies is assumed).
If the *p*-value is *greater than .05* (alpha), the null hypothesis is *not rejected* (a difference between the strategies is not assumed).

In SPSS the *p*-value is reported as "*sig.*"
The decision process for hypothesis testing is summarized in the following table.

p-value (reported as "*sig.*" in SPSS)	Decision
If $p \leq .05$	Reject the null hypothesis
If $p > .05$	Do not reject the null hypothesis

Consider the examples shown in the table below. The first example shows a *p*-value of .020. With an alpha of .05, what decision would be made about the null hypothesis? Since the *p*-value of .02 is less than .05, the null hypothesis is rejected. In examples 2 and 3, the null hypothesis would not be rejected since both *p*-values (.080 and .521) are greater than .05.

Example	*p*-value (reported as "*sig.*" in SPSS)	Decision (using an alpha of .05)	Interpretation
1	.020	Reject the null hypothesis	Side with the alternative hypothesis
2	.080	Do not reject the null hypothesis	Side with the null hypothesis
3	.521	Do not reject the null hypothesis	Side with the null hypothesis

While an alpha of .05 will be used in this text, if you wish to use another value (such as .01 or .001), all you have to do is adjust your decision rule. If alpha of .01 was used, for example, all three p-values in the preceding table would lead to the null hypothesis *not* being rejected since all values are greater than .01. As is shown in this example, the value of alpha (.05 vs. .01) can make a difference in the conclusion made about the null hypothesis (i.e., whether it is rejected or not).

For each of the chapters in this unit, we will examine a p-value, and using the process detailed above, we will either reject or not reject the null hypothesis. If the null hypothesis is rejected, the result is often referred to as being "significant" or "statistically significant." If the null hypothesis is not rejected, the result is referred to as "not significant."

Effect Sizes

While hypothesis testing is a powerful tool for making inferences about populations, it is important to recognize what hypothesis testing does and does not tell us. Considering our word strategy problem again, hypothesis testing allows us to conclude, with a reasonable degree of assurance, whether or not the two strategies are *different* in the population. What hypothesis testing fails to indicate, however, is *how different* the groups are (i.e., hypothesis testing indicates that the groups are different but doesn't indicate whether the difference is small, moderate, or large). One way to describe the degree of difference between the groups is by calculating an effect size. **Effect sizes** indicate the magnitude of the results in our study. Effect sizes are described further in Chapter 5 and will be illustrated for several of the procedures described in Unit II.

This concludes our introduction to Unit II. Next we'll begin with the one-sample t test in Chapter 5.

The One-Sample *t* Test

The one-sample *t* test is used when the mean of one sample is compared to some known or estimated population mean. The sample is typically different from the population in some way, and the question of interest is whether the mean of the sample differs significantly from the mean of the population on a dependent variable of interest. An example of a one-sample *t* test is presented below.

Example

An industrial psychologist hired by a leading accounting firm wanted to know if the average number of hours worked per week at the firm was significantly different from the (hypothetical) national average of 52 hours for accountants. The industrial psychologist randomly sampled 16 people from different divisions within the firm and recorded the average number of hours they worked per week over a three-month period. The dependent variable in this study is the number of hours worked per week.

Objective and Data Requirements of the One-Sample *t* Test

The One-Sample *t* Test

Objective	Data Requirements	Example
To determine whether the mean of a sample differs significantly from some known or estimated population mean.	One sample of participants One continuous dependent variable	Accountants at leading accounting firm Dependent variable • Number of hours worked per week

Null and Alternative Hypotheses

The null hypothesis (H_0) states that the number of hours worked per week at the leading accounting firm is equal to the national average (μ) of 52 hours:

$$H_0: \mu = 52$$

The alternative hypothesis (H_1) states that the number of hours worked per week at the leading accounting firm is not equal to the national average of 52 hours:

$$H_1: \mu \neq 52$$

Evaluation of the Null Hypothesis

The one-sample *t* test provides a test of the null hypothesis that the number of hours worked per week at the accounting firm is equal to 52 hours. If the *t* test produces results that seem unlikely if the null hypothesis is true (results that occur less than 5% of the time), then the null hypothesis is rejected. If the *t* test produces results that seem fairly likely if the null hypothesis is true (results that occur greater than 5% of the time), then the null hypothesis is not rejected.[1]

Research Question

The fundamental question of interest in a research study can also be expressed in the form of a research question, such as:

> "Is the number of hours worked per week for employees at a leading accounting firm different from the national average of 52 hours?"

The Data

The data for the 16 participants are presented in Figure 5.1.

Participant	Hours worked per week
1	54
2	48
3	68
4	53
5	60
6	45
7	57
8	62
9	71
10	60
11	55
12	63
13	68
14	64
15	56
16	60

Figure 5.1 **The number of hours worked per week by the 16 employees at the leading accounting firm. (*Note*: The participant variable is included for illustration but will not be entered into SPSS.)**

Data Entry and Analysis in SPSS

Steps 1 and 2 below describe how to enter the data in SPSS. The data file is also available online at www.routledge.com/cw/yockey under the name *hours worked.sav* in the Chapter 5 folder. If you prefer to open the file from the web site, skip to Step 3.

Step 1: Create the Variable

1. Start SPSS.
2. Click the *Variable View* tab.

In SPSS, one variable will be created for the number of hours worked per week by the employees at the leading accounting firm. The variable will be named **hoursweek**.

3. Enter the name **hoursweek** and press the down arrow key (↓). Under *Measure*, classify **hoursweek** as scale. See Figure 5.2 for details.

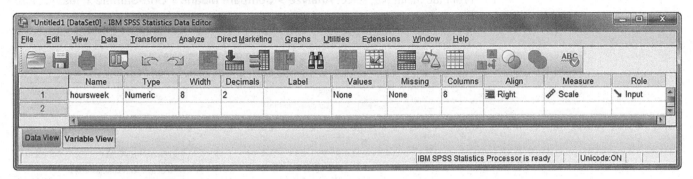

Figure 5.2 The *Variable View* window with the variable hoursweek entered.

Step 2: Enter the Data

1. Click the *Data View* tab. The variable **hoursweek** appears in the first column of the *Data View* window.
2. To enter the data for **hoursweek**, make sure the first cell in the upper left-hand corner of the window is active (if it isn't active, then click on it). Enter the number of hours worked for each of the participants, beginning with the first participant's value (*54*) and continuing until the last participant's value (*60*) has been entered. (After entering the value for a participant, press either the down-arrow key (↓) or the *Enter* button to move to the next row in the *Data View* window.) The completed data file in presented in Figure 5.3.

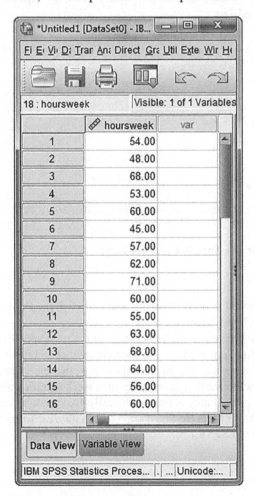

Figure 5.3 The completed data file for the one-sample *t* test example.

Step 3: Analyze the Data

1. From the menu bar, select **Analyze > Compare Means > One-Sample T Test** . . . (see Figure 5.4).

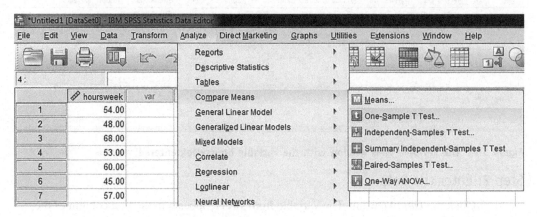

Figure 5.4 **Menu commands for the one-sample *t* test.**

2. A *One-Sample T Test* dialog box appears with the variable **hoursweek** on the left-hand side of the dialog box (see Figure 5.5).

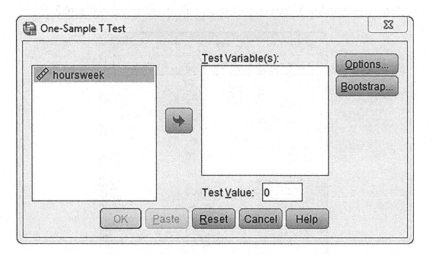

Figure 5.5 **The *One-Sample T Test* dialog box.**

3. Select the dependent variable, **hoursweek**, and click the right-arrow button (➡) to move it into the *Test Variable(s)* box.
4. In the *Test Value* box, enter *52*. This is the value that is specified in the null hypothesis. See Figure 5.6 for details. [*Note*: This step is critical and is often overlooked. If the default value of zero is left in the *Test Value* box, the one-sample *t* would test whether the employees at the leading accounting firm work significantly different from *zero* hours per week (which they certainly should!). Be sure to always enter the value specified in the null hypothesis (in this case, 52) into the *Test Value* box when performing a one-sample *t* test in SPSS.]
5. Click *OK*.

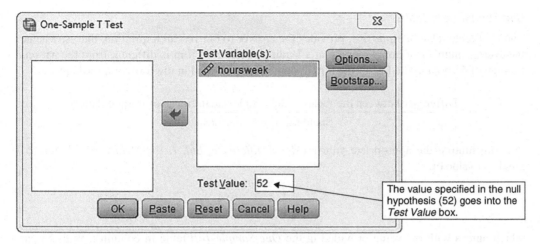

Figure 5.6 **The *One-Sample T Test* dialog box (continued).**

The one-sample *t* test procedure runs in SPSS and the results are presented in the *Viewer* window.

One-Sample Statistics

	N	Mean	Std. Deviation	Std. Error Mean
hoursweek	16	59.0000	7.14609	1.78652

> The *Mean Difference* of 7.00 is equal to the difference between the mean number of hours worked per week at the leading accounting firm (59), and the value of 52 (the population for accountants) specified in the null hypothesis.

One-Sample Test

	Test Value = 52					
				Mean Difference	95% Confidence Interval of the Difference	
	t	df	Sig. (2-tailed)		Lower	Upper
hoursweek	3.918	15	.001	7.00000	3.1921	10.8079

> Since the *p*–value of .001 is less than .05, the null hypothesis is rejected.

Figure 5.7 **Output for the one-sample *t* test.**

Step 4: Interpret the Results

The output of the one-sample *t* test is displayed in Figure 5.7.

One-Sample Statistics Table

The first table of output, *One-Sample Statistics*, displays the sample size (*N*), mean, standard deviation, and standard error of the mean for the sample. Notice that the average number of hours worked per week at the leading accounting firm is 59, which is seven hours more than the national average of 52. Whether this difference (of seven hours) is large enough to be statistically significant will be considered next.

One-Sample Test Table

The next table, *One-Sample Test*, provides the answer to our research question, that is, whether the average number of hours worked at a leading accounting firm is different from the national average of 52 hours. The test of the null hypothesis is provided in the form of a *t*, where:

$$t = \frac{\text{Difference between the mean of the sample and the mean of the population}}{\text{Standard error of the mean}}$$

Substituting the appropriate values (*Mean Difference, Std. Error Mean*) from Figure 5.7 yields a *t* value of:

$$t = \frac{7}{1.78652} = 3.918$$

which agrees with the value provided in the *One-Sample Test* table in column *t*. With 16 participants, the degrees of freedom (*df*) are equal to 15 (number of participants − 1), with a corresponding *p*-value of .001. Because the *p*-value of .001 is less than .05, the null hypothesis that the average number of hours worked per week at the leading accounting firm is equal to 52 is rejected. Since the test is significant, inspecting the mean (once again) for the 16 participants from the *One-Sample Statistics* table shows that the average number of hours worked at the accounting firm (59) was significantly higher than the national average of 52.

Effect Sizes

As was described in the Unit II introduction, hypothesis testing indicates whether or not there is a significant difference between the groups (answering a yes/no question), while effect sizes provide an indication of the *magnitude* of the results (answering a "To what degree?" question). In the current example, with hypothesis testing we concluded that there was a difference in the number of hours worked between the employees at the leading accounting firm and the national average. An effect size will now be calculated to express how large that difference is.

A commonly used effect size statistic for the one-sample *t* test is Cohen's *d*, where

$$d = \frac{\text{Difference between the mean of the sample and the mean of the population}}{\text{Standard deviation}}$$

Substituting the appropriate values from Figure 5.7 (*Mean Difference, Std. Deviation*) yields a *d* of

$$d = \frac{7}{7.15} = .98$$

Jacob Cohen (1988), a pioneer in the development of effect size measures, provided guidelines for what constitutes small, medium, and large effect sizes in practice. While the guidelines provided by Cohen are in widespread use (and will also be used in this text), it should be noted that they are only approximations (a sentiment stressed by Cohen) and can vary considerably across disciplines.

Cohen's guidelines for small, medium, and large effect sizes for the one-sample *t* test are .20, .50, and .80, respectively. These values indicate the amount of difference between the sample mean and the population mean in terms of standard deviation units. Therefore, a value of .20 indicates one-fifth of a standard deviation difference between the groups, .50 indicates one-half of a standard deviation difference, and .80 indicates eight-tenths of a standard deviation difference. Using Cohen's conventions, a *d* of .98 corresponds to a large effect in practice and indicates a difference of almost one standard deviation in the number of hours worked between the employees at the leading accounting firm and the national average for accountants (with the employees at the leading accounting firm working more).[2]

Expression of the Results in APA Format

For each of the chapters in Unit II, a write-up of the results will be provided using the format of the American Psychological Association (APA). Specific guidelines for APA format may be found in the *Publication Manual of the American Psychological Association* (2009).[3]

In writing the results, the conclusion of the hypothesis test, the degrees of freedom, the *t* value, the *p*-value, and effect size are reported along with the mean and standard deviation of the sample. An example of a brief write-up in APA format is presented next.

Written Results

Employees at a leading accounting firm ($M = 59.00$, $SD = 7.15$) work significantly more hours per week than the national average of 52 hours, $t(15) = 3.92$, $p < .05$, $d = 0.98$.

Assumptions of the One-Sample *t* Test

For each of the chapters in Unit II, the assumptions of the statistical procedures will be described. Assumptions are important because, if they are not met, the results of a given statistical procedure can be untrustworthy (i.e., the *p*-values can be inaccurate). Whether a test is compromised by an assumption violation, however, depends both on the specific assumption that is violated (some assumptions are much worse than others to violate) and the degree to which the assumption is not met. The assumptions of the one-sample *t* test are described next.

1. *The observations are independent.*
   This assumption should be satisfied by designing your study so the participants do not influence each other in any way. Violating this assumption can seriously compromise the accuracy of the one-sample *t* test. If there is reason to believe the independence assumption has been violated, the one-sample *t* test should not be used.
2. *The dependent variable is normally distributed in the population.*
   This assumption means that the number of hours worked per week should be normally distributed in the population. For moderate to large samples sizes ($N \geq 30$), most types of nonnormal distributions tend to have relatively little impact on the accuracy of the *t* test, although some nonnormal distributions can adversely affect the power of the *t* test. One remedy for nonnormal data is to perform a nonlinear transformation on the data; nonlinear transformations, however, are beyond the scope of this text [the interested reader is referred to Tabachnick and Fidell (2007) for more information on nonlinear transformations].

Summary of Steps for Conducting a One-Sample *t* Test in SPSS

I. **Data Entry and Analysis**
   1. Create one variable in SPSS.
   2. Enter the data.
   3. Select **Analyze > Compare Means > One-Sample T Test . . .**
   4. Move the dependent variable to the *Test Variable(s)* box.
   5. In the *Test Value* box, enter the value specified in the null hypothesis.
   6. Click *OK*.

II. Interpretation of the Results

1. Check the *p*-value [reported as "*Sig.*" (*2-tailed*)] in the *One-Sample Test* table.
   - If $p \le .05$, the null hypothesis is rejected. Compare the mean of the sample to the mean of the population and write the results indicating whether the sample mean is greater than or less than the population mean.
   - If $p > .05$, the null hypothesis is not rejected. Write the results indicating that there is not a significant difference between the mean of the sample and the mean of the population.

Exercises

1. For a research project, a student wanted to test whether people who claim to be successful at picking winning teams in football are able to select "winners" at different than chance levels (i.e., picking winners more or less than 50% of the time). She identifies 15 people who advertise their ability to pick "winners" and records the percentage of correct picks for each person over an entire football season. The percentage of correct picks for the 15 "prognosticators" is presented in Figure 5.8.

Prognosticator	Percentage of correct picks
1	45
2	46
3	47
4	52
5	51
6	43
7	47
8	38
9	53
10	51
11	52
12	50
13	48
14	47
15	51

Figure 5.8 **Percentage of correct picks for the 15 prognosticators.**

Enter the data in SPSS and perform the appropriate analyses to answer the questions below (name the variable **success**). (*Hint*: For this problem, use a *Test Value* of 50 and do not include a % sign when entering the data.)

a. State the null and alternative hypotheses.
b. State a research question for the data.
c. Do the prognosticators pick winners at a rate different from 50%? Test at $\alpha = .05$.
d. What is the effect size? Would you characterize the effect size as small, medium, or large?
e. Write the results of the study using APA format as appropriate.

2. The mean score on a standardized math skills test is known to be 50 for the entire U.S. population of fourth graders (with higher scores indicating better performance). A new math skills training program was recently implemented at a local school district, and an administrator was charged with the task of evaluating whether the children under the new program have performance that is different than the national average (preferably the performance is *higher* than the national average, but test for either

possibility). Twenty-five fourth graders who were instructed using the new math skills program were administered the standardized math exam. The exam scores for the students are provided in the file *Chapter 5_Exercise 2.sav* in the Chapter 5 folder online at www.routledge.com/cw/yockey (the variable is named **mathscore**). Open the file in SPSS and perform the appropriate analyses to answer the questions below.

    a.   State the null and alternative hypotheses.

    b.   State a research question for the data.

    c.   Are the scores on the math exam for the fourth graders different from the national average? Test at $\alpha = .05$.

    d.   What is the effect size? Would you characterize the effect size as small, medium, or large?

    e.   Write the results of the study using APA format as appropriate.

3.   A researcher wanted to examine whether students were either in favor of or opposed to a presidential candidate. Fifty students were asked to indicate which of the following statements best reflects their opinion about the candidate.

Statement	Numeric value in the data file
I am strongly in favor of the candidate.	1
I am somewhat in favor of the candidate.	2
I am neither in favor of nor opposed to the candidate.	3
I am somewhat opposed to the candidate.	4
I am strongly opposed to the candidate.	5

The responses of the 50 participants are provided in the file *Chapter 5_ Exercise 3.sav* in the Chapter 5 folder online at www.routledge.com/cw/yockey (the variable is named **score**). Open the file in SPSS and perform the appropriate analyses to answer the questions below. (*Hint*: To investigate students' attitudes toward the candidate, test to see whether they are different from a neutral response—which implies a value of "3" in the *Test Value* box.)

    a.   State the null and alternative hypotheses.

    b.   State a research question for the data.

    c.   Are the students either in favor of or opposed to the candidate? Test at $\alpha = .05$.

    d.   What is the effect size? Would you characterize the effect size as small, medium, or large?

    e.   Write the results of the study using APA format as appropriate.

Notes

1. This assumes $\alpha = .05$ is used. If, on the other hand, $\alpha = .01$ was used, then 'unlikely' results would be those that occurred less than 1% of the time when the null hypothesis was true.

2. An alternative measure of effect in this example would be to simply state the difference in hours worked between the employees at the leading accounting firm and the national average (employees from the leading firm worked seven more hours per week on average). When the dependent variable makes sense intuitively, this is a reasonable practice (although *d* can still be reported as well). However, when the dependent variable doesn't have intuitive meaning (such as a measure of assertiveness on a 10 to 50 scale), then a standardized measure such as *d* is better.

3. While reporting the exact p-value in the written results is recommended in the 6th edition of the APA Publication Manual, the tradition of reporting "$p < .05$" is used in this text to provide continuity with classes (e.g., introductory statistics) where SPSS analyses supplement hand calculations. For those reporting results in research papers or presentations, reporting the specific p-value is recommended. For example, if a p-value of .003 is reported in SPSS, then report "$p = .003$" instead of "$p < .05$" in your written results. If a p-value of .000 is output in SPSS, report "$p < .001$."

The Independent-Samples *t* Test

The independent-samples *t* test is used when the means of two independent groups are compared on a continuous dependent variable of interest. An example of an independent-samples *t* test is presented next.

Example

A clinical psychologist wanted to investigate the relative effectiveness of cognitive-behavioral therapy and psychoanalytic therapy on depression. Thirty people suffering from depression were randomly assigned to receive one of the two therapies, with 15 people receiving cognitive-behavioral therapy and 15 receiving psychoanalytic therapy. After two months of therapy, the depression score for each participant was recorded. The independent variable in this study is the type of therapy (cognitive-behavioral, psychoanalytic) and the dependent variable is depression, with higher scores representing greater depression levels (the range of possible scores on the depression scale is from 10 to 70).

Objective and Data Requirements of the Independent-Samples *t* Test

Independent-Samples *t* Test

Objective	Data Requirements	Example
To test whether the means of two groups differ significantly on a dependent variable of interest.	One independent variable with two separate groups	Independent variable • Type of therapy (cognitive-behavioral, psychoanalytic)
	One continuous dependent variable	Dependent variable • Depression

Null and Alternative Hypotheses

The null hypothesis states that the mean depression scores for the two groups are equal in the population:

$$H_0 : \mu_{\text{psychoanalytic}} = \mu_{\text{cognitive-behavioral}}$$

The alternative hypothesis states that the mean depression scores for the two groups are not equal in the population:

$$H_1 : \mu_{\text{psychoanalytic}} \neq \mu_{\text{cognitive-behavioral}}$$

Evaluation of the Null Hypothesis

The independent-samples *t* test provides a test of the null hypothesis that the population means for the two groups are equal. If the *t* test produces results that seem unlikely if the null hypothesis is true (results that occur less than 5% of the time), then the null hypothesis is rejected. If *t* test produces results that seem fairly likely if the null hypothesis is true (results that occur greater than 5% of the time), then the null hypothesis is not rejected.

Research Question

The fundamental question of interest in a research study can also be expressed in the form of a research question, such as:

> "Is there a difference in the average depression levels between those who received cognitive-behavioral therapy and those who received psychoanalytic therapy?"

The Data

The data for the 30 participants are presented in Figure 6.1. The participants who received psychoanalytic therapy are assigned a "1" and those who received cognitive-behavioral therapy are assigned a "2."

Participant	Therapy	Depression	Participant	Therapy	Depression
1	1	57	16	2	47
2	1	61	17	2	42
3	1	67	18	2	59
4	1	63	19	2	37
5	1	51	20	2	35
6	1	55	21	2	42
7	1	45	22	2	38
8	1	62	23	2	49
9	1	41	24	2	61
10	1	36	25	2	43
11	1	55	26	2	47
12	1	57	27	2	49
13	1	70	28	2	37
14	1	62	29	2	41
15	1	58	30	2	48

Figure 6.1 **The data for the independent-samples t test example. (Note: The participant variable is included for illustration but will not be entered into SPSS.)**

Data Entry and Analysis in SPSS

Steps 1 and 2 below describe how to enter the data in SPSS. The data file is also available online at www.routledge.com/cw/yockey under the name *therapy.sav* in the Chapter 6 folder. If you prefer to open the file from the web site, skip to Step 3.

Step 1: Create the Variables

1. Start SPSS.
2. Click the *Variable View* tab.

In SPSS, two variables will be created, one for the different therapy groups (the independent variable) and one for the depression scores (the dependent variable). The variables will be named **therapy** and **depression**, respectively.

3. Enter the variable names **therapy** and **depression**, respectively, in the first two rows of the *Variable View* window. Under *Measure*, classify **therapy** as nominal and **depression** as scale (see Figure 6.2 for details).

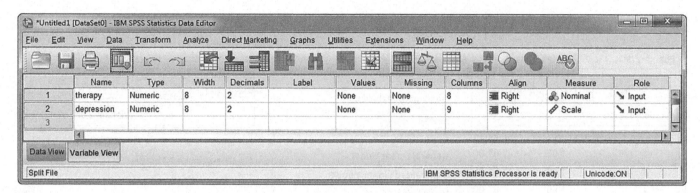

Figure 6.2   The *Variable* View window with the variables therapy and depression entered.

4. Using the process described in Chapter 1, create value labels for the variable **therapy**. For **therapy**, 1 = "psychoanalytic" and 2 = "cognitive-behavioral."

Step 2: Enter the Data

1. Click the *Data View* tab. The variables **therapy** and **depression** appear in the first two columns of the *Data View* window.
2. Consulting Figure 6.1, enter the values for each of the participants on the two variables of interest. For the first participant, enter the values *1* and *57* for the variables **therapy** and **depression**, respectively. Using this approach, enter the data for all 30 participants. The completed data set is presented in Figure 6.3.

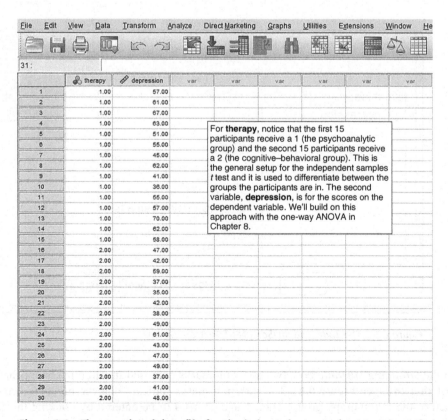

For **therapy**, notice that the first 15 participants receive a 1 (the psychoanalytic group) and the second 15 participants receive a 2 (the cognitive–behavioral group). This is the general setup for the independent samples *t* test and it is used to differentiate between the groups the participants are in. The second variable, **depression**, is for the scores on the dependent variable. We'll build on this approach with the one-way ANOVA in Chapter 8.

Figure 6.3   The completed data file for the independent-samples *t* test example.

Step 3: Analyze the Data

1. From the menu bar, select **Analyze > Compare Means > Independent-Samples T Test** (see Figure 6.4).

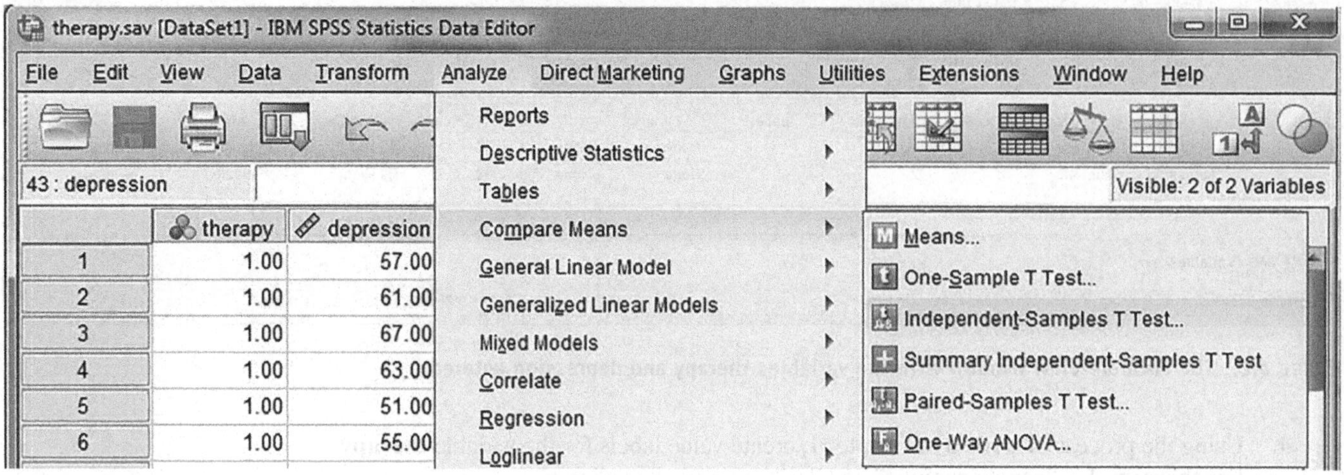

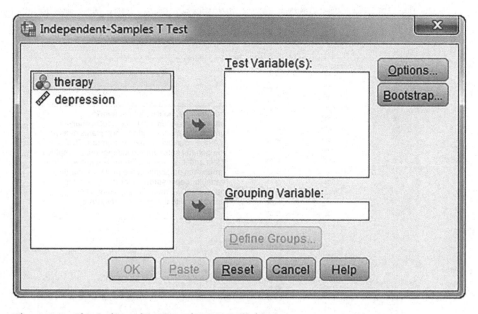

Figure 6.4   **Menu commands for the independent-samples *t* test.**

An *Independent-Samples T Test* dialog box appears with the variables **therapy** and **depression** in the left-hand side of the dialog box (see Figure 6.5).

2. Select the dependent variable, **depression**, and click the upper right-arrow button (➡) to move it into the *Test Variable(s)* box.
3. Select the independent variable, **therapy**, and click the lower right-arrow button (➡) to move it into the *Grouping Variable* box.

Figure 6.5   **The *Independent-Samples T* Test dialog box.**

In the *Grouping Variable* box, two question marks enclosed in parentheses appear to the right of **therapy** (see Figure 6.6). The question marks indicate that the numbers originally assigned to the two therapy groups (i.e., 1 and 2) need to be entered by clicking the *Define Groups* button.

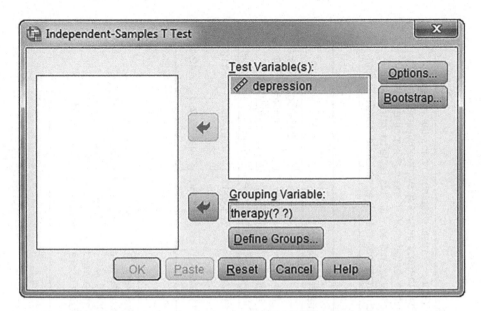

Figure 6.6   The *Independent-Samples T* Test dialog box (continued).

4. Click *Define Groups*.
5. The *Define Groups* dialog box opens. Enter a *1* to the right of *Group 1* (the number assigned to the psychoanalytic group), and a *2* to the right of *Group 2* (the number assigned to the cognitive-behavioral group). See Figure 6.7 for details.

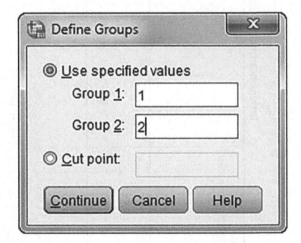

Figure 6.7   The *Define Groups* dialog box.

6. Click *Continue*.
7. Click *OK*.

The independent-samples *t* test procedure runs in SPSS and the results are presented in the *Viewer* window.

Step 4: Interpret the Results

The output of the independent samples *t* test is displayed in Figure 6.8 on page 76.

Group Statistics Table

The first table of output, *Group Statistics*, displays the descriptive statistics including the sample size, mean, standard deviation, and standard error for each of the therapy groups. Notice that the cognitive-behavioral group had a lower mean depression score (mean = 45.00) than the

t–Test

Group Statistics

	therapy	N	Mean	Std. Deviation	Std. Error Mean
depression	psychoanalytic	15	56.0000	9.41883	2.43193
	cognitive-behavioral	15	45.0000	7.63451	1.97122

The *Group Statistics* table provides the means of the two therapy groups (psychoanalytic and cognitive–behavioral). If the null hypothesis is rejected, we will consult this table to determine which group has the lower mean depression score.

Independent Samples Test

		Levene's Test for Equality of Variances		t-test for Equality of Means					95% Confidence Interval of the Difference	
		F	Sig.	t	df	Sig. (2-tailed)	Mean Difference	Std. Error Difference	Lower	Upper
depression	Equal variances assumed	.311	.582	3.514	28	.002	11.00000	3.13050	4.58747	17.41253
	Equal variances not assumed			3.514	26.850	.002	11.00000	3.13050	4.57507	17.42493

The *p*-value for Levene's test of equal variances. If *p* ≤ .05, we assume the variances are *not* equal (and read the bottom row of results for *t*). If *p* > .05, we assume the variances are equal (and read the top row of results for *t*). Since the *p*-value of .582 is greater than .05, we assume the variances are equal and interpret the results of the *t* test using the *Equal Variances Assumed* row.

Since the *p*-value of .002 is less than .05, the null hypothesis that the means are equal for the two groups is rejected. Consult the *Group Statistics* table to determine which group has the lower mean depression score (cognitive–behavioral is lower).

Figure 6.8 **The output for the independent-samples *t* test.**

psychoanalytic group (mean = 56.00). Whether the difference between the two groups is large enough to be statistically significant will be considered shortly.

Independent Samples Test Table

The second table, *Independent-Samples Test*, presents the results for *Levene's Test for Equality of Variances* followed by the *t-test for Equality of Means*. These tests will be discussed separately below.

Levene's Test for Equality of Variances

Levene's Test for Equality of Variances tests whether the population variances are equal for the two therapy groups, an assumption of the independent-samples *t* test. SPSS uses a procedure developed by Levene to test for the assumption of equal variances.

The null and alternative hypotheses for Levene's test are

H_0: $\sigma^2_{psychoanalytic} = \sigma^2_{cognitive-behavioral}$ (The population variances are equal for the two groups.)

H_1: $\sigma^2_{psychoanalytic} \neq \sigma^2_{cognitive-behavioral}$ (The population variances are not equal for the two groups.)

The equal variances assumption is assessed by examining the *p*-value (*Sig.*) reported under *Levene's Test for Equality of Variances* in the output. If $p \leq .05$, the null hypothesis is rejected, and it is assumed that the population variances are *not* equal. If $p > .05$, the null hypothesis is not rejected, and it is assumed that the population variances are equal.

The results from the *Independent Samples Test* table shows that Levene's test produced an *F* of .311 (*F* tests will be discussed in Chapter 8) with a *p*-value of .582. Since the *p*-value of .582 is greater than .05, the null hypothesis that the variances are equal is not rejected. Therefore, based on the results of Levene's test, we'll assume that the population variances are equal for the two groups. The decision rule for assessing the assumption of equal variances is summarized in Figure 6.9.

t-Test for Equality of Means

The next section of the table, *t-test for Equality of Means*, provides the answer to our research question, that is, whether there is a difference in the depression levels for the two therapy groups. In SPSS, two sets of results are presented, one assuming equal variances between the groups and the other assuming unequal variances between the groups. Since Levene's test was not significant (recall that the *p*-value for Levene's test was greater than .05), the values from the first row of the table, labeled *Equal variances assumed*, will be used. [If, on the other hand, Levene's test was significant (i.e., $p \leq .05$), the values from the second row of the table, labeled *Equal variances not assumed*, would be used.]

The test of the null hypothesis that the means are equal is provided in the form of a *t*, where:

$$t = \frac{\text{Difference between the two sample means}}{\text{Standard error of the difference between the two means}}$$

Substituting the appropriate values (*Mean Difference, Std. Error Difference*) from the *Independent-Samples Test* table yields a *t* value of:

$$t = \frac{11}{3.1305} = 3.514$$

which agrees with the value provided in the *Independent-Samples Test* table in column *t*. With 30 participants, the degrees of freedom (*df*) are equal to 28 (total number of participants − 2), with a corresponding *p*-value of .002. Because the *p*-value of .002 is less than .05, the null hypothesis that the means are equal is rejected, and it is concluded that the depression scores are significantly different for the two therapy groups. Since the test is significant, inspecting the means (once again) from the *Group Statistics* table indicates that the cognitive-behavioral therapy group had lower average depression scores (mean = 45.00) than the psychoanalytic group (mean = 56.00). (If, on the other hand, the *t* test had *not* been significant, we would have assumed that any difference between the means in the *Group Statistics* table was due to sampling error.)

Assessing the Assumption of Equal Variances:

Levene's Result	Decision	Conclusion
$p > .05$	Fail to reject H_0	Assume the variances are equal in the population.
$p \le .05$	Reject H_0	Assume the variances are not equal in the population.
Our data		
$p = .582; .582 > .05$	Fail to reject H_0	Assume the variances are equal in the population.

Figure 6.9   **Decision rule for assessing the assumption of equal variances.**

Effect Sizes

A popular estimate of effect size for the independent-samples t test is given by d, where:

$$d = t \sqrt{\frac{N_1 + N_2}{N_1 N_2}}$$

N_1 and N_2 are the samples sizes for groups 1 and 2, and t is the value of the t statistic reported in Figure 6.8.[1]

Inserting the appropriate values from the *Independent-Samples Test* in Figure 6.8 yields an effect size of:

$$d = 3.514 \sqrt{\frac{15 + 15}{15 * 15}}$$

$$d = 1.28$$

Cohen (1988) gave estimates of values of d of .20, .50, and .80 as corresponding to small, medium, and large effect sizes, respectively, in the behavioral sciences. Based on Cohen's guidelines, the effect size of 1.28 would be considered very large in practice and indicates that the cognitive-behavioral group has depression scores that are 1.28 standard deviations lower, on average, than the psychoanalytic group.

Expression of the Results in APA Format

In writing the results for the independent-samples t test, the conclusion of the hypothesis test, the degrees of freedom, the t value, the p-value, and the effect size are reported along with the mean and standard deviation for each of the groups. An example of a brief write-up in APA format is presented next.

Written Results

Those who received cognitive-behavioral therapy ($M = 45.00$, $SD = 7.63$) had significantly lower depression scores than those who received psychoanalytic therapy ($M = 56.00$, $SD = 9.42$), $t(28) = 3.51$, $p < .05$, $d = 1.28$.

Assumptions of the Independent-Samples t Test

1. *The observations are independent.*
   Violating this assumption can seriously compromise the accuracy of the independent-samples t test. This assumption should be satisfied by designing your study so the participants do not influence each other in any way (participants working together in answering the depression measure would be an example of violating the independence assumption). If there is reason to believe the independence assumption has been violated, the independent-samples t test should not be used.
2. *The dependent variable is normally distributed for each of the groups in the population.*
   This assumption means that the depression scores should be normally distributed in the population (they should resemble a bell-shaped curve when plotted) for both therapy

groups. For moderate to large sample sizes, most types of nonnormal distributions tend to have relatively little impact on the accuracy of the *t* test, although some nonnormal distributions can adversely affect the power of the *t* test.

3. *The variances for each of the groups are equal in the population.*
   Violating the equal variances assumption can compromise the accuracy of the independent-samples *t* test, particularly when the group sample sizes are unequal. Interpreting the results of Levene's test in SPSS and reading the appropriate results for *t* from the output addresses this assumption.

Summary of Steps for Conducting an Independent-Samples *t* Test in SPSS

I. **Data Entry and Analysis**
   1. Create two variables in SPSS (one for the independent variable and one for the dependent variable).
   2. Enter the data.
   3. Create value labels for the independent variable. In the *Value Labels* dialog box, enter the numeric values and labels as appropriate. Click *OK*.
   4. Select **Analyze > Compare Means > Independent-Samples T Test . . .**
   5. Move the dependent variable to the *Test Variable(s)* box and the independent variable to the *Grouping Variable* box.
   6. Click *Define Groups*. Enter a *1* for group 1 and a *2* for group 2. Click *Continue*.
   7. Click *OK*.

II. **Interpretation of the Results**
   1. Check the results of Levene's test for the equality of variances.
      - If $p > .05$ for Levene's test, equal population variances are assumed for the two groups. Interpret the first row of values for the *t* test, labeled *Equal variances assumed.*
      - If $p \leq .05$ for Levene's test, equal population variances are not assumed for the two groups. Interpret the second row of values for the *t* test, labeled *Equal variances not assumed.*
   2. Check the *p*-value (*Sig.*) in the *t-test for Equality of Means* section of the *Independent-Samples Test* table.
      - If $p \leq .05$ the null hypothesis is rejected. Inspect the means from the *Group Statistics* table and write the results indicating the nature of the difference between the groups.
      - If $p > .05$ the null hypothesis is not rejected. Write the results indicating that there is not a significant difference between the groups.

Exercises

1. Recent advances in surgical technology have led to an increase in the use of minimally invasive surgery (MIS), which involves making one or more small incisions (using small instruments) to perform a surgery, as opposed to making a considerably larger incision (using larger instruments) that traditional surgery requires. One of the claims advocates of MIS make is that the patient experiences less pain following the surgery. To investigate this claim, a researcher followed 30 people who were scheduled to undergo cardiovascular surgery, with 15 receiving MIS and 15 receiving traditional surgery. The reported pain level of each surgical patient was recorded 24 hours following surgery and is presented in Figure 6.10. The pain scale ranged from 1 to 10, with higher scores indicating a greater degree of pain.

Procedure	Pain
Minimally invasive	5, 4, 7, 2, 3, 5, 4, 6, 2, 5, 6, 8, 4, 5, 5
Traditional	6, 7, 5, 8, 9, 7, 8, 6, 6, 7, 8, 8, 6, 3, 9

Figure 6.10 **The postoperative pain scores for the two groups.**

Enter the data into SPSS and perform the appropriate analyses to answer the questions below. Name the variables **procedure** and **pain**.

    a.   State the null and alternative hypotheses.

    b.   State a research question for the data.

    c.   Test for the assumption of equal variances. Do the data suggest unequal variances between the groups?

    d.   Is there a significant difference in the reported pain levels between the groups? Test at $\alpha = .05$.

    e.   What is the effect size for the study? Would you characterize the effect size as small, medium, or large?

    f.   Write the results of the study using APA format as appropriate.

2.   Two different methods were compared for helping people overcome snake phobia (ophidiophobia). Twenty people who suffered from excessive fear of snakes were randomly assigned to receive one of two treatments: systematic desensitization (small, progressive steps are made toward overcoming the snake phobia) or implosion therapy (the participant is overwhelmed or "flooded" with the fear with the goal of overcoming it).[2] After three weeks of treatment, the snake anxiety score for each participant was obtained using a measure of snake fear (with higher scores representing greater fear of snakes). The data are in the file *Chapter 6_ Exercise 2.sav* in the Chapter 6 folder online at www.routledge.com/cw/yockey (the variables in the file are named **therapy** and **snakefear**; for **therapy**, 1 = "systematic desensitization" and 2 = "implosion" and 2). Open the file in SPSS, and perform the appropriate analyses to answer the questions below.

    a.   State the null and alternative hypotheses.

    b.   State a research question for the data.

    c.   Test for the assumption of equal variances. Do the data suggest unequal variances between the groups?

    d.   Is there a significant difference in the reported snake fear between the groups? Test at $\alpha = .05$.

    e.   What is the effect size for the study? Would you characterize the effect size as small, medium, or large?

    f.   Write the results of the study using APA format as appropriate.

3.   A researcher wanted to investigate whether there was a difference in satisfaction with nursing homes between residents who had access to a community pet and those who did not. Satisfaction was measured on a 5 to 25 scale, with higher scores indicating greater satisfaction. Sixty nursing home residents participated in the study, with 30 residents participating from a home with a pet and 30 participating from a home without a pet. The satisfaction scores for the residents are located in the file *Chapter 6_Exercise 3.sav* in the Chapter 6 folder online at www.routledge.com/cw/yockey (the variables in the file are named **group** and **satisfaction**; for **group**, 1 = "pet" and 2 = "no pet"). Open the file in SPSS, and perform the appropriate analyses to answer the questions below.

    a.   State the null and alternative hypotheses.

    b.   State a research question for the data.

    c.   Test for the assumption of equal variances. Do the data suggest unequal variances between the groups?

    d.   Is there a significant difference in the reported satisfaction levels between the residents? Test at $\alpha = .05$.

    e.   What is the effect size for the study? Would you characterize the effect size as small, medium, or large?

    f.   Write the results of the study using APA format as appropriate.

Notes

1. An alternative solution for *d* may be found by taking the mean difference between the two groups divided by the pooled standard deviation. While this formula is more appealing intuitively, since SPSS does not provide the pooled standard deviation in the output, the formula is not presented here.

2. It is the responsibility of the researcher to ensure that the guidelines of the American Psychological Association have been followed regarding the ethical treatment of research participants.

The Dependent-Samples *t* Test

The dependent-samples *t* test (also known as paired-samples *t*, repeated-measures *t*, or matched-subjects *t*) is used when the mean of one sample is compared to the mean of another sample, *where the two samples are related in some way*. With the dependent-samples *t* test, the two samples may consist of either the same people measured on two occasions or related people who are each measured once (e.g., identical twins on IQ, husbands and wives on quality of communication). The key to correctly identifying the dependent-samples *t* test is to remember that the two samples are naturally related in some way. An example of a dependent-samples *t* test is presented next.

Example

A worker for a national polling organization was charged with the task of surveying the public to determine which issue was more important to voters, the economy or national security. Twenty-five potential voters were asked to indicate the importance of *each of the two issues* on a 1 to 7 scale (where 1 = not important at all and 7 = extremely important). The independent variable is the voter issue (economy, national security) and the dependent variable is the importance rating.[1]

Objective and Data Requirements of the Dependent-Samples *t* Test

The Dependent-Samples *t* Test

Objective	Data Requirements	Example
To test whether the means of two related groups differ significantly on a dependent variable of interest.	One independent variable with two related groups or categories One continuous dependent variable	Independent variable • Voter issues (economy, national security) Dependent variable • Importance rating (on a 1 to 7 scale)

Null and Alternative Hypotheses

The null hypothesis states that the difference in the importance ratings for the economy and national security is equal to zero in the population:

$$H_0: \mu_{\text{economy}} - \mu_{\text{national security}} = 0$$

The alternative hypothesis states that the difference in the importance ratings is not equal to zero in the population:

$$H_1: \mu_{\text{economy}} - \mu_{\text{national security}} \neq 0$$

Evaluation of the Null Hypothesis

The dependent-samples t test provides a test of the null hypothesis that the difference between the two population means is equal to zero. If the t test produces results that seem unlikely if the null hypothesis is true (results that occur less than 5% of the time), then the null hypothesis is rejected. If t test produces results that seem fairly likely if the null hypothesis is true (results that occur greater than 5% of the time), then the null hypothesis is not rejected.

Research Question

The fundamental question of interest in a research study can also be expressed in the form of a research question, such as:

> "Is there a difference in the perceived importance of the economy and national security for voters?"

The Data

The data for the 25 participants are presented in Figure 7.1.

Participant	Economy	National Security
1	5	7
2	6	4
3	5	2
4	6	3
5	5	5
6	7	7
7	7	6
8	4	5
9	7	3
10	5	4
11	4	6
12	6	4
13	7	5
14	4	7
15	6	4
16	7	5
17	7	5
18	6	7
19	6	4
20	6	2
21	6	4
22	3	1
23	5	2
24	7	6
25	7	7

Figure 7.1 **The data for the dependent-samples t test. (*Note*: The participant variable is included for illustration but will not be entered into SPSS.)**

Data Entry and Analysis in SPSS

Steps 1 and 2 describe how to enter the data in SPSS. The data file is also available online at www.routledge.com/cw/yockey under the name *opinion.sav* in the Chapter 7 folder. If you prefer to open the file from the web site, skip to Step 3.

Step 1: Create the Variables

1. Start SPSS.
2. Click the *Variable View* tab.

In SPSS, two variables will be created, one for the ratings on the economy and one for national security. The variables will be named **economy** and **security**, respectively.

3. Enter the variable names **economy** and **security** in the first two rows of the *Variable View* window. Under *Measure*, classify both variables as scale (see Figure 7.2).

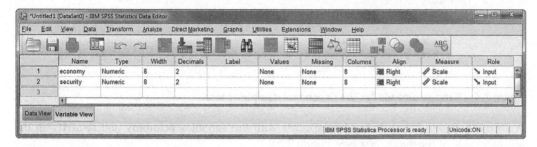

Figure 7.2 **The *Variable View* window with the variables economy and security entered.**

Step 2: Enter the Data

1. Click the *Data View* tab. The variables **economy** and **security** appear in the first two columns of the *Data View* window.
2. Consulting Figure 7.1, enter the importance ratings for each of the participants on the two variables of interest. For the first participant, enter the ratings *5* and *7* for **economy** and **security**, respectively. Using this approach, enter the data for all 25 participants. The completed data set is presented in Figure 7.3.

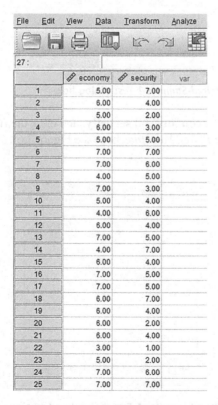

Figure 7.3 **The completed data file for the dependent-samples *t* test example.**

Step 3: Analyze the Data

1. From the menu bar select: **Analyze > Compare Means > Paired-Samples T Test** . . . (see Figure 7.4).

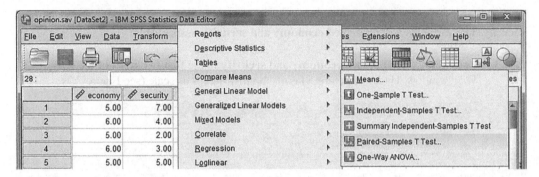

Figure 7.4 **Menu commands for the dependent-samples *t* test.**

A *Paired-Samples T Test* dialog box appears with the variables **economy** and **security** in the left-hand side of the dialog box (see Figure 7.5).

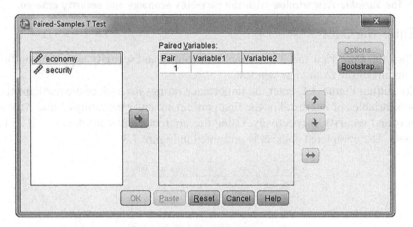

Figure 7.5 **The *Paired-Samples T Test* dialog box.**

2. Select the variables, **economy** and **security**, and click the right-arrow button (🔍) to move them into the *Paired Variables* box (see Figure 7.6).
3. Click *OK*.

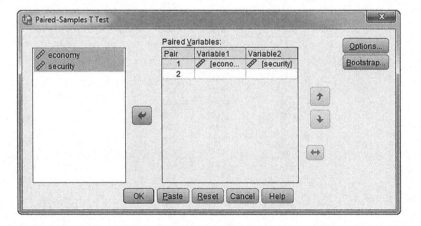

Figure 7.6 **The *Paired-Samples T Test* dialog box (continued).**

The dependent samples *t* test procedure runs in SPSS and the results are presented in the *Viewer* window.

Step 4: Interpret the Results

The output of the dependent-samples *t* test is displayed in Figure 7.7.

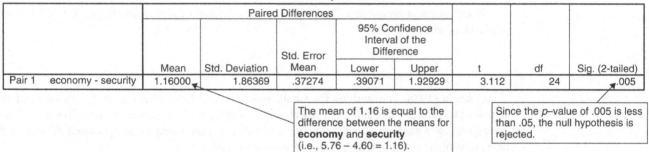

Paired Samples Statistics

		Mean	N	Std. Deviation	Std. Error Mean
Pair 1	economy	5.7600	25	1.16476	.23295
	security	4.6000	25	1.77951	.35590

The *Paired Samples Statistics* table provides the means of the two variables (**economy** and **security**). If the null hypothesis is rejected, we'll consult this table to determine which variable has the higher mean rating.

Paired Samples Correlations

		N	Correlation	Sig.
Pair 1	economy & security	25	.253	.222

Paired Samples Test

		Paired Differences							
					95% Confidence Interval of the Difference				
		Mean	Std. Deviation	Std. Error Mean	Lower	Upper	t	df	Sig. (2-tailed)
Pair 1	economy - security	1.16000	1.86369	.37274	.39071	1.92929	3.112	24	.005

The mean of 1.16 is equal to the difference between the means for **economy** and **security** (i.e., 5.76 − 4.60 = 1.16).

Since the *p*–value of .005 is less than .05, the null hypothesis is rejected.

Figure 7.7 **Output for the Dependent-Samples *t* Test.**

Paired Samples Statistics

The first table of output, *Paired Samples Statistics*, displays the descriptive statistics for **economy** and **security**, including the mean, sample size (*N*), standard deviation, and standard error of the mean. Notice that the economy has a higher mean importance rating (mean = 5.76) than national security (mean = 4.60). Whether the difference in the mean ratings (5.76 vs. 4.60) is large enough to be statistically significant will be considered shortly.

Paired Samples Correlations

The *Paired Samples Correlations* table is not critical to interpreting the results of the paired-samples *t* test and therefore will not be discussed, except to mention that the correlation is equal to the Pearson correlation coefficient between the economy and national security ratings for the 25 respondents (the Pearson correlation coefficient is discussed in Chapter 12).

Paired Samples Test

The *Paired Samples Test* table provides the answer to our research question, that is, whether there is a difference in the importance ratings for the economy and national security. The test of the null hypothesis is provided in the form of a *t*, where:

$$t = \frac{\text{Mean difference between the ratings on the economy and security}}{\text{Standard error of the mean of the difference scores}}$$

Substituting the appropriate values (*Mean, Std. Error Mean*) from the *Paired Samples Test* table yields a *t* of:

$$t = \frac{1.16}{.37274} = 3.112$$

which agrees with the value provided in the *Paired Samples Test* table in column *t*. With 25 participants, the degrees of freedom (*df*) are equal to 24 (number of participants in the sample − 1), with a corresponding *p*-value of .005.

Because the *p*-value of .005 is less than .05, the null hypothesis that the means are equal is rejected, and it is concluded that the importance ratings for the economy and national security are significantly different. Since the test is significant, inspecting the means (once again) from the *Paired Samples Statistics* table indicates that the economy had a higher mean importance rating (mean = 5.76) than national security (mean = 4.60). (If the *t* test had *not* been significant, on the other hand, we would have assumed that any difference between the means in the *Paired Samples Statistics* table was due to sampling error.)

Effect Sizes

A commonly used effect size statistic for the dependent-samples *t* test is *d*, where:

$$d = \frac{\text{Mean difference}}{\text{Standard deviation of the difference scores}}$$

Inserting the appropriate values from the *Paired Samples Test* table (*Mean, Std. Deviation*) produces an effect size of:

$$d = \frac{1.16}{1.86} = .62$$

Cohen's (1988) conventions for small, medium, and large effect sizes for the dependent samples *t* test are .20, .50, and .80, respectively. Using Cohen's conventions, the effect size of .62 corresponds to a medium effect in practice and indicates that the economy was rated .62 standard deviations higher in importance than was national security.

Expression of the Results in APA Format

In writing the results, the conclusion of the hypothesis test, the degrees of freedom, the *t* value, the *p*-value, and the effect size are reported along with the mean and standard deviation for each of the variables. An example of a brief write-up in APA format is presented below.

Written Results

Voters view the economy (*M* = 5.76, *SD* = 1.16) as significantly more important than national security (*M* = 4.60, *SD* = 1.78), *t*(24) = 3.11, *p* < .05, *d* = 0.62.

Assumptions of the Dependent-Samples *t* Test

The assumptions of the dependent-samples *t* test are provided below. The second assumption is concerned with difference scores rather than the original scores shown in Figure 7.1. Difference scores are equal to the difference between the two measures taken for each participant (i.e., the difference between the economy and national security ratings for each person). For example, the difference score for the first individual in the data set shown in Figure 7.1 would be equal to −2 (i.e., 5 − 7 = −2).

1. *Observations are independent within groups.*
   Violating the assumption of independence *within* groups can seriously compromise the accuracy of the dependent-samples *t* test. This assumption should be satisfied by designing your study so the participants do not influence each other in any way (participants working together in determining their ratings for the importance of the economy would be an example of violating the independence assumption). If there is reason to believe the independence assumption has been violated *within* groups, the dependent-samples *t* test should not be used. It is important to note that independence *between* groups is not an assumption of the dependent-samples *t* test (we expect a

dependency between the two ratings for the *same* person, as it is the reason for using the dependent-samples *t* test in the first place).

2. *The difference scores are normally distributed in the population.*
   This assumption means that the difference between the ratings should be normally distributed in the population. For moderate to large sample sizes, most types of non-normal distributions tend to have relatively little impact on the accuracy of the *t* test, although some nonnormal distributions can adversely affect the power of the *t* test.

Summary of Steps for Conducting a Dependent Samples *t* Test in SPSS

I. **Data Entry and Analysis**
    1. Create two variables in SPSS.
    2. Enter the data.
    3. Select **Analyze > Compare Means > Paired-Samples T Test . . .**
    4. Move the two variables to the *Paired Variables* box.
    5. Click *OK*.

II. **Interpretation of the Results**
    1. Check the *p*-value (*"Sig."*) in the far right-hand column of the *Paired Samples Test* table.
       - If $p \leq .05$, the null hypothesis is rejected. Inspect the means from the *Paired Samples Statistics* table and write the results indicating the nature of the difference between the two groups.
       - If $p > .05$, the null hypothesis is not rejected. Write the results indicating that there is not a significant difference between the two groups.

Exercises

1. The impact of a campaign film on attitudes toward a political candidate was investigated. Prior to showing the film, the attitudes of 15 people toward the candidate were assessed using a political likability scale. After completing the scale, the participants were shown a 20-minute campaign film in favor of the candidate, and then they completed the likability scale a second time. The scores for the participants across the two administrations of the likability scale are reported in Figure 7.8 (scores on the scale range from 20 to 100, with higher scores indicating more favorable attitudes toward the candidate).

Participant	Before film	After film
1	75	80
2	25	26
3	50	58
4	45	65
5	48	59
6	88	93
7	55	52
8	78	92
9	52	59
10	46	52
11	48	52
12	48	53
13	57	61
14	55	59
15	42	41

Figure 7.8 **Attitude ratings toward a political candidate before and after viewing the campaign film.**

Enter the data in SPSS and perform the appropriate analyses to answer the questions below. Name the variables **beforefilm** and **afterfilm**.
   a.   State the null and alternative hypotheses.
   b.   State a research question for the data.
   c.   Did attitudes toward the candidate change after viewing the campaign film? Test at $\alpha = .05$.
   d.   What is the effect size? Would you characterize the effect size as small, medium, or large?
   e.   Write the results of the study using APA format as appropriate.
2.   Air traffic controllers often experience a high degree of on-the-job stress. In an effort to help air traffic controllers cope with their stress, the impact of a relaxation exercise program was investigated. Thirty air traffic controllers were selected from some of the busiest airports in the country and were administered a scale measuring job-related stress (the scale ranged from 10 to 50, with higher scores indicating greater stress levels). Following the administration of the stress scale, the air traffic controllers were trained in a relaxation technique for four weeks and were then administered the job-related stress scale a second time. The data are in the file *Chapter 7_Exercise 2.sav* in the Chapter 7 folder online at www.routledge.com/cw/yockey (the variables are named **prerelax** and **postrelax**). Open the file in SPSS and perform the appropriate analyses to answer the questions below.
   a.   State the null and alternative hypotheses.
   b.   State a research question for the data.
   c.   Are the stress levels different after the relaxation exercise training as compared to before? Test at $\alpha = .05$.
   d.   What is the effect size? Would you characterize the effect size as small, medium, or large?
   e.   Write the results of the study using APA format as appropriate.
3.   A researcher investigated the impact of receiving training from a sports psychologist on the accuracy of shots of college tennis players. The shot accuracy of 15 tennis players was recorded before and after receiving eight weeks of training from a sports psychologist (accuracy scores ranged from 0 to 100, with higher scores indicating greater accuracy). The data are in the file *Chapter 7_Exercise 3.sav* in the Chapter 7 folder online at www.routledge.com/cw/yockey (the variables are named **beforetraining** and **aftertraining**). Open the file in SPSS and perform the appropriate analyses to answer the questions below.
   a.   State the null and alternative hypotheses.
   b.   State a research question for the data.
   c.   Is there a difference in the accuracy of the tennis players' shots after receiving training as compared to before? Test at $\alpha = .05$.
   d.   What is the effect size? Would you characterize the effect size as small, medium, or large?
   e.   Write the results of the study using APA format as appropriate.

Note

1. The term independent variable used in this text is not necessarily meant to imply a variable that is actively manipulated by the researcher but is instead used to help identify the characteristics of each statistical procedure. Whether the variable is a true independent variable, quasi-experimental, or non-experimental will not affect the calculations of the *t* test; it will, however, affect the type of conclusions that may be drawn from the study.

The One-Way between Subjects Analysis of Variance (ANOVA)

The one-way between subjects analysis of variance (ANOVA) is used when the means of two or more independent groups are compared on a dependent variable of interest. With the one-way between subjects ANOVA, the independent variable is a between subjects factor, where each participant receives *only one* level of the factor (i.e., each person is in a single group).[1] An example of a one-way between subjects ANOVA is presented below.

Example

As part of a class-required research project, a student was interested in investigating whether there was a difference between three different learning strategies (strategies A, B, and C) on word recall. Thirty students who agreed to participate in the study were randomly assigned to receive one of the three strategies (with 10 students in each strategy group). After learning the strategy of interest, the students were shown a list of 15 words for five minutes and were asked to remember as many of the words as possible using the new strategy. After a brief delay, each student wrote down as many of the words as he or she could remember from the list, with the researcher recording the number of words correctly recalled for each participant. The independent variable in this study is the type of learning strategy (A, B, and C) and the dependent variable is the number of words correctly recalled.

Objective and Data Requirements of the One-Way between Subjects ANOVA

The One-Way between Subjects ANOVA

Objective	Data Requirements	Example
To test whether the means of two or more groups differ significantly on a dependent variable of interest.	Independent variable • Between subjects factor with two or more separate groups or categories	Independent variable • Learning strategy (strategies A, B, and C)
	Dependent variable • Continuous	Dependent variable • Number of words correctly recalled

Null and Alternative Hypotheses

The null hypothesis states that the mean number of words recalled for the three groups is equal in the population:

$$H_0 : \mu_{\text{Strategy A}} = \mu_{\text{Strategy B}} = \mu_{\text{Strategy C}}$$

In order for the null hypothesis to be false, it is not necessary for all the groups to be different from each other (although this is one possibility); all that is required is that the null hypothesis be false in some way (i.e., there is a difference *somewhere* between the groups). Therefore, rather than generate all possible ways the null hypothesis could be false (which would become increasingly tedious as the number of groups increased), a general statement that the means differ in some way will be made:

H_1: At least one of the population means is different from the others.

Evaluation of the Null Hypothesis

The one-way between subjects ANOVA provides a test of the null hypothesis that the population means for the three groups are equal. If the test produces results that seem unlikely if the null hypothesis is true (results that occur less than 5% of the time), then the null hypothesis is rejected. If the test produces results that seem fairly likely if the null hypothesis is true (results that occur greater than 5% of the time), then the null hypothesis is not rejected.

Research Question

The fundamental question of interest in a research study can also be expressed in the form of a research question, such as:

"Does the number of words recalled depend on the type of learning strategy used?"

The Data

The data for the 30 participants are presented in Figure 8.1. The participants who received strategy A are assigned a "1," those who received strategy B are assigned a "2," and those who received strategy C are assigned a "3."

Participant	Strategy	Word recall	Participant	Strategy	Word recall	Participant	Strategy	Word recall
1	1	8	11	2	12	21	3	6
2	1	10	12	2	10	22	3	4
3	1	9	13	2	9	23	3	5
4	1	7	14	2	10	24	3	6
5	1	9	15	2	9	25	3	4
6	1	7	16	2	8	26	3	2
7	1	10	17	2	12	27	3	5
8	1	8	18	2	10	28	3	3
9	1	12	19	2	10	29	3	7
10	1	9	20	2	12	30	3	5

Figure 8.1 **The data for the one-way between subjects ANOVA example. (*Note*: The participant variable is included for illustration but will not be entered into SPSS.)**

Data Entry and Analysis in SPSS

Steps 1 and 2 describe how to enter the data in SPSS. The data file is also available online at www.routledge.com/cw/yockey under the name *word recall.sav* in the Chapter 8 folder. If you prefer to open the file from the web site, skip to Step 3.

Step 1: Create the Variables

1. Start SPSS.
2. Click the *Variable View* tab.

In SPSS, two variables will be created, one for the different strategy groups (the independent variable) and one for the number of words recalled (the dependent variable). The variables will be named **strategy** and **wordrecall**, respectively.

3. Enter the variable names **strategy** and **wordrecall** in the first two rows of the *Variable View* window. Under *Measure*, classify **strategy** as nominal and **wordrecall** as scale (see Figure 8.2).

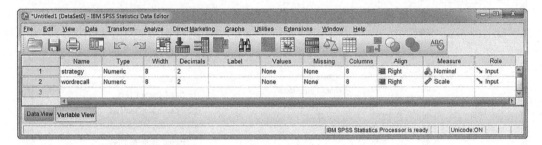

Figure 8.2 **The *Variable View* window with the variables strategy and wordrecall entered.**

4. Using the process described in Chapter 1, create value labels for the variable **strategy**. For **strategy**, 1 = "Strategy A," 2 = "Strategy B," and 3 = "Strategy C."

Step 2: Enter the Data

1. Click the *Data View* tab. The variables **strategy** and **wordrecall** appear in the first two columns of the *Data View* window.
2. Consulting Figure 8.1, enter the values for each of the participants on the two variables of interest. For the first participant, enter the values *1* and *8* for the variables **strategy** and **wordrecall**, respectively. Using this approach, enter the data for all 30 participants. The completed data set is presented in Figure 8.3.

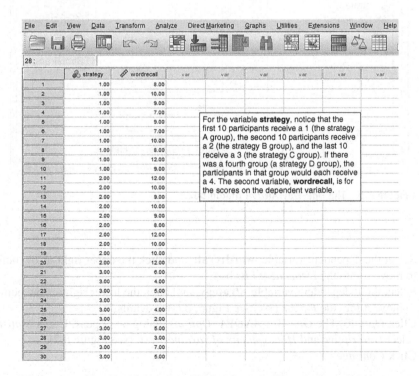

Figure 8.3 **The completed data file for the one-way ANOVA example.**

Step 3: Analyze the Data

1. From the menu bar, select **Analyze > Compare Means > One-Way ANOVA** . . . (see Figure 8.4).

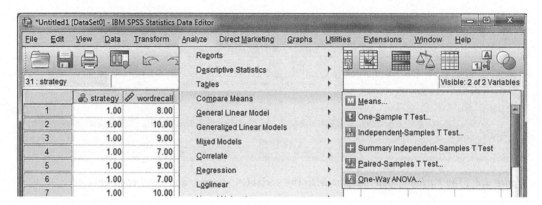

Figure 8.4 **Menu commands for the one-way ANOVA procedure.**

A *One-Way ANOVA* dialog box appears with the variables **strategy** and **wordrecall** in the left-hand side of the dialog box (see Figure 8.5).

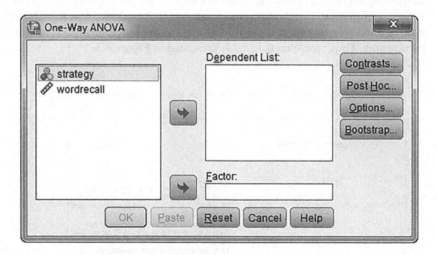

Figure 8.5 **The *One-Way ANOVA* dialog box.**

2. Select the dependent variable, **wordrecall**, and click the upper right-arrow button ( ) to move it into the *Dependent List* box.
3. Select the independent variable, **strategy**, and click the lower right-arrow button ( ) to move it into the *Factor* box. See Figure 8.6 for details.
4. Click *Options*. The *One-Way ANOVA: Options* dialog box opens. Under *Statistics* select *Descriptive* and *Homogeneity of variance test*[2] (see Figure 8.7).
5. Click *Continue*.

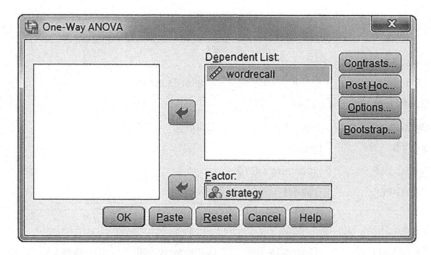

Figure 8.6 The *One-Way ANOVA* dialog box (continued).

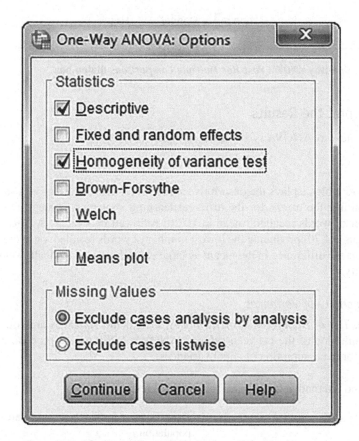

Figure 8.7 The *One-Way ANOVA: Options* dialog box.

6. Click *Post Hoc*. The *One-Way ANOVA: Post Hoc Multiple Comparisons* dialog box opens. Under *Equal Variance Assumed* select *Tukey* (not *Tukey's b*).[3] See Figure 8.8 on page 94 for details.
7. Click *Continue*.
8. Click *OK*.

The one-way ANOVA procedure runs in SPSS and the results are presented in the *Viewer* window.

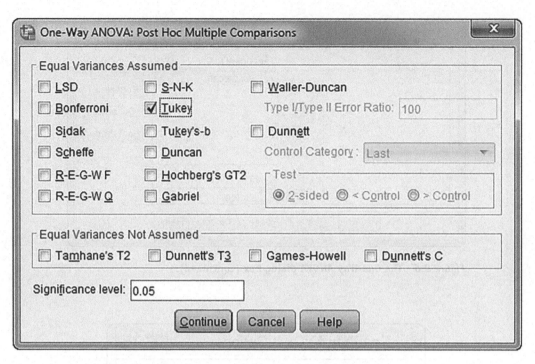

Figure 8.8 **The *One-Way ANOVA: Post Hoc Multiple Comparisons* dialog box.**

Step 4: Interpret the Results

The output of one-way ANOVA is displayed in Figure 8.9.

Descriptives

The *Descriptives* table displays the descriptive statistics for each of the groups (and for the total sample). Examining the means for the different learning strategies, strategy B had the highest average number of words recalled (mean = 10.20) followed by strategy A (mean = 8.90) with strategy C (mean = 4.70) producing the lowest number of words recalled, on average, of the three groups. Whether the difference in the means is large enough to be statistically significant will be discussed shortly.

Test of Homogeneity of Variances

The next table, *Test of Homogeneity of Variances,* tests if the variances are equal for the three groups, an assumption of the between subjects ANOVA. SPSS uses a procedure developed by Levene to test for the assumption of equal variances.

The null and alternative hypotheses for Levene's test are:

H_0: $\sigma^2_{\text{strategy A}} = \sigma^2_{\text{strategy B}} = \sigma^2_{\text{strategy C}}$ (The variances for the three groups are equal in the population.)

H_1: At least one of the variances is different from the others.

The equal variances assumption is assessed by examining the *p*-value (*Sig.*) reported in the *Test of Homogeneity of Variances* table in the output. If $p \leq .05$ the null hypothesis is rejected, and it is assumed that the population variances are not equal. If $p > .05$ the null hypothesis is not rejected, and it is assumed that the population variances are equal for the three groups.

For our data, Levene's test produced an *F* of .021 (SPSS labels this value *Levene Statistic*) and a *p*-value of .980 (see Figure 8.9). Since .980 is greater than .05, the null hypothesis of equal

One way

Descriptives

wordrecall

| | N | Mean | Std. Deviation | Std. Error | 95% Confidence Interval for Mean | | Minimum | Maximum |
					Lower Bound	Upper Bound		
Strategy A	10	8.9000	1.52388	.48189	7.8099	9.9901	7.00	12.00
Strategy B	10	10.2000	1.39841	.44222	9.1996	11.2004	8.00	12.00
Strategy C	10	4.7000	1.49443	.47258	3.6309	5.7691	2.00	7.00
Total	30	7.9333	2.77841	.50727	6.8959	8.9708	2.00	12.00

Test of Homogeneity of Variances

wordrecall

Levene Statistic	df1	df2	Sig.
.021	2	27	.980

The p–value for the test of equal variances, an assumption of ANOVA. Since .980 is greater than .05, the null hypothesis is *not* rejected and equal variances for the three strategies *are* assumed.

ANOVA

wordrecall

	Sum of Squares	df	Mean Square	F	Sig.
Between Groups	165.267	2	82.633	38.073	.000
Within Groups	58.600	27	2.170		
Total	223.867	29			

The p–value for the test of whether the means are equal in the population. Since the p–value (*sig.*) is less than .05, the null hypothesis that the means are equal for the three strategy groups is rejected.

Post Hoc Tests

Multiple Comparisons

Dependent Variable: wordrecall
Tukey HSD

| (I) strategy | (J) strategy | Mean Difference (I-J) | Std. Error | Sig. | 95% Confidence Interval | |
					Lower Bound	Upper Bound
Strategy A	Strategy B	-1.30000	.65884	.138	-2.9335	.3335
	Strategy C	4.20000*	.65884	.000	2.5665	5.8335
Strategy B	Strategy A	1.30000	.65884	.138	-.3335	2.9335
	Strategy C	5.50000*	.65884	.000	3.8665	7.1335
Strategy C	Strategy A	-4.20000*	.65884	.000	-5.8335	-2.5665
	Strategy B	-5.50000*	.65884	.000	-7.1335	-3.8665

*. The mean difference is significant at the .05 level.

Homogeneous Subsets

wordrecall

Tukey HSD[a]

| strategy | N | Subset for alpha = .05 | |
		1	2
Strategy C	10	4.7000	
Strategy A	10		8.9000
Strategy B	10		10.2000
Sig.		1.000	.138

Since strategy C does not share a column with A and B, it is significantly different (lower) than strategies A and B.

Strategies A and B are *not* significantly different since they share the same column.

Means for groups in homogeneous subsets are displayed.
a. Uses Harmonic Mean Sample Size = 10.000.

Figure 8.9 **Output for the One-Way between Subjects ANOVA.**

variances is *not* rejected. Therefore, based on the results of Levene's test, we'll assume the population variances are equal for the three groups. The decision rule for assessing the assumption of equal variances is summarized in Figure 8.10 on page 96.

Levene's result	Decision	Conclusion
$p > .05$	Fail to reject H_0	Assume the variances are equal in the population.
$p \leq .05$	Reject H_0	Assume the variances are *not* equal in the population.
Our data		
$p = .980;\ .980 > .05$	Fail to reject H_0	Assume the variances are equal in the population.

Figure 8.10   **Decision rule for assessing the assumption of equal variances.**

ANOVA—The Test of the Null Hypothesis that the Means of the Three Strategies are Equal

The next table, *ANOVA*, provides the answer to our research question, that is, whether or not the number of words correctly recalled differs for the three strategy groups. ANOVA produces an *F* test, which is a ratio of two variances, with each variance represented as a mean square (*MS*) in the output:

$$F = \frac{MS\ Between\ Groups}{MS\ Within\ Groups}$$

Substituting the appropriate values from the ANOVA table in Figure 8.9 produces an *F* of:

$$F = \frac{82.633}{2.170} = 38.073$$

which agrees with the value reported in column *F* of the ANOVA table.

This test produces two degrees of freedom, (*df*) between groups (number of groups – 1) and *df* within groups (total sample size – the number of groups). The *df* between groups and *df* within groups from the ANOVA table are 2 and 27, respectively.

The *p*-value in the ANOVA table under the column "*Sig.*" is .000 (which is read as "less than .001" not "zero"). Since the *p*-value is less than .05, the null hypothesis that the means are equal is rejected, and it is concluded that at least one of the strategies is different from the others.

Post Hoc Tests—Assessing Which Groups Are Different

While the null hypothesis of equal means for the three groups was rejected, the alternative hypothesis is nonspecific, stating only that the means differ in some way. In order to explore *how* the groups differ, further testing is required.

One common approach is to test all possible pairs of groups, commonly referred to as testing all pairwise comparisons. While many different tests of pairwise comparisons are available in SPSS, one of the more commonly used tests is Tukey's post hoc procedure. (Post hoc means "after the fact"; Tukey's test is typically interpreted only *after* a significant result for the overall ANOVA is obtained, i.e., the null hypothesis is rejected.) In the current example with three groups, Tukey's procedure will produce three separate tests: A vs. B, A vs. C, and B vs. C.[4]

By default, SPSS provides two different tables of output for Tukey's test, *Multiple Comparisons* and *Homogeneous Subsets*. While either table can be used to interpret the results of the pairwise comparisons, the results will be described first using the latter table, *Homogenous Subsets*. In the *Homogeneous Subsets* table in Figure 8.9, two different columns, labeled "*1*" and "*2*," are presented. When interpreting the results of the *Homogenous Subsets* table, groups that share the same column are *not* significantly different from one another, while groups that do not share the same column *are* significantly different. In our example, since strategies A and B share the same column (column 2), they are *not* significantly different from each other (any observed difference between A and B is considered to be due to sampling error). However, since strategy C does not share a column with strategies A and B, C *is* significantly different from A and B.

Inspecting the means for the three groups provided in the table shows that the number of words recalled for strategy C (mean = 4.7) is lower than A (mean = 8.9) and B (mean = 10.2).

The following table summarizes the results of Tukey's test from the *Homogeneous Subsets* table.

Test	Do the groups share the same column?	Result
A vs. B	Yes	Not significant; assume A and B are equal.
A vs. C	No	Significant; A recalled more words than C.
B vs. C	No	Significant; B recalled more words than C.

Alternatively, the results of the pairwise comparisons could have been interpreted using the *Multiple Comparisons* table. In the *Multiple Comparisons* table presented in Figure 8.9, the two groups being tested are presented in the first two columns of the table followed by the mean difference between the groups, the standard error, the *p*-value (Sig.), and the 95% confidence interval. Reading across the first row of the table, Strategy A is tested against Strategy B, which produces a mean difference of –1.3 (mean of strategy A – mean of strategy B) and a *p*-value of .138. Since the *p*-value is greater than .05, strategies A and B are *not* significantly different from one another. The next pairwise comparison (reading diagonally) is Strategy A vs. Strategy C, which produces a mean difference of 4.2 (mean of strategy A – mean of strategy C), and a *p*-value less than .001 (reported as .000 in SPSS due to rounding). Since the *p*-value is less than .05, A and C are significantly different. Inspecting the means from the *Descriptives* table in Figure 8.9 shows that those using strategy A (mean = 8.9) recalled more words on average than those using strategy C (mean = 4.7).

The potentially confusing part of the multiple comparisons table is that each of the pairwise comparisons is presented twice. Following the test of A and C, the test of strategies A and B is presented again; the only difference between the two tests is that this time strategy B is presented first. Since the test of B vs. A is exactly the same as A vs. B (notice the identical *p*-value of .138 for both tests), it makes no difference which of the two tests is reported. The multiple comparisons table always produces this redundancy, with each pairwise comparison presented twice. Therefore, when interpreting the results, be sure to report the result of each pairwise comparison only once. Summarizing the findings so far, we've reported the results of A vs. B and A vs. C, with only the test of B vs. C remaining. Looking diagonally across the next row, we see that B and C are significantly different, with a *p*-value less than .001 (once again reported as .000 in SPSS due to rounding). The means from the *Descriptives* table shows that strategy B (mean = 10.2) is significantly higher than strategy C (mean = 4.7). In summary, the results of the two tables are the same: A and B are not significantly different from each other, and both A and B are significantly higher than C.

Effect Sizes

The measure of effect size commonly used with ANOVA is eta-square (η^2). The formula for eta-square is:

$$\eta^2 = \frac{\text{Sum of squares between groups}}{\text{Sum of squares total}}$$

The values for sum of squares between groups and the sum of squares total can be found in the *ANOVA* table in Figure 8.9.[5] Inserting the appropriate values into the above formula produces an eta-square value of:

$$\eta^2 = \frac{165.267}{223.867} = .74$$

Cohen's (1988) conventions for small, medium, and large effect sizes for eta-square are .01, .06, and .14, respectively. Eta-square can be expressed in terms of the percentage of variance in the dependent variable that is accounted for by the independent variable. A value of .74 corresponds to a very large effect in practice and indicates that the learning strategies accounted for 74% of the variance in word recall.

Expression of the Results in APA Format

In writing the results for the one-way between subjects ANOVA, the conclusion of the hypothesis test, the degrees of freedom (*df*), the *F* value, the *p*-value, and the effect size are reported along with the means and standard deviations of the three strategy groups (the means and standard deviations may be reported in a separate table if desired). An example of a brief write-up in APA format is presented next.

Written Results

The number of words recalled varied by the learning strategy used, $F(2, 27) = 38.07$, $p < .05$, $\eta^2 = .74$, Tukey's post hoc procedure indicated that those who used strategy A ($M = 8.90$, $SD = 1.52$) and those who used strategy B ($M = 10.20$, $SD = 1.40$) recalled significantly more words than those who used strategy C ($M = 4.70$, $SD = 1.49$). There was not a significant difference in the number of words recalled between strategies A and B.

Assumptions of the One-Way between Subjects ANOVA

1. *The observations are independent.*
   Violating this assumption can seriously compromise the accuracy of the ANOVA test. This assumption should be satisfied by designing your study so the participants do not influence each other in any way (participants working together in generating their word lists would be an example of violating the independence assumption). If there is reason to believe the independence assumption has been violated, the between subjects ANOVA should not be used.
2. *The dependent variable is normally distributed for each of the groups in the population.*
   This assumption means that the number of words recalled should be normally distributed in the population for each of the strategy groups. For moderate to large sample sizes, most types of nonnormal distributions tend to have relatively little impact on the accuracy of the ANOVA test, although some nonnormal distributions can adversely affect the power of ANOVA.
3. *The variances for each of the groups are equal in the population.*
   Violating the equal variances assumption can compromise the accuracy of the ANOVA test, particularly when the sample sizes of the groups are unequal. Interpreting the results of Levene's test in SPSS and selecting and reporting the results of an alternative procedure (the Brown-Forsythe test or Welch test) if the variances are not equal (followed by an appropriate post hoc test if necessary such as Dunnett's T3) addresses this assumption. (See the summary below for more information on these procedures.)

Summary of Steps for Conducting a One-Way between Subjects ANOVA in SPSS

I. **Data Entry and Analysis**
   1. Create two variables in SPSS (one for the independent variable and one for the dependent variable).
   2. Enter the data.
   3. Create value labels for the independent variable. In the *Value Labels* dialog box, enter the numeric values and labels as appropriate. Click *OK*.
   4. Select **Analyze > Compare Means > One-Way ANOVA . . .**
   5. Move the dependent variable to the *Dependent List* box and the independent variable to the *Factor* box.
   6. Click *Options*. Select *Descriptive* and *Homogeneity of variance test*. Click *Continue*.
   7. Click *Post Hoc*. Select *Tukey*. Click *Continue*.
   8. Click *OK*.

II. Interpretation of the Results

1. Check the results of Levene's test of homogeneity of variances:
   a. If $p > .05$ for Levene's test, equal population variances are assumed. Interpret the ANOVA *F*.
      - If the ANOVA is significant (i.e., $p \le .05$), interpret the results of Tukey's post hoc procedure.
      - If the ANOVA is not significant (i.e., $p > .05$), stop. Write the results stating that there is not a significant difference between the groups.
   b. If $p \le .05$ for Levene's test, equal population variances are not assumed. Rerun the analysis selecting either the *Brown-Forsythe* or the *Welch* procedure (by clicking on the *Options* button), and select one of the post hoc tests that does not assume equal variances between the groups (e.g., Dunnett's T3) by clicking on *Post Hoc*. Unlike the ANOVA and Tukey's test, these tests do not require the assumption of equal variances.
      - If the overall test (*Brown-Forsythe* or *Welch*) is significant (i.e., $p \le .05$), interpret the results of the post hoc procedure.
      - If the overall test (*Brown-Forsythe* or *Welch*) is not significant (i.e., $p > .05$), stop. Write the results stating that there is not a significant difference between the groups.

Exercises

1. A medical researcher wanted to investigate the effect of different pain medications on people suffering from migraine headaches. Twenty-one people who had recently seen a doctor for migraine headaches were randomly assigned to receive one of three pills: drug A, drug B, or a placebo. While taking the appropriate pill, each participant recorded their pain level three times a day at regular intervals for one week (pain was recorded on a 1 to 10 scale, with higher scores indicating greater pain). The average pain level over the one-week period was calculated for each participant and is reported in Figure 8.11.

Drug	Pain
A	5.2, 4.1, 5.8, 6.85, 4.75, 1.75, 4
B	3.05, 6.15, 5.5, 6.15, 1.85, 6.4, 3.1
C	8.15, 7.15, 6.2, 7.85, 9.45, 9.25, 6.3

Figure 8.11   **The pain levels for the three groups.**

   Enter the data in SPSS and perform the appropriate analyses to answer the questions below. Name the variables **drug** and **pain**.
   a. State the null and alternative hypotheses.
   b. State a research question for the data.
   c. Test for the assumption of equal variances. Do the data suggest unequal variances between the groups? Test at $\alpha = .05$.
   d. Is there a significant difference in the reported pain levels between the groups? Test at $\alpha = .05$.
   e. What is the effect size for the overall ANOVA? Would you characterize the effect size as small, medium, or large?
   f. If the overall ANOVA is significant, briefly summarize the results of Tukey's post hoc procedure.
   g. Write the results of the study using APA format as appropriate (be sure to include the results of Tukey's test if the overall ANOVA is significant).
2. A researcher wanted to know whether the level of frustration over high gas prices differed for different types of vehicle owners. Following a sharp increase in the price

of gas, the researcher asked 30 people to indicate their level of frustration with prices at the pump (frustration scores ranged from 1 to 10, with higher scores indicating greater frustration). Ten people were surveyed who owned a motorcycle as their primary means of transportation (coded a 1 in the data file), 10 were surveyed who owned a hybrid vehicle (coded a 2 in the data file), and 10 were surveyed who owned a nonhybrid vehicle (coded a 3 in the data file). The data are provided in the file *Chapter 8_Exercise 2.sav* in the Chapter 8 folder online at www.routledge.com/cw/yockey (the variables are named **vehicle** and **frustration**). Open the file in SPSS and perform the appropriate analyses to answer the questions below.

a. State the null and alternative hypotheses.
b. State a research question for the data.
c. Test for the assumption of equal variances. Do the data suggest unequal variances between the groups? Test at $\alpha = .05$.
d. Is there a significant difference in the frustration levels of vehicle owners? Test at $\alpha = .05$.
e. What is the effect size for the overall ANOVA? Would you characterize the effect size as small, medium, or large?
f. If the overall ANOVA is significant, briefly summarize the results of Tukey's post hoc procedure.
g. Write the results of the study using APA format as appropriate (be sure to include the results of Tukey's test if the overall ANOVA is significant).

3. A market researcher hired by an alarm company examined whether companies differed in their response time to alarm calls. Three of the leading companies were investigated for the study. The response time (in seconds) of each of the companies to 15 randomly selected calls was recorded and is presented in the file *Chapter 8_Exercise 3.sav* in the Chapter 8 folder online at www.routledge.com/cw/yockey (the variables are named company and time; for **company**, 1 = "company A," 2 = "company B," and 3 = "company C"). Open the file in SPSS and perform the appropriate analyses to answer the questions below.

a. State the null and alternative hypotheses.
b. State a research question for the data.
c. Test for the assumption of equal variances. Do the data suggest unequal variances between the groups? Test at $\alpha = .05$.
d. Is there a significant difference in the response time for the alarm companies? Test at $\alpha = .05$.
e. What is the effect size for the overall ANOVA? Would you characterize the effect size as small, medium, or large?
f. If the overall ANOVA is significant, briefly summarize the results of Tukey's post hoc procedure.
g. Write the results of the study using APA format as appropriate (be sure to include the results of Tukey's test if the overall ANOVA is significant).

Notes

1. "Factor" is another name for an independent variable in ANOVA. "Level" is another name for a category or group. The factor gender, for example, has two levels: male and female.
2. *Brown-Forsythe* and *Welch* (shown in Figure 8.7) are alternative tests to ANOVA when the variances are not equal between the groups. If Levene's test suggests unequal variances, then one of these tests can be used in place of the standard one-way ANOVA (both Levene's test and assumption of equal variances will be discussed shortly).
3. If Levene's test suggests unequal variances, a post hoc test under *Equal Variances Not Assumed* should be used (instead of Tukey's).
4. Tukey's post hoc procedure has a built-in control so that the overall alpha (Type I error rate) for the three tests combined does not exceed .05. More will be said about controlling the overall alpha for follow-up tests in Chapters 10 and 11.
5. Eta-square can be calculated in SPSS using the *General Linear Model—Univariate* procedure. The *General Linear Model* procedure (and the calculation of eta-square using it) is illustrated in Chapter 9.

The Two-Way between Subjects Analysis of Variance (ANOVA)

The two-way between subjects analysis of variance (ANOVA) is used when two independent variables are evaluated on a continuous dependent variable of interest. In the two-way between subjects ANOVA, both of the independent variables are between subjects factors, consisting of two or more levels each, where each participant receives *only one level* of each factor. An example of a two-way between subjects ANOVA is presented next.

Example

A researcher wanted to investigate the effect of physical therapy and relaxation exercise on back pain. Twenty-four people suffering from acute back pain were recruited from a local orthopedic clinic for the study. Two different types of physical therapy and relaxation exercises were investigated. For physical therapy, half (12) of the participants used stretching exercises and the other half (12) used strengthening exercises. For relaxation exercise, half (12) of the participants used muscle relaxation (tensing and relaxing muscles starting with the head and moving to the toes) and half (12) used guided imagery (a structured visual technique intended to aid in relaxation).

The study design (illustrated in Figure 9.1) is an example of a completely crossed design where the levels of physical therapy are crossed with the levels of relaxation exercise. The study design resulted in four different conditions (with six participants in each condition): stretching and muscle relaxation (cell a), stretching and guided imagery (cell b), strengthening and muscle relaxation (cell c), and strengthening and guided imagery (cell d). This type of design is commonly referred to as a 2 × 2 ("two by two") ANOVA, with two levels of physical therapy and two levels of relaxation exercise, resulting in four different conditions.

	Relaxation exercise		
	muscle relaxation	guided imagery	Total
stretching	6 participants (cell a)	6 participants (cell b)	12
strengthening	6 participants (cell c)	6 participants (cell d)	12
Total	12	12	24

Physical therapy (row label)

Figure 9.1 **Study design of the two-way between subjects ANOVA example.**

The study lasted six weeks, with the participants receiving weekly training in the appropriate procedures. At the end of the six-week period, the participants completed a 10-item questionnaire assessing their current level of pain (total possible scores on the questionnaire ranged from 0 to 60, with 0 indicating no pain and 60 indicating a very high degree of pain). The dependent variable in this study is the pain level reported at the end of the six-week period, and the independent variables are physical therapy and relaxation exercise.

Objectives and Data Requirements of the Two-Way between Subjects ANOVA

Two-Way between Subjects ANOVA

Objectives	Data Requirements	Example
1. To test for main effects • Is there a difference in pain between the stretching and strengthening conditions? • Is there a difference in pain between the muscle relaxation and guided imagery conditions?	Independent variables • Two between subjects factors with two or more levels each	Independent variables • Physical therapy (stretching, strengthening) • Relaxation exercise (muscle relaxation, guided imagery)
2. To test for an interaction effect • Does the impact of physical therapy on pain depend on the type of relaxation exercise used?	Dependent variable • Continuous	Dependent variable • Reported pain level (after the six-week period)

Null and Alternative Hypotheses

Three different null hypotheses are tested in the two-way between subjects ANOVA. One null hypothesis is tested for each of the independent variables (known as tests of main effects), and one for the combined effect of the two independent variables (known as a test of an interaction effect). The hypotheses are described below.

Hypothesis 1. Test of Physical Therapy: Stretching vs. Strengthening

The null hypothesis for physical therapy states that the mean pain level for stretching and strengthening exercises are equal in the population:

$$H_0: \mu_{\text{stretching}} = \mu_{\text{strengthening}} \tag{H.1}$$

The alternative hypothesis states that the two population means are not equal:

$$H_1: \mu_{\text{stretching}} \neq \mu_{\text{strengthening}}$$

Hypothesis 2. Test of Relaxation Exercise: Muscle Relaxation vs. Guided Imagery

The null hypothesis for relaxation exercise states that the mean pain level for muscle relaxation and guided imagery are equal in the population:

$$H_0: \mu_{\text{muscle relaxation}} = \mu_{\text{guided imagery}} \tag{H.2}$$

The alternative hypothesis states that the two population means are not equal:

$$H_1: \mu_{\text{muscle relaxation}} \neq \mu_{\text{guided imagery}}$$

Hypothesis 3. Test of the Interaction Effect of Physical Therapy and Relaxation Exercise

The null hypothesis states that there is not an interaction between the two variables:

$$H_0: \text{There is not a physical therapy} \times \text{relaxation exercise interaction.} \tag{H.3}$$

The alternative hypothesis states there is an interaction between the two variables:

H_1: There is a physical therapy × relaxation exercise interaction.

Evaluation of the Null Hypothesis

The two-way between subjects ANOVA tests the three null hypotheses discussed previously. For a given hypothesis of interest, if the test produces results that seem unlikely if the null hypothesis is true (results that occur less than 5% of the time), then the null hypothesis is rejected. If the test produces results that seem fairly likely if the null hypothesis is true (results that occur greater than 5% of the time), then the null hypothesis is not rejected.

Research Questions

The fundamental questions of interest in a two-way ANOVA can also be expressed in the form of research questions, such as:

For Physical Therapy

"Does the reported pain level differ for those who used stretching exercises versus those who used strengthening exercises?"

For Relaxation Exercise

"Does the reported pain level differ for those who used muscle relaxation versus those who used guided imagery?"

For the Interaction of Physical Therapy and Relaxation Exercise

"Does the reported pain level for physical therapy depend on whether muscle relaxation or guided imagery was used?"

The Data

The data for the 24 participants are presented in Figure 9.2. For physical therapy, those who received stretching exercises are assigned a "1," while those who received strengthening exercises are assigned a "2." For the relaxation exercise, those who received muscle relaxation are assigned a "1," while those who received guided imagery are assigned a "2."

Participant	Physical therapy	Relaxation exercise	Pain level	Participant	Physical therapy	Relaxation exercise	Pain level
1	1	1	30	13	2	1	40
2	1	1	22	14	2	1	50
3	1	1	25	15	2	1	38
4	1	1	28	16	2	1	52
5	1	1	20	17	2	1	45
6	1	1	20	18	2	1	50
7	1	2	50	19	2	2	50
8	1	2	45	20	2	2	55
9	1	2	35	21	2	2	50
10	1	2	40	22	2	2	45
11	1	2	30	23	2	2	47
12	1	2	45	24	2	2	43

Figure 9.2 **The data for the two-way between subjects ANOVA example. (*Note*: The participant variable is included for illustration but will not be entered into SPSS.)**

Data Entry and Analysis in SPSS

Steps 1 and 2 describe how to enter the data into SPSS. The data file is also available online at www.routledge.com/cw/yockey under the name *back pain.sav* in the Chapter 9 folder. If you prefer to open the file from the web site, skip to Step 3.

Step 1: Create the Variables

1. Start SPSS.
2. Click the *Variable View* tab.

In SPSS, three variables will be created, one each for physical therapy and relaxation exercise (the independent variables), and one for the reported pain level (the dependent variable). The variables will be named **phyther**, **relax**, and **pain**, respectively.

3. Enter the names **phyther**, **relax**, and **pain**, respectively, in the first three rows of the *Variable View* window. Under *Measure*, classify **phyther** and **relax** as nominal and **pain** as scale (see Figure 9.3).

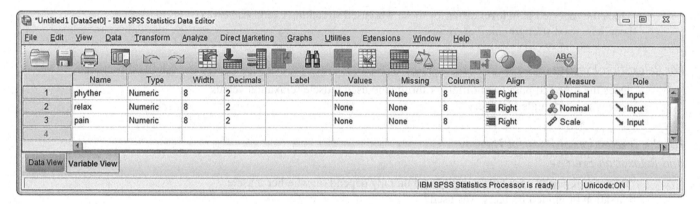

Figure 9.3 The *Variable View* window with the variables phyther, relax, and pain entered.

4. Using the process described in Chapter 1, create value labels for **phyther** and **relax**. For **phyther**, 1 = "stretching" and 2 = "strengthening." For **relax**, 1 = "muscle relaxation" and 2 = "guided imagery."

Step 2: Enter the Data

1. Click the *Data View* tab. The variables **phyther**, **relax**, and **pain** appear in the first three columns of the *Data View* window.
2. Consulting Figure 9.2, enter the values for each of the participants on the three variables of interest. For the first participant, enter the values *1*, *1*, and *30*, for the variables **phyther**, **relax**, and **pain**, respectively. Using this approach, enter the data for all 24 participants. The completed data set is shown in Figure 9.4.

Step 3: Analyze the Data

1. From the menu bar, select **Analyze > General Linear Model > Univariate** . . . (see Figure 9.5).

A *Univariate* dialog box appears with the variables **phyther**, **relax**, and **pain** in the left-hand side of the dialog box (see Figure 9.6).

2. Select the dependent variable, **pain**, and click the upper right-arrow button (▶) to move it into the *Dependent Variable* box.

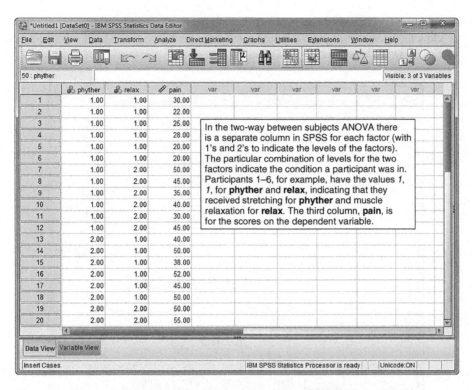

Figure 9.4   **The completed data file for the two-way between subjects ANOVA.**

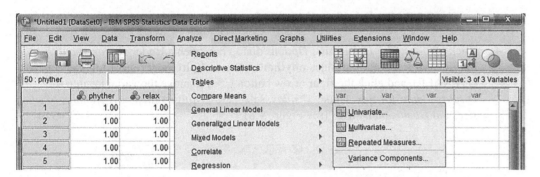

Figure 9.5   **Menu commands for the two-way between subjects ANOVA.**

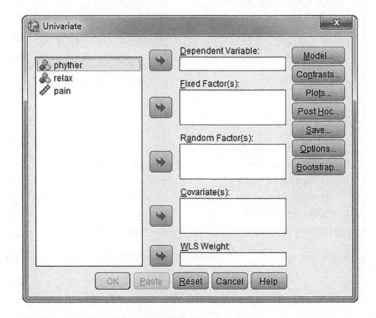

Figure 9.6   **The *Univariate* dialog box.**

3. With the *Ctrl* key held down, select the independent variables **phyther** and **relax**, and click the second right-arrow button (➥) from the top to move them into the *Fixed Factor(s)* box[1] (see Figure 9.7).

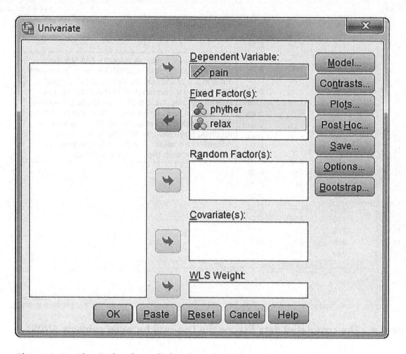

Figure 9.7 The *Univariate* dialog box (continued).

4. Click *Options*. The *Univariate: Options* dialog box opens. Under *Factor(s) and Factor Interactions* select the variables **phyther**, **relax,** and **phyther*relax** (don't select OVERALL), and click the right-arrow button (➥) to move the variables into the *Display Means for* box. Under *Display*, select *Descriptive statistics*, *Estimates of effect size*, and *Homogeneity tests* (see Figure 9.8).

Figure 9.8 The *Univariate: Options* dialog box.

5. Click *Continue.*
6. Click *Plots.* The *Univariate: Profile Plots* dialog box opens. Select **phyther** and click
    the upper right-arrow button (⬆) to move it into the *Horizontal Axis* box. Select **relax**
    and click the middle right-arrow button (⬆) to move it into the *Separate Lines* box
    (see Figure 9.9).

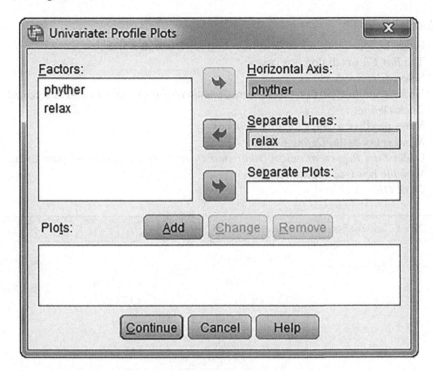

Figure 9.9   *Univariate: Profile Plots* dialog box.

7. Click *Add.* The interaction term **phyther × relax** is displayed under *Plots* in the dialog
    box (see Figure 9.10).
8. Click *Continue.*
9. Click *OK.*

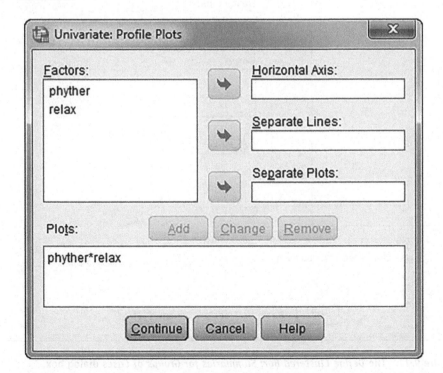

Figure 9.10   The *Univariate: Profile Plots* dialog box (continued).

The two-way ANOVA procedure runs in SPSS and the results are presented in the *Viewer* window.

Prior to discussing the results of the ANOVA, a bar chart will be created. A bar chart is an alternative to the profile plot for displaying an interaction effect. The commands for producing a bar chart for the two-way ANOVA are provided next (see Chapter 3 for more information on bar charts).

To produce a bar chart

1. From the menu bar, select **Graphs > Legacy Dialogs > Bar . . .**
2. The *Bar Charts* dialog box opens.
3. Select *Clustered*.
4. Under *Data in Chart are*, make sure *Summaries for groups of cases* is selected.
5. Click *Define*.
6. Move **phyther** to the *Category Axis* box.
7. Move **relax** to the *Define Clusters by* box.
8. Under *Bars Represent*, select *Other statistic (e.g., mean)* and move **pain** to the *Variable* box (see Figure 9.11).
9. Click *OK*.

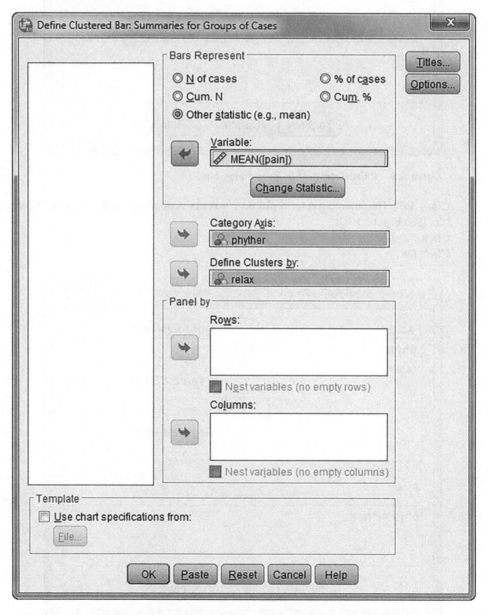

Figure 9.11 The *Define Clustered Bar: Summaries for Groups of Cases* dialog box.

The bar chart procedure runs in SPSS and the results are presented in the *Viewer* window.

Step 4: Interpret the Results

The output of the two-way between subjects ANOVA is displayed in Figure 9.12, and the output of the bar chart is displayed in Figure 9.13 (on page 111).

Univariate Analysis of Variance

Between-Subjects Factors

		Value Label	N
phyther	1.00	stretching	12
	2.00	strengthening	12
relax	1.00	muscle relaxation	12
	2.00	guided imagery	12

Descriptive Statistics

Dependent Variable: pain

phyther	relax	Mean	Std. Deviation	N
stretching	muscle relaxation	24.1667	4.21505	6
	guided imagery	40.8333	7.35980	6
	Total	32.5000	10.41415	12
strengthening	muscle relaxation	45.8333	5.81091	6
	guided imagery	48.3333	4.27395	6
	Total	47.0833	5.03548	12
Total	muscle relaxation	35.0000	12.30669	12
	guided imagery	44.5833	6.94731	12
	Total	39.7917	10.93053	24

Levene's Test of Equality of Error Variances[a]

Dependent Variable: pain

F	df1	df2	Sig.
1.238	3	20	.322

> The *p*–value (*sig.*) for the test of equal variances, an assumption of ANOVA. Since .322 is greater than .05, the null hypothesis is *not* rejected and equal variances for the four cells *are* assumed.

Tests the null hypothesis that the error variance of the dependent variable is equal across groups.

a. Design: Intercept + phyther + relax + phyther * relax

Tests of Between-Subjects Effects

Dependent Variable: pain

Source	Type III Sum of Squares	df	Mean Square	F	Sig.	Partial Eta Squared
Corrected Model	2128.125[a]	3	709.375	22.889	.000	.774
Intercept	38001.042	1	38001.042	1226.170	.000	.984
phyther	1276.042	1	1276.042	41.174	.000	.673
relax	551.042	1	551.042	17.780	.000	.471
phyther * relax	301.042	1	301.042	9.714	.005	.327
Error	619.833	20	30.992			
Total	40749.000	24				
Corrected Total	2747.958	23				

a. R Squared = .774 (Adjusted R Squared = .741)

> Our three tests of interest.

> All three tests are significant, since the *p*-values are less than .05.

(continued)

Estimated Marginal Means

1. phyther

Dependent Variable: pain

phyther	Mean	Std. Error	95% Confidence Interval	
			Lower Bound	Upper Bound
stretching	32.500	1.607	29.148	35.852
strengthening	47.083	1.607	43.731	50.436

Since **phyther** was significant, the marginal means table is inspected to determine which condition resulted in less pain. (Stretching resulted in less pain, with a mean of 32.50.)

2. relax

Dependent Variable: pain

relax	Mean	Std. Error	95% Confidence Interval	
			Lower Bound	Upper Bound
muscle relaxation	35.000	1.607	31.648	38.352
guided imagery	44.583	1.607	41.231	47.936

Relax was significant; the marginal means table shows that muscle relaxation resulted in less pain than guided imagery.

3. phyther * relax

Dependent Variable: pain

phyther	relax	Mean	Std. Error	95% Confidence Interval	
				Lower Bound	Upper Bound
stretching	muscle relaxation	24.167	2.273	19.426	28.907
	guided imagery	40.833	2.273	36.093	45.574
strengthening	muscle relaxation	45.833	2.273	41.093	50.574
	guided imagery	48.333	2.273	43.593	53.074

Profile Plots

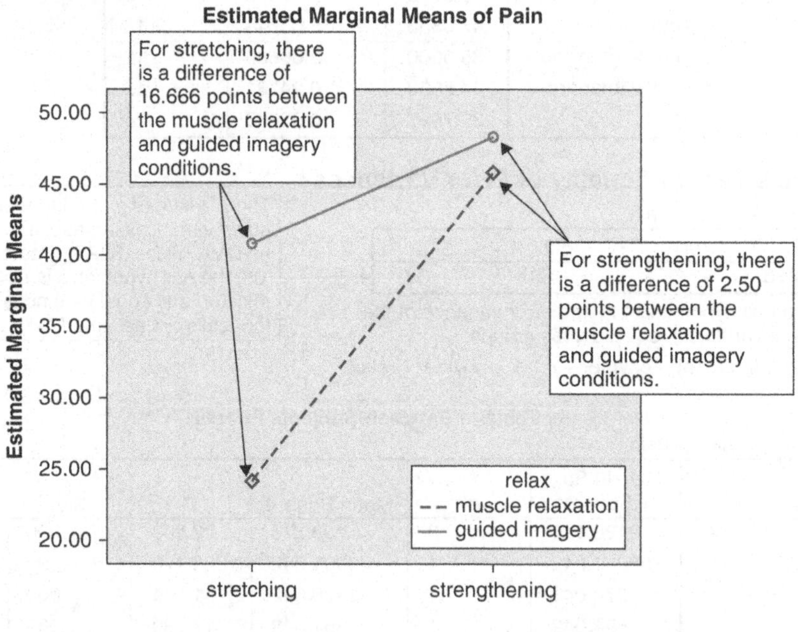

For stretching, there is a difference of 16.666 points between the muscle relaxation and guided imagery conditions.

For strengthening, there is a difference of 2.50 points between the muscle relaxation and guided imagery conditions.

Figure 9.12 **The output for the two-way between subjects ANOVA procedure.**

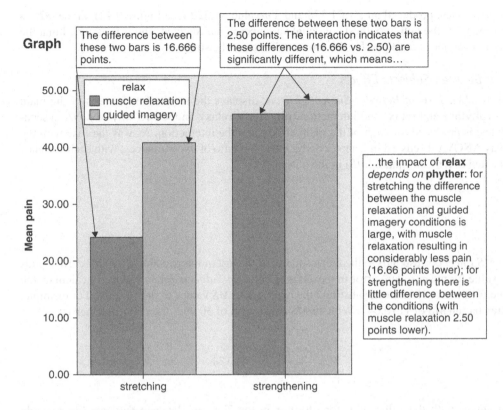

Graph

The difference between these two bars is 16.666 points.

The difference between these two bars is 2.50 points. The interaction indicates that these differences (16.666 vs. 2.50) are significantly different, which means…

…the impact of **relax** *depends on* **phyther**: for stretching the difference between the muscle relaxation and guided imagery conditions is large, with muscle relaxation resulting in considerably less pain (16.66 points lower); for strengthening there is little difference between the conditions (with muscle relaxation 2.50 points lower).

Figure 9.13 **Output for the *Bar Chart* procedure.**

Between-Subjects Factors

The *Between-Subjects Factors* table displays the factors included in the study (the independent variables), the number of levels of each factor, the value labels, and the sample size for each level of the variables. Notice that there are 12 participants for each level of **phyther** and **relax**, which is consistent with our study design.

Descriptive Statistics

The *Descriptive Statistics* table shows the mean, standard deviation, and sample size (*N*) for each of the conditions in the study (and for the levels of each factor). While we'll focus our attention on the *Estimated Marginal Means* tables later in the output for interpreting mean differences between groups, we will use the standard deviations from this table in the write-up of our results.

Levene's Test of Equality of Error Variances

The next table, *Levene's Test of Equality of Error Variances*, provides a test of whether the variances are equal for the four cells (conditions) in our study, an assumption of the two-way between subjects ANOVA (see Chapter 8 for more information on the equal variance assumption).

The null and alternative hypotheses for Levene's test are:

$H_0: \sigma_{1,1}^2 = \sigma_{1,2}^2 = \sigma_{2,1}^2 = \sigma_{2,2}^2$ (The variances for the four cells are equal in the population.)

H_1: At least one of the variances is different from the others.

The equal variances assumption is assessed by examining the *p*-value (*Sig.*) reported under the *Levene's Test of Equality of Error Variances* table in the output. If $p \leq .05$, the null hypothesis is rejected, and it is assumed that the population variances are *not* equal. If $p > .05$, the null hypothesis is *not* rejected, and it *is* assumed that the population variances are equal for the four cells in the study.

Levene's test produced an F of 1.238 and a p-value of .322 (see Figure 9.12). Since .322 is greater than .05, the null hypothesis of equal variances is *not* rejected, and it *is* assumed that the population variances are equal for the four conditions in the study.

Tests of Between-Subjects Effects

The next table, *Tests of Between-Subjects Effects*, displays the results for the tests of the main effects (**phyther** and **relax**) and interaction (**phyther** × **relax**)[2] In the two-way ANOVA, a separate F test is produced for each of the main effects and the interaction. As was the case with the one-way ANOVA discussed in Chapter 8, the F test is a ratio of two variances, with each variance represented as a mean square (MS) in the output:

$$F = \frac{MS\ Effect}{MS\ Error}$$

where *MS Effect* corresponds to the mean square for the test of interest and *MS Error* corresponds to the value for mean square error in the *Tests of Between-Subjects Effects* table. To calculate the F value for the test of interest, substitute the appropriate MS values in the formula. For example, **phyther** has an MS of 1276.042. With an *MS Error* term of 30.992, the F for **phyther** is:

$$F = \frac{1276.042}{30.992} = 41.174$$

which agrees with the value of F for **phyther** in the *Tests of Between-Subjects Effects* table reported in Figure 9.12.

This test produces two degrees of freedom (df) for **phyther** (df = number of levels of **phyther** – **1**) and df for error (df = total sample size – the number of cells in the study). For the test of **phyther**, the df are 1 and 20, respectively.

The reported p-value found in the ANOVA table for **phyther** under the column "*Sig.*" is .000 (which should be read as "less than .001"). Since the p-value is less than .05, the null hypothesis is rejected, and it is concluded that the reported pain levels for the stretching and strengthening conditions are significantly different (which group is lower for **phyther** will be discussed in the next section on marginal means).

The next test presented in the *Tests of Between-Subjects Effects* table is for **relax**. The test of **relax** produces an F value of 17.78 (551.042/30.992) with 1 (number of levels of **relax** – 1) and 20 (df error) degrees of freedom. The reported p-value in the ANOVA table for **relax** under the column "*Sig.*" is .000. Since the p-value is less than .05, the null hypothesis is rejected, and it is concluded that the reported pain levels for the muscle relaxation and guided imagery conditions are significantly different (which group is lower for **relax** will be discussed in the next section on marginal means).

The last test of interest, the test of **phyther** × **relax**, produced an F of 9.714 (301.042/30.992) on 1 [(number of levels of **phyther** – 1) × (number of levels of **relax** – 1)] and 20 (df error) degrees of freedom. The p-value for the test of the interaction is .005, which, since it is less than .05, leads us to reject the null hypothesis and conclude that there is a significant interaction between **phyther** and **relax**.

Estimated Marginal Means

The *Estimated Marginal Means* results produce a series of tables, one for each of the factors and one for the interaction (the marginal means tables are displayed whether the tests are significant or not). The marginal means tables are useful for interpreting the direction of *significant* results. Since all three tests are significant in our example, each of the marginal means tables will be discussed below. (If a given test was not significant, on the other hand, any differences between the marginal means for that test would be considered due to sampling error and would not be described.)

The first table, *phyther*, presents the marginal means for the two physical therapy conditions. Since **phyther** was significant, we'll inspect the means to see which group had lower reported pain levels. The marginal means table shows that those in the stretching condition (mean = 32.50) had significantly lower reported pain levels than those in the strengthening condition (mean = 47.08).

The second table, *relax*, presents the marginal means for the two relaxation exercise conditions. Since the test for **relax** was significant, we'll inspect the means to see which group had lower reported pain levels. The marginal means table shows that those who used muscle relaxation (mean = 35.00) had significantly lower reported pain levels than those who used guided imagery (mean = 44.58).

The last table of marginal means, phyther × relax, shows the means for the significant, interaction effect. Each of the four cell means from the study are presented, with each mean representing the average pain level of the six participants for the cell of interest. To more clearly identify the interaction effect, the table has been reproduced in a slightly modified form in Figure 9.14.

	Stretching	Strengthening	Marginal means for relax
Muscle relaxation	24.167	45.833	35.000
Guided imagery	40.833	48.333	44.583
Mean difference	**16.666**	**2.500**	**9.583**

Figure 9.14 **Cell means for the four conditions in the study, the marginal means for relax, and the mean *difference* between the relaxation exercise conditions for stretching, strengthening, and for the marginal means for relax.**

The first column of values in Figure 9.14 shows that, for those in the stretching condition, the pain level for muscle relaxation (24.167) was 16.666 points lower on average than for guided imagery (40.833). The next column presents the means for the strengthening condition and shows that the average pain level for muscle relaxation was only 2.50 points lower than for guided imagery (45.833 vs. 48.333). These mean differences illustrate the interaction effect: For stretching, the difference between muscle relaxation and guided imagery was large (16.666), while for strengthening the difference between muscle relaxation and guided imagery was small (2.50). A significant interaction effect indicates that these differences (16.666 vs. 2.50) are themselves significantly different. Looking at the mean pain levels across the four conditions, Figure 9.14 clearly shows the beneficial impact of combining the muscle relaxation and stretching conditions on pain (the participants had the lowest average pain level in this condition with a mean of 24.167).

Graphical Displays of the Interaction Effect

While we've just examined the interaction effect by inspecting the difference between cell means, it can be also useful to create a graph to display the results. We'll consider two different types of graphs for displaying the interaction effect: profile plots and bar charts. These two graphs are shown in Figures 9.12 and 9.13, respectively.

Profile Plots

The *Profile Plots* graph (shown in Figure 9.12) displays the cell means of the four conditions in the study. In the plot, the levels of physical therapy are on the X-axis, with stretching on the left and strengthening on the right. The lines of the plot correspond to the different levels of **relax**, with the top line in the plot for guided imagery and the bottom line for muscle relaxation. On the left-hand side of the plot, the difference between the two points represents the difference between muscle relaxation and guided imagery for stretching (the 16.666-point difference discussed previously). The difference between the two points on the right side of the plot corresponds to the difference between muscle relaxation and guided imagery for strengthening (the 2.50-point difference). Recall that the interaction indicated that these two differences (16.666 and 2.50) are themselves significantly different. When the means are plotted, this difference results in (significantly) nonparallel lines, which is another way of describing an interaction.

Graph—Bar Chart

The bar chart shown in Figure 9.13 is an alternative to the *Profile Plot* for producing a graph of a significant interaction effect. The profile plot and bar chart present the same information—the cell means for the four conditions under study; they just present the information in different ways. In the bar chart in Figure 9.13, **phyther** is on the horizontal (*X*) axis and the levels of **relax** are plotted as separate bars. The average pain level for each of the four conditions is equal to the height of the bar on the vertical (*Y*) axis. The first two bars on the left show that, for stretching, muscle relaxation resulted in considerably lower pain scores than guided imagery (the 16.666-point difference), resulting in a substantial difference in height between the adjacent bars for the stretching condition. The two bars on the right are for the strengthening condition. Notice that these two bars are very close in height, with muscle relaxation slightly lower than guided imagery, reflecting the small (2.50) difference in reported pain between these two conditions. Viewed from the perspective of the bar chart, a significant interaction indicates that the difference in height between adjacent bars is not the same across all levels of the *X*-axis variable (which is another way of stating that 16.666 is significantly different than 2.50).

Interpreting the Main Effects When the Interaction Effect Is Significant

When the interaction effect is significant, significant main effects can be misleading (depending on the nature of the results), and as a result should be interpreted with caution. This point is illustrated in Figure 9.14. The first two means in the far right-hand column of Figure 9.14 correspond to the marginal means for **relax**. The significant *main effect* for **relax** indicates that muscle relaxation and guided imagery are significantly different, with pain levels for muscle relaxation that are 9.583 points lower on average than guided imagery (35.000 vs. 44.583). This is the difference that the main effect predicts for **relax**, and it may be obtained by averaging the mean differences for the stretching and strengthening conditions [(16.666 + 2.500)/2 = 9.583]. However, the significant interaction effect implies that the difference between the relaxation conditions *depends on* the type of physical therapy received: For stretching, the difference is larger than predicted by the main effect (16.666 actual versus a predicted value of 9.583), while for strengthening the difference is smaller (2.500 actual versus a predicted value of 9.583). Thus, using the main effect (in isolation) to describe the difference between the relaxation exercise conditions mischaracterizes both values, underestimating the difference for stretching and overestimating the difference for strengthening.[3] If there was not a significant interaction, however, the main effect(s) would adequately describe the differences between the groups.

Simple Effects

When a significant interaction effect is present, further testing of the effect is possible using simple effects analyses. Simple effects analyses compare the effects of one factor *at a single level* of the other factor (such as testing the difference between stretching and strengthening at guided imagery). Simple effects analyses may be performed using the LMATRIX command in SPSS or by conducting independent samples *t* tests for the tests of interest. While simple effects are not covered in this chapter due to space considerations, an example of simple effects testing is illustrated in Chapter 11.

Effect Sizes

The measure of effect size commonly used with a two-way between subjects ANOVA is partial eta-square (η^2). To calculate partial eta-square, the sum of squares (*SS*) from the *Tests of Between-Subjects Effects* table is used (named *Type III Sum of Squares* in the output). The formula for partial eta-square is:

$$\text{partial}\,\eta^2 = \frac{SS_{\text{Effect}}}{SS_{\text{Effect}} + SS_{\text{Error}}}$$

where SS_{Effect} corresponds to the sum of squares for the effect of interest and SS_{Error} corresponds to the sum of squares for error. To calculate the partial eta-square for a given test of interest, substitute the appropriate SS values found in Figure 9.12 in the above formula. For example, **phyther** has an SS of 1276.04 and an SS_{Error} of 619.83. Substituting the values into the formula produces a partial eta-square of:

$$\text{partial}\,\eta^2 = \frac{1276.04}{1276.04 + 619.83} = .67$$

which agrees with the value for **phyther** provided in Figure 9.12. Partial eta-square ranges from 0 to 1, with the larger the value of partial eta-square, the more variance the effect explains in the dependent variable. Conventional effect size measures for partial eta-square have not been provided.

Expression of the Results in APA Format

In writing the results for the two-way between subjects ANOVA, the conclusion of the hypothesis test, the degrees of freedom (df), the F value, the p-value, and the effect size are reported along with the means and standard deviations (the means and standard deviations may be reported in a separate table if desired). If the interaction is significant, a bar chart or profile plot would also typically be provided. A sample write-up of the results in APA format is presented next.

Written Results

A 2 × 2 between-subjects ANOVA was conducted with back pain as the dependent variable and physical therapy (stretching/strengthening) and relaxation exercise (muscle relaxation/guided imagery) as the independent variables. The results indicated that there was a significant main effect for physical therapy, $F(1, 20) = 41.17$, $p < .05$, partial $\eta^2 = .67$, with those using stretching exercises ($M = 32.50$, $SD = 10.41$) reporting significantly less pain that those using strengthening exercises ($M = 47.08$, $SD = 5.04$). There was also a significant main effect for relaxation exercise, $F(1, 20) = 17.78$, $p < .05$, partial $\eta^2 = .47$, with those using muscle relaxation ($M = 35.00$, $SD = 12.31$) reporting significantly less pain than those using guided imagery ($M = 44.58$, $SD = 6.95$). There was also a significant physical therapy by relaxation exercise interaction, $F(1, 20) = 9.71$, $p < .05$, partial $\eta^2 = .33$. For strengthening, there was little difference in pain between the muscle relaxation and guided imagery conditions, while for stretching, the difference in pain between the muscle relaxation and guided imagery conditions was large, with muscle relaxation resulting in substantially lower pain (see the profile plot in Figure 9.12 or the bar chart in Figure 9.13 for more details). Overall, the participants who received the combined effect of stretching and muscle relaxation reported substantially less pain than the other conditions.

Assumptions of the Two-Way Between Subjects ANOVA

1. *The observations are independent.*
   The independence assumption should be satisfied by designing your study so the participants do not influence each other in any way (an example of a *violation* of this assumption would be if people received *both* muscle relaxation and guided imagery). Violating the independence assumption can seriously compromise the accuracy of the ANOVA test. If there is reason to believe the independence assumption has been violated, the between subjects ANOVA should not be used.
2. *The dependent variable is normally distributed for each of the cells in the population.*
   This assumption means that the dependent variable should be normally distributed in the population for each of the cells in the study. For moderate to large sample sizes, most

types of nonnormal distributions tend to have relatively little impact on the accuracy of the ANOVA test, although some nonnormal distributions can adversely affect the power of ANOVA.

3. *The variances for each of the cells are equal in the population.*
    This assumption means that the variances in each of the cells (the four conditions in the study) should be equal in the population. Violating the equal variances assumption can compromise the accuracy of the ANOVA test, particularly when the group sample sizes are unequal. Interpreting the results of Levene's test in SPSS addresses this assumption. If the equal variance assumption is violated and the sample sizes are fairly unequal in the cells, the two-way ANOVA should not be used (unlike the one-way ANOVA in Chapter 8, SPSS does not currently have a built-in procedure for unequal variances in the two-way ANOVA).

Summary of Steps for Conducting a Two-Way between Subjects ANOVA in SPSS

I. **Data Entry and Analysis**
    1. Create three variables in SPSS (one for each independent variable and one for the dependent variable).
    2. Create value labels for each independent variable. In the *Value Labels* dialog box, enter the numeric values and labels as appropriate. Click *OK*.
    3. Enter the data.
    4. Select **Analyze > General Linear Model > Univariate . . .**
    5. Move the dependent variable to the *Dependent Variable* box and the independent variables to the *Fixed Factor(s)* box.
    6. Click *Options*. Move the factors and the interaction term to the *Display Means for* box. Select *Descriptive statistics*, *Estimates of effect size*, and *Homogeneity tests*. Click *Continue*.
    7. Click *Plots*. Move the factor with the greater number of levels (if relevant) to the *Horizontal Axis* box and the other factor to the *Separate Lines* box. Click *Add*. Click *Continue*. (As an alternative to the profile plot, a bar chart may be created.)
    8. If there are any factors with three or more levels, Click *Post Hoc*. Move the factor with three or more levels to the *Post Hoc Tests for* box. Select *Tukey* (not *Tukey's b*). Click *Continue*.
    9. Click *OK*.

II. **Interpretation of the Results**
    1. Check Levene's test of equality of error variances.
        a. If $p > .05$ for Levene's test, equal variances are assumed. Proceed with intepreting the ANOVA test.
            *   Interpret the results of each of the factors, indicating the nature of the differences for significant main effects with two levels. For significant main effects with three or more levels, interpret the results of Tukey's test.
            *   If the interaction is significant, describe the nature of the relationship between the two variables.
        b. If $p \leq .05$ for Levene's test, equal population variances are *not* assumed. Since SPSS does not have a two-way procedure for unequal variances, if your sample sizes are equal or nearly equal, running the traditional two-way ANOVA should result in fairly accurate p-values (how accurate they are depends on the degree of inequality in the sample sizes and the variances). If the difference in the sample sizes is moderate to large, one option is to run two separate one-way ANOVAs (for factors with three or more levels) or t tests (for factors with two levels), testing for equal variances for each factor (if two separate tests are run, however, an interaction effect cannot be tested).

For factors with two levels, read the bottom row from the *t-test for Equality of Means* table to interpret the results (see Chapter 6 for more details). For factors with three or more levels and equal variances, run the traditional one-way ANOVA followed by Tukey's test. For factors with three or more levels and unequal variances, use either the Brown-Forsythe or Welch's test and select a post hoc test that does not assume equal variances (see Chapter 8 for more details).

- For significant factors with two levels (i.e., the *t* test), inspect the means in the *Group Statistics* table to describe the nature of the differences between the groups. For significant factors with three or more levels, interpret the results of the post hoc procedure for the factor(s) of interest.
- For nonsignificant factors, do not describe any mean differences between the groups. Write the results stating that there is not a significant difference between the groups for the factor(s) of interest.

Exercises

1. A researcher investigated the impact of gender and cell phone usage on driving performance. Each of the 24 people (12 males and 12 females) who agreed to participate in the study drove a car on a closed course where their driving accuracy was assessed (driving accuracy was measured on a 0 to 50 scale, with higher scores indicating better driving performance). While driving on the closed course, half of the participants (6 males and 6 females) spoke on a cell phone, while the other half did not. The data are provided in Figure 9.15.

Gender	Cellphone	Driving score	Gender	Cellphone	Driving score
1	1	34	2	1	35
1	1	29	2	1	32
1	1	38	2	1	27
1	1	34	2	1	26
1	1	33	2	1	37
1	1	30	2	1	24
1	2	45	2	2	48
1	2	44	2	2	47
1	2	46	2	2	40
1	2	42	2	2	46
1	2	47	2	2	50
1	2	40	2	2	39

Figure 9.15 **The data for Exercise 1. For gender, 1 = "male" and 2 = "female." For cellphone, 1 = "spoke on cell phone" and 2 = "didn't speak on cell phone."**

Enter the data in SPSS and perform the appropriate analyses to answer the questions below. Name the variables **gender**, **cellphone**, and **drivingscore**.

a. State the null and alternative hypotheses for each test of interest.
b. State a research question for each test of interest.
c. Test for the assumption of equal variances. Do the data suggest unequal variances between the conditions? Test at $\alpha = .05$.
d. Test for main effects of gender, cell phone use, and for a gender × cell phone interaction (use $\alpha = .05$ for each test). Which tests, if any, are significant? Which tests, if any, are not significant?
e. Report the effect size for each of the tests. Which of the tests has the largest effect size?
f. Write the results of the study using APA format as appropriate.

2. A psychologist investigated the impact of two different teaching methods (methods A and B) and majors in college (broadly classified as natural science and social science) on math anxiety. Forty college students (20 from each major) were included in the study, with half of the students (10 from each major) receiving teaching method A and half receiving teaching method B. After six weeks of instruction using the appropriate method, a math anxiety scale was administered. Scores on the scale ranged from 20 to 80, with higher scores indicating greater math anxiety. The data are provided in the file *Chapter 9_Exercise 2.sav* in the Chapter 9 folder online at www.routledge. com/cw/yockey. In the file, the variables are named **method** (1 = "method A" and 2 = "method B"), **major** (1 = "natural science" and 2 = "social science"), and **mathanxiety**. Open the file in SPSS, and perform the appropriate analyses to answer the questions below.

   a. State the null and alternative hypotheses for each test of interest.
   b. State a research question for each test of interest.
   c. Test for the assumption of equal variances. Do the data suggest unequal variances between the conditions? Test at α = .05.
   d. Test for main effects of method, major, and for a method × major interaction (use α = .05 for each test). Which tests, if any, are significant? Which tests, if any, are not significant?
   e. Report the effect size for each of the tests. Which of the tests has the largest effect size?
   f. Write the results of the study using APA format as appropriate.

3. Shown in Figure 9.16 is a plot of a significant interaction effect examining the impact of diet (whole grain, nonwhole grain), and the number of pounds overweight at the beginning of the study (11–30 pounds, 31–50 pounds) on weight loss. For diet, the two diets were identical with the exception that one used whole grains (e.g., whole wheat

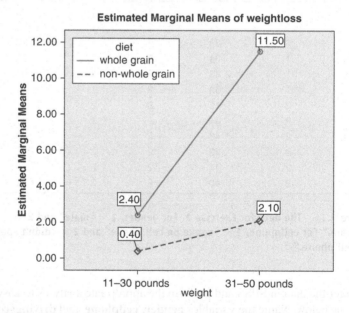

Figure 9.16 The weight × diet interaction plot.

pasta) while the other did not (e.g., white pasta). The dependent variable is the amount of weight lost in the study, with a positive value indicating that weight was *lost* (the means are displayed for each of the four conditions in the plot in Figure 9.16). Using the information in the plot, answer the questions below.

   a. Which of the four conditions experienced the greatest weight loss in the study? Which experienced the least?

b. Describe the significant interaction plot. Make sure that your description characterizes the interaction effect present in the graph (e.g., don't limit yourself to describing how those who were more overweight lost more weight, on average, than those who were less overweight, as this is a description of a main effect).

Notes

1. A fixed factor is an independent variable where the levels were specifically chosen for the study with the intent not to generalize to other possible levels. A random factor, on the other hand, consists of an independent variable whose levels were randomly selected from a larger number of potential levels with the intent to generalize the findings to the wider population of levels. Fixed factors are more common than random factors in most areas of study, although random factors do occur with some regularity in certain disciplines.
2. In the *Tests of Between-Subjects Effects* table, the corrected total sum of squares is equal to the sum of squares for **phyther, relax, phyther*relax,** and error. The corrected model sum of squares is equal to the sum of squares for **phyther, relax,** and **phyther*relax.** The intercept and total are usually not of interest in the two-way ANOVA.
3. The presence of a significant interaction does not necessarily mean the main effects should uniformly not be interpreted, but instead indicates that they *can be* misleading. If main effects are interpreted, they should be done so *in light of* the interaction.

The One-Way within Subjects Analysis of Variance (ANOVA)

The one-way within subjects analysis of variance (ANOVA) is used when the means of an independent variable are compared on a continuous dependent variable of interest. In a within subjects ANOVA, the independent variable is a within subjects factor with two or more levels, where *each participant receives all levels* of the independent variable.[1] An example of a one-way within subjects ANOVA is presented next.

Example

A school psychologist wanted to evaluate the potential effectiveness of a new social skills program, which was designed to teach children skills for fostering good relationships with their peers. Twenty-five fourth graders who were having difficulties in their peer relations were enrolled in the social skills program for a period of 16 weeks. The social skills of the 25 children (as rated by the teachers) were measured immediately before the start of the program, at eight weeks, and at the conclusion of the program (at 16 weeks). A 10-item social skills scale was used to measure social skills in children. The scale ranged from 6 to 60, with higher scores indicating more socially appropriate behaviors. The independent variable in this study is time (before, eight weeks, and after) and the dependent variable is the social skills scores.

Objectives and Data Requirements of the One-Way within Subjects ANOVA

One-Way within Subjects ANOVA

Objective	Data Requirements	Example
To test whether the means of two or more related groups differ significantly on a dependent variable of interest.	Independent variable • Within subjects factor with two or more levels Dependent variable • Continuous	Independent variable • Time (before, eight weeks, after) Dependent variable • Social skills scores

Null and Alternative Hypotheses

The null hypothesis states that the mean social skills scores for the three time occasions are equal in the population:

$$H_0: \mu_{\text{before}} = \mu_{\text{8weeks}} = \mu_{\text{after}}$$

In order for the null hypothesis to be false, it is not necessary that all three means be different from one another (although this is one possibility); all that is required is that the null hypothesis is false in some way (i.e., there is a difference *somewhere* between the groups). Therefore, rather than generate all possible ways the null hypothesis could be false (which would become increasingly tedious as the number of groups increased), a general statement that the means differ in some way will be made.

H_1: At least one of the means is different from the others.

Evaluation of the Null Hypothesis

The one-way within subjects ANOVA provides a test of the null hypothesis that the population means for the three time occasions are equal. If the test produces results that seem unlikely if the null hypothesis is true (results that occur less than 5% of the time), then the null hypothesis is rejected. If the test produces results that seem fairly likely if the null hypothesis is true (results that occur greater than 5% of the time), then the null hypothesis is not rejected.

Research Question

The fundamental question of interest in a research study can also be expressed in the form of a research question, such as:

"Is there a difference in social skills before, during, or after a 16-week social skills training program?"

The Data

The data for the 25 participants are presented in Figure 10.1. The three time occasions, before, eight weeks, and after, correspond to the social skills scores immediately before, halfway through, and immediately following the conclusion of the program.

Participant	Before	8 Weeks	After	Participant	Before	8 Weeks	After
1	20	24	26	14	32	30	31
2	25	26	25	15	34	32	36
3	28	31	30	16	22	25	29
4	18	16	17	17	16	19	22
5	24	25	30	18	31	28	31
6	30	28	31	19	14	14	18
7	18	22	25	20	13	10	14
8	14	17	21	21	15	14	16
9	12	15	16	22	31	32	32
10	9	11	10	23	35	32	36
11	15	15	19	24	28	29	31
12	17	16	20	25	26	25	25
13	35	32	31				

Figure 10.1   **The data for the one-way within subjects ANOVA. (*Note*: The participant variable is included for illustration but will not be entered into SPSS.)**

Data Entry and Analysis in SPSS

Steps 1 and 2 describe how to enter the data in SPSS. The data file is also available online at www.routledge.com/cw/yockey under the name *social skills.sav* in the Chapter 10 folder. If you prefer to open the file from the web site, skip to Step 3.

Step 1: Create the Variables

1. Start SPSS.
2. Click the *Variable View* tab.

In SPSS, three variables will be created, one for each of the time occasions social skills scores were measured. The variables will be named **before**, **week8**, and **after**, respectively.

3. Enter the variable names **before**, **week8**, and **after**, respectively, in the first three rows of the *Variable View* window. Under *Measure*, classify all three variables as scale (see Figure 10.2).

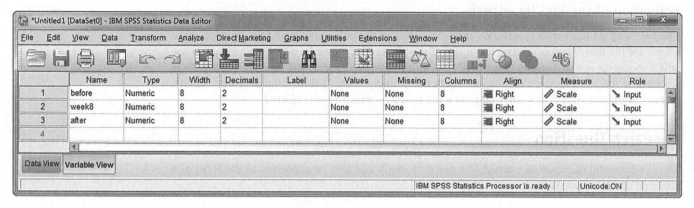

Figure 10.2   The *Variable View* window in SPSS with the variables before, week8, and after entered.

Step 2: Enter the Data

1. Click the *Data View* tab. The variables **before**, **week8**, and **after** appear in the first three columns of the *Data View* window.
2. Consulting Figure 10.1, enter the scores for each of the participants on the three variables of interest. For the first participant, enter the scores *20*, *24*, and *26* on the variables **before**, **week8**, and **after**, respectively. Using this approach, enter the data for all 25 participants. The completed data set is presented in Figure 10.3.

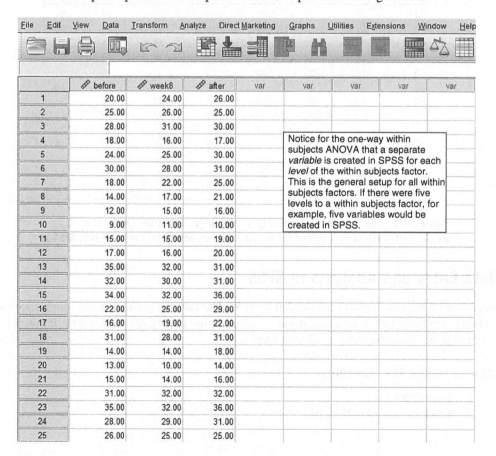

Figure 10.3   The data file for the one-way within subjects ANOVA example.

Step 3: Analyze the Data

1. From the menu bar, select **Analyze > General Linear Model > Repeated Measures** . . . (see Figure 10.4).

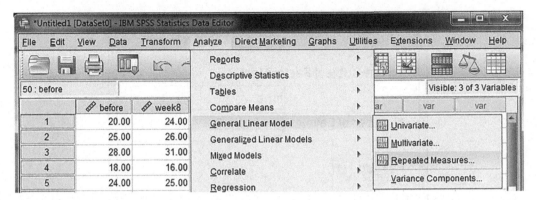

Figure 10.4   **Menu commands for the one-way within subjects ANOVA procedure.**

The *Repeated Measures Define Factor(s)* dialog box opens (see Figure 10.5). This dialog box is used to provide a name for the within subjects factor and to enter the number of levels of the factor.

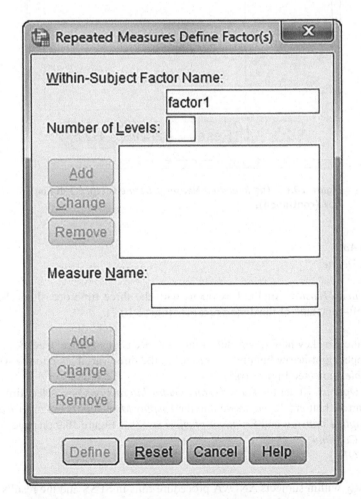

Figure 10.5   **The *Repeated Measures Define Factor(s)* dialog box.**

2. Double-click the name "factor1" in the *Within Subject Factor Name* text box (*factor1* is the default name provided by SPSS for the within subjects factor). Enter the name, **time**.
3. In the text box to the right of *Number of Levels*, enter a *3*. This corresponds to the number of levels (**before**, **week8**, **after**) of the within subjects factor. See Figure 10.6 for details.

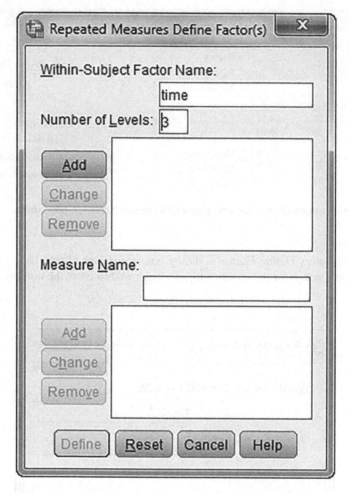

Figure 10.6 The *Repeated Measures Define Factor(s)* dialog box (continued).

4. Click *Add*.
5. Click *Define*.

The *Repeated Measures* dialog box opens with the three time occasions (**before**, **week8**, **after**) on the left-hand side of the dialog box (see Figure 10.7).

6. With the *Ctrl* key held down, select the time occasions **before**, **week8**, and **after**. Click the upper right-arrow button (➡) to move the three variables into the *Within-Subjects Variables* box (see Figure 10.8).[2]
7. Click *Options*. Under the *Factor(s) and Factor Interactions* box, select **time**, and click the right-arrow button (➡) to move it to the *Display Means for* box. Under *Display*, select *Descriptive statistics* and *Estimates of effect size* (see Figure 10.9 on page 126 for details).
8. Click *Continue*.
9. Click *OK*.

The one-way within subjects ANOVA procedure runs in SPSS and the results are presented in the *Viewer* window.

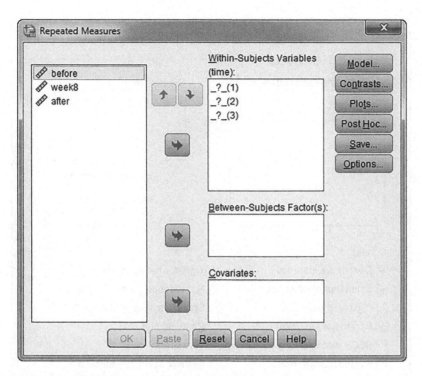

Figure 10.7 **The *Repeated Measures* dialog box.**

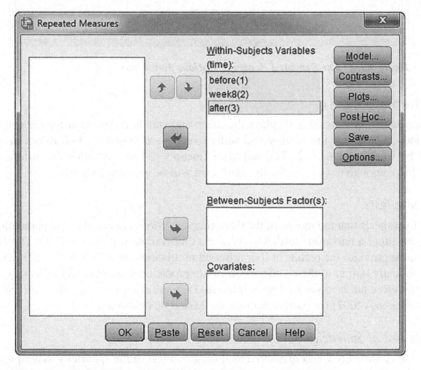

Figure 10.8 **The *Repeated Measures* dialog box (continued).**

Step 4: Interpret the Results

The output for the one-way within subjects ANOVA is displayed in Figure 10.10 on page 127.

Within-Subjects Factors

The first table, *Within-Subjects Factors*, lists the three time occasions the participants were measured, including before the program (**before**), eight weeks into the program (**week8**), and at the conclusion of the program (**after**).

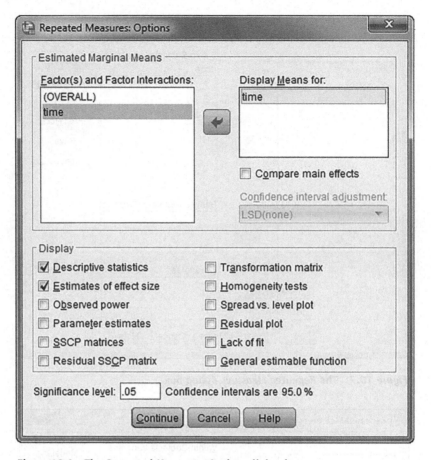

Figure 10.9   The *Repeated Measures: Options* dialog box.

Descriptive Statistics

The *Descriptive Statistics* table displays the mean and standard deviation for each of the three time periods. Notice that the mean social skills scores were lowest for **before** (mean = 22.48), followed by **week8** (mean = 22.72), and **after** (mean = 24.88). Whether the difference in the means is large enough to be statistically significant will be examined shortly.

Multivariate Tests

The null hypothesis that the means of the three time occasions are equal in the population can be tested using either a univariate test (ANOVA) or a multivariate test (MANOVA). The *Multivariate Tests* table provides the results of four different multivariate tests. While the multivariate tests are automatically output in the results, multivariate procedures are beyond the scope of this text and will therefore not be discussed here. Interested readers are referred to Maxwell and Delaney (2004) or Stevens (2002) for more details on the MANOVA procedure.

Mauchly's Test of Sphericity

The next table, *Mauchly's Test of Sphericity*, provides a test of the sphericity assumption, which is an assumption of the within subjects ANOVA when there are three or more levels to the within subjects factor.[3] While a test of this assumption is provided in the *Mauchly's Test of Sphericity* table (the *p*-value for the test is .056), this test can be inaccurate (see Howell, 2007, or Maxwell and Delaney, 2004, for more details) and therefore will not be considered (an alternative solution to testing the assumption of sphericity will be provided).[4]

If the assumption of sphericity is not met, the standard ANOVA *F* test (reported as *Sphericity Assumed* in the *Tests of Within-Subjects Effects* table) is inaccurate, yielding results that lead to rejecting a true null hypothesis more often than is warranted. As a result of the inaccuracy of the *F* test when the assumption of sphericity is violated, several alternative *F* tests that adjust for the lack of sphericity have been proposed. There are three such "adjustment procedures" in

General Linear Model

Within-Subjects Factors

Measure: MEASURE_1

time	Dependent Variable
1	before
2	week8
3	after

Descriptive Statistics

	Mean	Std. Deviation	N
before	22.4800	8.10411	25
week8	22.7200	7.35142	25
after	24.8800	7.20139	25

Multivariate Tests[b]

Effect		Value	F	Hypothesis df	Error df	Sig.
time	Pillai's Trace	.569	15.155[a]	2.000	23.000	.000
	Wilks' Lambda	.431	15.155[a]	2.000	23.000	.000
	Hotelling's Trace	1.318	15.155[a]	2.000	23.000	.000
	Roy's Largest Root	1.318	15.155[a]	2.000	23.000	.000

a. Exact statistic

b. Design: Intercept
   Within Subjects Design: time

Mauchly's Test of Sphericity[b]

Measure: MEASURE_1

Within Subjects Effect	Mauchly's W	Approx. Chi-Square	df	Sig.	Epsilon[a] Greenhouse-Geisser	Huynh-Feldt	Lower-bound
time	.779	5.751	2	.056	.819	.871	.500

Tests the null hypothesis that the error covariance matrix of the orthonormalized transformed dependent variables is proportional to an identity matrix.

a. May be used to adjust the degrees of freedom for the averaged tests of significance. Corrected tests are displayed in the Tests of Within-Subjects Effects table.

b. Design: Intercept Within Subjects Design: time

Tests of Within-Subjects Effects

Measure: MEASURE_1

Source		Type III Sum of Squares	df	Mean Square	F	Sig.	Partial Eta Squared
time	Sphericity Assumed	87.360	2	43.680	14.298	.000	.373
	Greenhouse-Geisser	87.360	1.638	53.343	14.298	.000	.373
	Huynh-Feldt	87.360	1.741	50.166	14.298	.000	.373
	Lower-bound	87.360	1.000	87.360	14.298	.001	.373
Error(time)	Sphericity Assumed	146.640	48	3.055			
	Greenhouse-Geisser	146.640	39.305	3.731			
	Hunh-Feldty	146.640	41.794	3.509			
	Lower-bound	146.640	24.000	6.110			

> The *p*–value for the test that the social skills scores are equal across the 3 time occasions. Use either the *Greenhouse–Geisser* or *Sphericity Assumed* values (both are significant since $p < .05$ for each test).

(continued)

Tests of Within-Subjects Contrasts

Measure: MEASURE_1

Source	time	Type III Sum of Squares	df	Mean Square	F	Sig.	Partial Eta Squared
time	Linear	72.000	1	72.000	16.457	.000	.407
	Quadratic	15.360	1	15.360	8.853	.007	.269
Error(time)	Linear	105.000	24	4.375			
	Quadratic	41.640	24	1.735			

Tests of Between-Subjects Effects

Measure: MEASURE_1

Transformed Variable: Average

Source	Type III Sum of Squares	df	Mean Square	F	Sig.	Partial Eta Squared
Intercept	40926.720	1	40926.720	247.336	.000	.912
Error	3971.280	24	165.470			

Estimated Marginal Means

time

Measure: MEASURE_1

time	Mean	Std. Error	95% Confidence Interval Lower Bound	Upper Bound
1	22.480	1.621	19.135	25.825
2	22.720	1.470	19.685	25.755
3	24.880	1.440	21.907	27.853

Figure 10.10 **Output for the one-way within subjects ANOVA procedure.**

the *Tests of Within-Subjects Effects* table: *Greenhouse-Geisser, Huynh-Feldt,* and *Lower-bound.* Each of these procedures attempts to adjust for the inaccuracy of the standard ANOVA *F* when the sphericity assumption has been violated. Since *Mauchly's Test of Sphericity* can be inaccurate, we'll bypass this test and take the more cautious approach of using one of the adjustment procedures printed out in SPSS (i.e., we'll assume the assumption of sphericity has been violated and proceed accordingly). Of the three adjustment procedures, the *Lower-bound* adjustment is overly cautious as it rejects the null hypothesis too infrequently (which is known as being conservative) and as a result is not recommended. When choosing an adjustment procedure, therefore, the choice is between the *Greenhouse-Geisser* and *Huynh-Feldt* procedures. While both procedures can provide fairly accurate adjustments when the assumption of sphericity has been violated, the *Greenhouse-Geisser* adjustment can be slightly conservative (i.e., it rejects the null hypothesis less often than is warranted) while the *Huynh-Feldt* adjustment can be slightly liberal (i.e., it rejects the null hypothesis more often than is warranted). We'll take the more cautious approach and interpret the *Greenhouse-Geisser* adjustment (although this will come at a slight sacrifice in power). While the *Greenhouse-Geisser* adjustment provides a more accurate result than the standard (sphericity assumed) *F* when the assumption of sphericity has been violated, because it is tedious to calculate by hand, its solution is usually considered only when conducting analyses by computer. Therefore, those who are using SPSS to confirm results of hand calculations will want to use the *Sphericity Assumed* values.

Tests of Within-Subjects Effects

The next table, *Tests of Within-Subjects Effects*, provides the answer to our research question, that is, whether or not the social skills scores differ for the three time occasions. ANOVA produces an *F* test, which is the ratio of two variances, with each variance represented as a mean square (*MS*) in the output:

$$F = \frac{MS\,Time}{MS\,Error\,(time)}$$

Substituting the values from the *Tests of Within-Subjects Effects* table under the row *Greenhouse-Geisser* yields an *F* of:

$$F = \frac{53.343}{3.731} = 14.298$$

which agrees with the value of *F* in the ANOVA table for the Greenhouse-Geisser solution. [The *Sphericity Assumed F* is also 14.298 (43.680/3.055).[5] As a reminder, if you are comparing the results to hand calculations you'll want to use the sphericity assumed values].

The ANOVA test produces two degrees of freedom (*df*) for **time** [(*df* = number of levels – 1) and *df* for error (*df* = (total sample size – 1)*(the number of levels – 1))], which results in values of 2 and 48, respectively, for the sphericity assumed values. To obtain the *df* for the *Greenhouse-Geisser* procedure, an adjustment is applied to the sphericity assumed degrees of freedom to compensate for the lack of sphericity in the data. In fact, if you look at the previous table, *Mauchly's Test of Sphericity*, you'll see that the value of a statistic called epsilon for *Greenhouse-Geisser* is .819. Multiplying the value of epsilon by the sphericity assumed degrees of freedom (2, 48) produces the degrees of freedom (within rounding error) of 1.638 and 39.305 that are reported for the *Greenhouse-Geisser* test.

The reported *p*-value found under the column "*Sig.*" for *Greenhouse-Geisser* is .000 (which is read as "less than .001"). Since the *p*-value is less than .05, the null hypothesis that the means of the three time occasions are equal is rejected (the null hypothesis would also be rejected using the sphericity assumed procedure, with a *p*-value less than .001 reported in the table). After discussing the remaining three tables of output, additional testing will be conducted to examine the nature of the differences among the three time occasions.

Test of Within-Subjects Contrasts and Tests of Between-Subjects Effects

The next two tables, *Test of Within-Subjects Contrasts* and *Tests of Between-Subjects Effects*, will not be used in our discussion of the one-way within subjects ANOVA. While the *Test of Within-Subjects Contrasts* can be used for conducting certain follow-up tests for **time**, we'll conduct dependent-samples *t* tests since, with only two levels of the within subjects factor tested at a time, the assumption of sphericity is not required.

The *Tests of Between-Subjects Effects* table displays the results for any between subjects factors included in the study. Since we don't have a between subjects factor in our study, this table is not relevant here (this table will be discussed in Chapter 11).

Estimated Marginal Means

The *Estimated Marginal Means* table provides the mean, standard error, and the 95% confidence interval for each of the three time occasions. While the *Descriptive Statistics* table discussed earlier also provided the mean for each group, the difference between the two tables is that the *Estimated Marginal Means* table displays the standard error and the 95% confidence interval for each of the groups, while the *Descriptive Statistics* table displays the standard deviation and the sample size.

Follow-up Tests after a Significant Result for the Overall ANOVA

Since the test for **time** was significant (see the *Tests of Within-Subjects Effects* section for a review), the null hypothesis that the social skills scores are equal across the three time occasions was rejected. Because the alternative hypothesis is nonspecific, however, stating only that the means differ in some way, follow-up testing is required to determine *which* of the time occasions are significantly different from one another. The approach we'll take for the follow-up tests is similar to that of the one-way between subjects ANOVA in Chapter 8. Recall for the between subjects ANOVA, if the overall test was significant, all pairwise comparisons were tested using Tukey's test. For the within subjects ANOVA, all pairwise comparisons will be tested using dependent-samples *t* tests, which is an appropriate follow-up procedure for the *within* subjects ANOVA. This would result in three pairwise *t* tests: **before** vs. **week8**, **before** vs. **after**, and **week8** vs. **after**. The commands for conducting the dependent samples *t* tests in SPSS are summarized next. (See Chapter 7 for more information on conducting dependent samples *t* tests.)

To conduct the three dependent-samples t tests in SPSS

1. From the menu bar select, **Analyze > Compare Means > Paired-Samples T Test . . .**
2. The *Paired-Samples T Test* dialog box opens. With the *Ctrl* key held down, select the variables *before* and *week8* and click the right-arrow button (➡) to move them to the *Paired Variables* box.
3. Repeat this procedure for **before** and **after** and **week8** and **after**. All three pairs should now be in the *Paired Variables* box (see Figure 10.11).

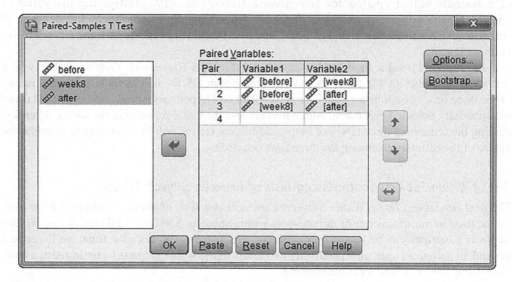

Figure 10.11   The *Paired-Samples T Test* dialog box.

4. Click *OK*.

The paired-samples *t* tests procedure runs in SPSS and the results are presented in the *Viewer* window. The output for the dependent-samples *t* tests is displayed in Figure 10.12.

T-Tests—Pairwise Comparisons of the Three Time Occasions

In conducting *t* tests of all possible pairwise comparisons, the following three null hypotheses were tested:

$$H_0: \mu_{before} = \mu_{week8}$$

$$H_0: \mu_{before} = \mu_{after}$$

$$H_0: \mu_{week8} = \mu_{after}$$

A common practice when conducting follow-up tests is to adjust the alpha level for each test so that the entire set of follow-up tests does not exceed .05 (the alpha used for each test is referred to as the alpha level per comparison). To find the alpha level for each test, take the overall alpha level for the set of tests (.05) and divide that by the number of follow-up tests conducted. For

T–Test

Paired Samples Statistics

		Mean	N	Std. Deviation	Std. Error Mean
Pair 1	before	22.4800	25	8.10411	1.62082
	week8	22.7200	25	7.35142	1.47028
Pair 2	before	22.4800	25	8.10411	1.62082
	after	24.8800	25	7.20139	1.44028
Pair 3	week8	22.7200	25	7.35142	1.47028
	after	24.8800	25	7.20139	1.44028

Paired Samples Correlations

		N	Correlation	Sig.
Pair 1	before & week8	25	.956	.000
Pair 2	before & after	25	.932	.000
Pair 3	week8 & after	25	.964	.000

Paired Samples Test

		Paired Differences							
					95% Confidence Interval of the Difference				
		Mean	Std. Deviation	Std. Error Mean`	Lower	Upper	t	df	Sig. (2-tailed)
Pair 1	before - week8	−.24000	2.40278	.48056	−1.23182	.75182	−.499	24	.622
Pair 2	before - after	−2.40000	2.95804	.59161	−3.62102	−1.17898	−4.057	24	.000
Pair 3	week8 - after	−2.16000	1.95107	.39021	−2.96536	−1.35464	−5.535	24	.000

For the test of the pairwise comparisons, before vs. after and week8 vs. after are both significant, since $p < .016$ for each test (before vs. week8 is not significant since its p–value of .622 is greater than .016).

Figure 10.12   **Output for the dependent-samples *t* follow-up tests.**

three tests and an alpha level of .05, the per comparison alpha level is .05/3 = .016 (rounded down so that the sum of the three tests does not exceed .05). This means that instead of evaluating each test against an alpha level of .05, the p-value for each test will be compared to an alpha level of .016. If the p-value is less than or equal to .016, the null hypothesis for the comparison of interest will be rejected. If the p-value is greater than .016, the null hypothesis will not be rejected.

This ensures that the probability of committing a Type I error (rejecting the null hypothesis when it is true) will be no greater than .05 for the entire *set* of follow-up tests. (If no adjustment was made and each follow-up test was conducted at .05, the overall alpha for the set of tests would *approach* the sum of the alpha levels for the three tests, or .15).

The results of the three pairwise comparisons are presented in the *Paired Samples Test* table. The results indicate that the first test, **before** vs. **week8**, is not significant, since the p-value of .622 is greater than .016. The remaining two tests, **before** vs. **after** and **week8** vs. **after**, are both significant, with reported p-values of .000 ($p < .001$). Since the latter two tests are significant, we'll inspect the means presented in the *Paired-Samples Statistics* table to determine which of the time occasions has the higher social skills scores. The

Paired-Samples Statistics table shows that social skills scores at **after** (24.88) are higher than both **before** (22.48) and **week8** (22.72). The results of the pairwise comparisons are summarized in Figure 10.13.

Test	Are the groups significantly different (is the *p*–value less than or equal to .016)?	Result
Before vs. 8 weeks	No	No significant difference between social skills scores before the program began and at 8 weeks
Before vs. after	Yes	Significant; at the end of the program children had higher social skills scores than before the program began
8 weeks vs. after	Yes	Significant; at the end of the program children had higher social skills scores than at 8 weeks

Figure 10.13 **Summary of the results of the three pairwise comparisons.**

Effect Sizes

The measure of effect size commonly used with one-way within subjects ANOVA is partial eta-square (η^2). To calculate partial eta-square, the sum of squares (*SS*) from the *Tests of Within-Subjects Effects* table are used (they are referred to as *Type III Sum of Squares* in the output). The formula for partial eta-square is:

$$\text{partial } \eta^2 = \frac{SS_{\text{Effect}}}{SS_{\text{Effect}} + SS_{\text{Error}}}$$

For **time**, the values for SS_{Effect} and SS_{Error} are reported in the *Tests of Within-Subjects Effects* table in Figure 10.10 as SS_{Time} and $SS_{\text{Error}(time)}$. Inserting the appropriate values from Figure 10.10 produces a partial eta-square of

$$\text{partial } \eta^2 = \frac{87.360}{87.360 + 146.640} = .373$$

which agrees with the value reported in the *Tests of Within-Subjects Effects* table for **time**.

While conventional effect size measures for small, medium, and large effect sizes for partial eta-square have not been provided, the larger the value of partial eta-square, the more variance the effect explains in the dependent variable.

Expression of the Results in APA Format

In writing the results for the one-way within subjects ANOVA, the conclusion of the hypothesis test, the degrees of freedom (*df*), the *F* value, the *p*-value, the effect size, and the results of the pair-wise comparisons are reported (assuming the overall ANOVA is significant) along with the mean and standard deviation for each of the time occasions social skills scores were measured (the mean and standard deviation for each of the groups may be reported in a separate table if desired). A sample write-up in APA format is presented next.

Written Results

The social skills scores for the children were significantly different across the time occasions, *Greenhouse-Geisser* adjusted $F(1.64, 39.31) = 14.30$, $p < .05$, partial $\eta^2 = .37$. Dependent samples *t* tests were conducted to assess which of the time occasions differed from one another, with each test conducted at an alpha level of .016. The results indicated that the social skills scores were significantly higher at the end of the program ($M = 24.88$, $SD = 7.20$) than at eight weeks ($M = 22.72$, $SD = 7.35$), $t(24) = -5.54$, $p < .016$, and at the end of the program as compared to before the program began ($M = 22.48$, $SD = 8.10$), $t(24) = -4.06$, $p < .016$. There was not a significant difference in social skills scores before the program began and at eight weeks, $t(24) = -.50$, $p > .016$.

[*Note:* If you prefer to use the sphericity assumed values, replace the *Geisser-Greenhouse* degrees of freedom (1.64, 39.31) with the sphericity assumed values (2, 48) and delete the phrase "*Geisser-Greenhouse* adjusted" from the results. All other results remain the same.]

Assumptions of the One-Way within Subjects ANOVA

1. *The observations are independent between the participants.*
   Violating this assumption can seriously compromise the accuracy of the within subjects ANOVA (teachers working together in determining their ratings of social skills scores for students is an example of a violation of the independence assumption). If there is reason to believe the independence assumption has been violated, the within subjects ANOVA should not be used.
2. *The dependent variable is normally distributed at each level of the independent variable in the population.*
   This assumption means that the social skills scores should be normally distributed in the population for each level of the independent variable (e.g., social skills scores should be normally distributed at before, eight weeks, and after). For moderate to large sample sizes, most types of nonnormal distributions tend to have relatively little impact on the accuracy of the ANOVA test, although some nonnormal distributions can adversely affect the power of the ANOVA test.
3. *Sphericity.*
   The sphericity assumption requires that the variances of the difference scores are equal for all pairs of levels of the within subjects factor in the population. For example, if you calculated the difference score between the first two levels of the within subjects factor for each of the participants (before – eight weeks) and then calculated the variance of those scores (recall that the variance is equal to the standard deviation squared) and repeated this procedure for all other combinations of levels (before – after and eight weeks – after), the sphericity assumption requires that these three variances are equal.

$$\sigma^2_{\text{before}-8\,\text{weeks}} = \sigma^2_{\text{before}-\text{after}} = \sigma^2_{8\,\text{weeks}-\text{after}}$$

Violating the assumption of sphericity can compromise the accuracy of the ANOVA test, resulting in the null hypothesis being rejected more often than is warranted. Using an alternative procedure that adjusts for the presence of sphericity (e.g., *Greenhouse-Geisser*) addresses a violation of this assumption. Because multivariate analysis of variance (MANOVA) does not require the assumption of sphericity, MANOVA is also a viable option, although a discussion of this procedure is beyond the scope of this text [see Maxwell and Delaney (2004) or Stevens (2002) for more details on the MANOVA procedure].

Summary of Steps for Conducting a One-Way within Subjects ANOVA in SPSS

I. Data Entry and Analysis

1. Create the number of variables in SPSS equal to the number of levels of the within subjects factor.
2. Enter the data.
3. Select **Analyze > General Linear Model > Repeated Measures . . .**
4. Enter the name of the within subjects factor in the *Within-Subject Factor Name* text box, and enter the number of levels in the *Number of Levels* box. Click *Add*. Click *Define*.
5. Move the variables (i.e., the levels of the within subjects factor) into the *Within-Subjects Variables* box.
6. Click *Options*. Move the within subjects factor to the *Display Means for* box. Under *Display*, click *Descriptive statistics* and *Estimates of effect size*. Click *Continue*.
7. Click *OK*.

II. Interpretation of the Results

1. Interpret the results for the overall ANOVA by examining the *p*-value either under *Greenhouse-Geisser* or the *Sphericity Assumed* rows (use the *Sphericity Assumed* values if comparing results to hand calculations).
   a. If the ANOVA is significant (i.e., $p \leq .05$), run dependent-samples *t* tests for all possible pairwise comparisons. Evaluate each *t* test at an alpha equal to .05 divided by the number of pairwise comparisons tested. Include the results for the overall ANOVA and the dependent-samples *t* tests in your write-up.
   b. If the ANOVA is not significant (i.e., $p > .05$), stop (do not conduct *t* tests). Write the results stating that there is not a significant difference between the groups.

Exercises

1. A school social worker examined the impact of a new truancy prevention program on the number of truancies at a local school. Fifteen children were enrolled in the new program, and the number of truancies for each child was tracked over a nine-month period, with the number of truancies recorded in three-month intervals. The data are provided in Figure 10.14.

0–3 months	3–6 months	6–9 months
30	28	20
36	30	24
39	37	34
45	40	35
21	24	17
36	44	20
30	28	17
36	34	28
33	36	27
42	37	26
36	39	38
30	35	36
21	20	10
24	18	20
36	30	30

Figure 10.14 **The number of truancies (at three-month intervals) for the children enrolled in the truancy program.**

Enter the data into SPSS and perform the appropriate analyses to answer the questions below. Name the variables **month3**, **month6**, and **month9**, respectively.
a. State the null and alternative hypotheses.
b. State a research question for the data.
c. Is there a significant difference in the number of truancies over the three time periods? Test at $\alpha = .05$.
d. What is the effect size for the ANOVA?
e. If the overall ANOVA is significant, perform follow-up tests as appropriate. Adjust alpha for each test so that the *set* of tests does not exceed .05.
f. Write the results of the study using APA format as appropriate.

2. A clinical psychologist wanted to investigate the effectiveness of psychoanalytic therapy over time. Fifteen people who checked into a treatment facility (and consented to participate) were enrolled in the study. Each of the participants received psychoanalytic therapy for a period of eight weeks. To measure the effectiveness of the therapy, the participants were administered a general measure of well-being before beginning therapy, four weeks into treatment, and after eight weeks. The well-being measure ranged from 10 to 50, with higher scores indicating greater well-being. The data are in the file *Chapter 10_Exercise 2.sav* in the Chapter 10 folder online at www.routledge.com/cw/yockey (the variables are named **beforetherapy**, **fourweeks**, and **eightweeks**). Open the data file in SPSS and perform the appropriate analyses to answer the questions below.
a. State the null and alternative hypotheses.
b. State a research question for the data.
c. Is there a significant difference in the well-being scores over time? Test at $\alpha = .05$.
d. What is the effect size for the ANOVA?
e. If the overall ANOVA is significant, perform follow-up tests as appropriate. Adjust alpha for each test so that the *set* of tests does not exceed .05.
f. Write the results of the study using APA format as appropriate.

3. A marketing researcher investigated the impact of offering different types of wifi Internet service on the likelihood of eating at a fast-food restaurant. The likelihood of dining at a fast-food restaurant was investigated under three different classifications: free wifi service, pay per use wifi service, and no wifi service. Ten people (who ate fast food at least once a month) were asked to rate on a 1 to 10 scale the likelihood (1 = least likelihood and 10 = greatest likelihood) that they would dine at a fast-food restaurant in each of the three conditions (free wifi, pay per use wifi, and no wifi). The data are provided in the file *Chapter 10_Exercise 3.sav* in the Chapter 10 folder online at www.routledge.com/cw/yockey (the variables are named **freewifi**, **payforwifi**, and **nowifi**). Open the data file in SPSS and perform the appropriate analyses to answer the questions below.
a. State the null and alternative hypotheses.
b. State a research question for the data.
c. Is there a significant difference in the likelihood of eating at a fast-food restaurant based on the type of wifi service offered? Test at $\alpha = .05$.
d. What is the effect size for the overall ANOVA?
e. If the overall ANOVA is significant, perform follow-up tests as appropriate. Adjust alpha for each test so that the *set* of tests does not exceed .05.
f. Write the results of the study using APA format as appropriate.

Notes

1. While within subjects factors most commonly consist of the same people measured on multiple occasions, they can also consist of related people each measured once (e.g., husbands and wives).
2. While **before, week8**, and **after** are entered as *variables* in SPSS, in the one-way within subjects ANOVA design they are *levels* of the within subjects factor **time.**
3. When there are only two levels to a within subjects factor, the assumption of sphericity is not required.

4. While Mauchley's test of sphericity won't be evaluated here, the approach for evaluating it is as follows: The null hypothesis is that the data are spherical in the population; if $p \leq .05$ for Mauchley's test, the null hypothesis is rejected and it is assumed that the sphericity assumption has *not* been satisfied. If $p > .05$, the null hypothesis is not rejected and it is assumed that the sphericity assumption has been satisfied.

5. While all four procedures in the *Tests of Within-Subjects Effects* table produce the same value for F, they frequently differ in their degrees of freedom (and subsequently in their p-values).

The One-between–One-within Subjects Analysis of Variance (ANOVA)

A one-between–one-within subjects ANOVA is used when two independent variables are evaluated on a dependent variable of interest. In the one-between–one-within ANOVA, one of the independent variables is a between subjects factor and the other is a within subjects factor. The between subjects factor consists of two or more levels, where each participant receives *only one* level of the treatment. The within subjects factor consists of two or more levels, where each participant receives *all* levels of the treatment.[1] An example of a one-between–one-within ANOVA is presented next.

Example

A researcher investigated whether a mentoring program designed for beginning high school teachers was effective at reducing stress. Twenty new teachers participated in the study, with 10 teachers receiving the mentoring program and 10 teachers serving as the control group (i.e., they did not receive any mentoring support). In the mentoring program, the new teachers were assigned a mentor whom they met with weekly to discuss aspects of their job that are particularly challenging as they begin their careers (e.g., classroom management issues). After agreeing to participate in the study, all the teachers were administered a teaching stress scale one week before beginning teaching (**before**), four weeks into the year (**week4**), and eight weeks into the year (**week8**). The teaching stress scale ranged from 20 to 80, with higher scores indicating greater teaching-related stress. In this study, support (two levels—mentor, no mentor) is the between subjects factor, time (three levels—before, four weeks, and eight weeks) is the within subjects factor, and the dependent variable is the reported level of teaching-related stress experienced by the new teachers.

Objectives and Data Requirements of the One-between–One-within ANOVA

One-between–One-within ANOVA

Objectives	Data Requirements	Example
To test for main effects	Independent variables	Independent variables
• Is there a difference in stress levels between mentored and nonmentored teachers?	• One-between subjects factor (with two or more levels)	• Support (mentor, no mentor)
• Is there a difference in stress levels before the program began, at four weeks, and at eight weeks?	• One-within subjects factor (with two or more levels)	• Time (before, four weeks, eight weeks)
To test for an interaction effect	Dependent variable	Dependent variable
• Does the impact of support (mentor, no mentor) depend on time (before, four weeks, eight weeks)?	• Continuous	• Teaching stress scores

Null and Alternative Hypotheses

There are three different null hypotheses for the one-between–one-within subjects ANOVA. One null hypothesis is tested for each of the independent variables (known as tests of main effects), and one for the combined effect of the two independent variables (known as a test for an interaction effect). Each of these hypotheses is described below.

Hypothesis 1. Test of Support: Mentoring vs. No Mentoring

The null hypothesis for support states that the mean stress levels for mentored and nonmentored teachers are equal in the population:

$$H_0: \mu_{\text{mentored}} = \mu_{\text{not mentored}}$$

The alternative hypothesis states that the mean stress levels for mentored and nonmentored teachers are not equal in the population:

$$H_1: \mu_{\text{mentored}} \neq \mu_{\text{not mentored}}$$

Hypothesis 2. Test of Time: Before, Four Weeks, and Eight Weeks

The null hypothesis for time states that the mean stress levels in the population are equal before the program began, at four weeks, and at eight weeks:

$$H_0: \mu_{\text{before}} = \mu_{4 \text{ weeks}} = \mu_{8 \text{ weeks}}$$

When there are three or more levels to a factor, the alternative hypothesis states that there is a difference somewhere between the levels of the factor:

$$H_1: \text{At least one of the population means is different from the others.}[2]$$

Hypothesis 3. Test of the Interaction Effect of Support and Time

The null hypothesis states that there is not an interaction between support and time:

$$H_0: \text{There is not a support} \times \text{time interaction.}$$

The alternative hypothesis states that there is an interaction between the two variables:

$$H_1: \text{There is a support} \times \text{time interaction.}$$

Evaluation of the Null Hypothesis

The one-between–one-within ANOVA provides a test of the three null hypotheses discussed above. For a given hypothesis of interest, if the test produces results that seem unlikely if the null hypothesis is true (results that occur less than 5% of the time), then the null hypothesis is rejected. If the test produces results that seem fairly likely if the null hypothesis is true (results that occur greater than 5% of the time), then the null hypothesis is not rejected.

Research Questions

The fundamental questions of interest in a one-between–one-within ANOVA can also be expressed in the form of research questions, such as:

For support

> "Do the reported stress levels differ for those who received mentoring versus those who did not?"

For time

> "Is there a difference in the reported stress levels before beginning teaching, at four weeks, and at eight weeks?"

For the interaction of time and support

> "Do the reported stress levels for time depend on whether or not mentoring was received?"

The Data

The data for the 20 participants are presented in Figure 11.1. For support, those who received mentoring are assigned a "1" and those who did not receive mentoring are assigned a "2." For time, **before**, **week4**, and **week8** correspond to teacher stress scores immediately before beginning teaching, four weeks into the school year, and eight weeks into the school year, respectively.

Participant	Support	Before	Week4	Week8	Participant	Support	Before	Week4	Week8
1	1	40	39	35	11	2	38	44	42
2	1	45	44	42	12	2	47	45	42
3	1	42	44	44	13	2	41	48	45
4	1	38	36	30	14	2	39	41	43
5	1	46	44	38	15	2	44	44	41
6	1	40	37	25	16	2	42	39	35
7	1	42	38	35	17	2	42	48	46
8	1	39	37	29	18	2	40	46	42
9	1	35	33	31	19	2	38	45	43
10	1	43	44	38	20	2	41	40	35

Figure 11.1 **The data for the one-between–one-within ANOVA. (*Note*: The participant variable is included for illustration but will not be entered into SPSS.)**

Data Entry and Analysis in SPSS

Steps 1 and 2 describe how to enter the data in SPSS. The data file is also available online at www.routledge.com/cw/yockey under the name *teaching stress.sav* in the Chapter 11 folder. If you prefer to open the file from the web site, skip to Step 3.

Step 1: Create the Variables

1. Start SPSS.
2. Click the *Variable View* tab.

In SPSS, four variables will be created, one for the support groups (mentor/no mentor) and one for each of the time occasions teaching stress was assessed. The variables will be named **support**, **before**, **week4**, and **week8**, respectively.

3. Enter the names **support**, **before**, **week4**, and **week8**, respectively, in the first four rows of the *Variable View* window. Under *Measure*, classify support as nominal, and **before**, **week4**, and **week8** as scale (see Figure 11.2).

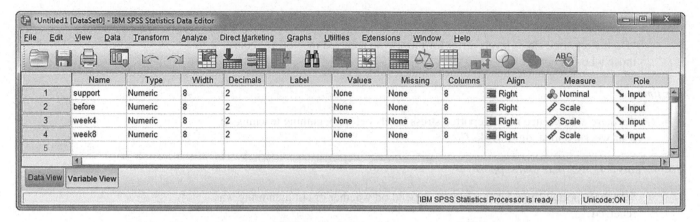

Figure 11.2   The *Variable View* window with the variables support, before, week4, and week8 entered.

4.   Using the process described in Chapter 1, create value labels for **support**. For **support**, 1 = "mentor" and 2 = "no mentor."

Step 2: Enter the Data

1.   Click the *Data View* tab. The variables **support**, **before**, **week4**, and **week8** appear in the first four columns of the *Data View* window.
2.   Consulting Figure 11.1, enter the values for each of the participants on the four variables of interest. For the first participant, enter the values *1*, *40*, *39*, and *35*, for the variables **support**, **before**, **week4** and **week8**, respectively. Using this approach, enter the data for all 20 participants. The completed data set is presented in Figure 11.3.

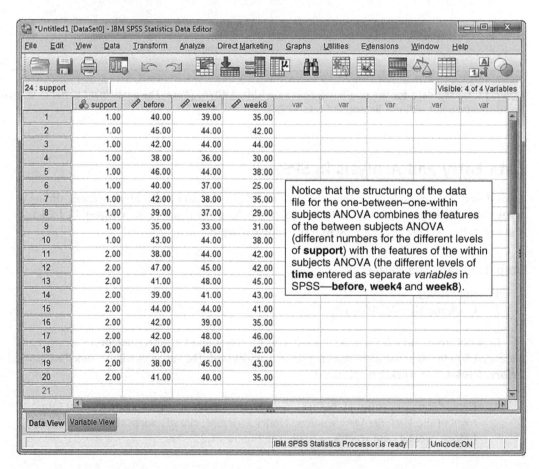

Figure 11.3   The completed data file for the one-between–one-within ANOVA.

Step 3: Analyze the Data

1. From the menu bar, select **Analyze > General Linear Model > Repeated Measures** . . . (see Figure 11.4).

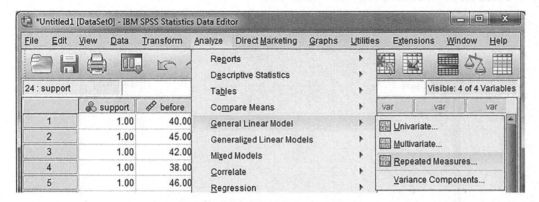

Figure 11.4 **Menu commands for the one-between–one-within subjects ANOVA procedure.**

A *Repeated Measures Define Factor(s)* dialog box opens (see Figure 11.5). This dialog box is used to provide a name for the within subjects factor and to enter the number of levels of the factor.[3]

2. Double-click "*factor1*" in the *Within Subject Factor Name* text box (*factor1* is the default name SPSS provides for the within subject factor). Enter the name **time**.
3. In the *Number of Levels* text box, enter the number *3*. This corresponds to the number of levels of **time** (**before**, **week4**, and **week8**). See Figure 11.6 for details.

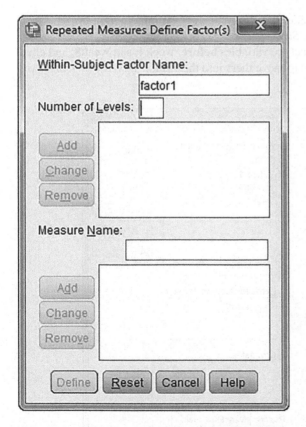

Figure 11.5 **The *Repeated Measures Define Factor(s)* dialog box.**

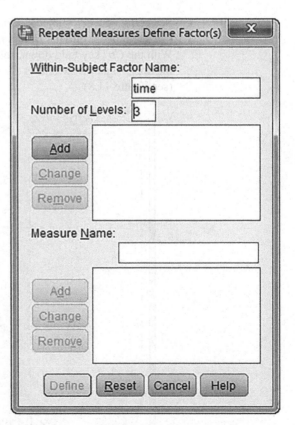

Figure 11.6 **The *Repeated Measures Define Factor(s)* dialog box (continued).**

4. Click *Add*.
5. Click *Define*.

The *Repeated Measures* dialog box opens with **support**, **before**, **week4**, and **week8** on the left-hand side of the dialog box (see Figure 11.7).

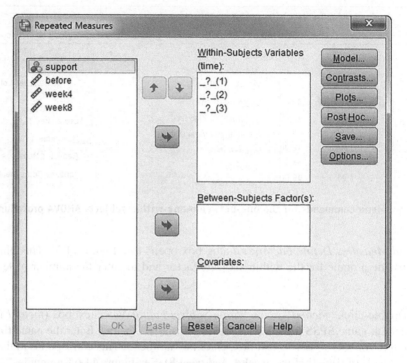

Figure 11.7 The *Repeated Measures* dialog box.

6. Select the between subjects variable, **support**, and click the middle right-arrow button (⮞) to move it into the *Between-Subjects Factor(s)* box.
7. With the *Ctrl* key held down, select the variables **before, week4**, and **week8**, and click the upper right-arrow button (⮞) to move them into the *Within-Subjects Variables* box (see Figure 11.8).

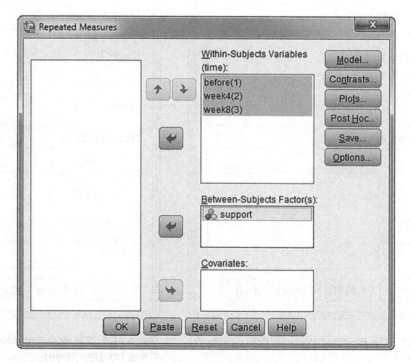

Figure 11.8 The *Repeated Measures* dialog box (continued).

8. Click *Options*. The *Repeated Measures: Options* dialog box opens. Under the *Factor(s) and Factor Interactions* box select **support**, **time**, and **support*time**, and click the right-arrow button (▶) to move them into the *Display Means for* box. Under *Display* select *Descriptive statistics* and *Estimates of effect size* (see Figure 11.9).

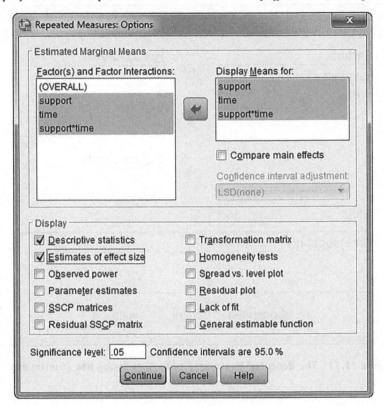

Figure 11.9   The *Repeated Measures: Options* dialog box.

9. Click *Continue*.
10. Click *Plots*. The *Repeated Measures: Profile Plots* dialog box opens. Select the factor, **time**, and click the upper right-arrow button (▶) to move it to the *Horizontal Axis* box. Select the factor, **support**, and click the middle right-arrow button (▶) to move it to the *Separate Lines* box. See Figure 11.10 for details.

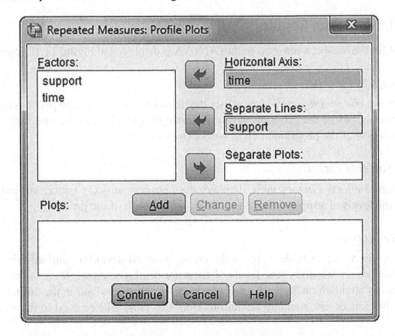

Figure 11.10   The *Repeated Measures: Profile Plots* dialog box.

11. Click *Add*. The interaction term **time*support** appears in the *Plots* box (see Figure 11.11).

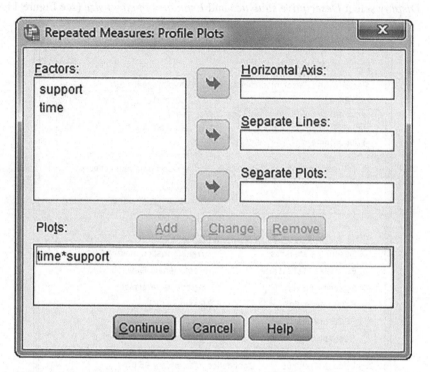

Figure 11.11 **The *Repeated Measures: Profile Plots* dialog box (continued).**

12. Click *Continue*.
13. Click *OK*.

The one-between–one-within ANOVA procedure runs in SPSS and the results are presented in the *Viewer* window.

Step 4: Interpret the Results

The output for the one-between–one-within ANOVA is displayed in Figure 11.12 (pages 145–147).

Within-Subjects Factors

The first table, *Within-Subjects Factors*, lists the three time occasions the participants were measured, including before the program began (**before**), four weeks into the program (**week4**), and at the conclusion of the program at eight weeks (**week8**).

Between-Subjects Factors

The *Between-Subjects Factors* table displays the between subjects factor, **support**, the value labels for the levels of **support**, and the sample size for each of the groups.

Descriptive Statistics

The *Descriptive Statistics* table displays the mean, standard deviation, and sample size for each of the conditions in the study (the levels of **time** are displayed under *Total* in the table). While we'll focus our attention on the *Estimated Marginal Means* tables later in the output for interpreting mean differences, the standard deviations from this table will be used in the write-up of our results.

Multivariate Tests

The null hypothesis for **time** and the **time*support** interaction may be tested either using a univariate test (ANOVA) or a multivariate test (MANOVA). The *Multivariate Tests* table provides the results of four different multivariate tests for **time** and **time*support**.[4] While the multivariate tests are automatically output in the results, multivariate procedures are beyond the scope of this text and will therefore not be discussed. Interested readers are referred to Maxwell and Delaney (2004) or Stevens (2002) for more details on the MANOVA procedure.

Mauchly's Test of Sphericity

The next table, *Mauchly's Test of Sphericity*, tests the sphericity assumption, which is an assumption of the one-between–one-within ANOVA when there are three or more levels to the within subjects factor.[5] While a test of this assumption is provided in the *Mauchly's Test of Sphericity* table in SPSS (the *p*-value for the test is .006), this test can be inaccurate (see Howell, 2007, or Maxwell and Delaney, 2004, for more details) and will therefore not be considered (an alternative approach to testing the assumption of sphericity will be provided).

General Linear Model

Within-Subjects Factors

Measure: MEASURE_1

time	Dependent Variable
1	before
2	week4
3	week8

Between-Subjects Factors

		Value Label	N
support	1.00	mentor	10
	2.00	no mentor	10

Descriptive Statistics

	support	Mean	Std. Deviation	N
before	mentor	41.0000	3.29983	10
	no mentor	41.2000	2.78089	10
	Total	41.1000	2.97180	20
week4	mentor	39.6000	4.08792	10
	no mentor	44.0000	3.12694	10
	Total	41.8000	4.20025	20
week8	mentor	34.7000	6.00093	10
	no mentor	41.4000	3.68782	10
	Total	38.0500	5.94249	20

Multivariate Tests[b]

Effect		Value	F	Hypothesis df	Error df	Sig.	Partial Eta Squared
time	Pillai's Trace	.704	20.183[a]	2.000	17.000	.000	.704
	Wilks' Lambda	.296	20.183[a]	2.000	17.000	.000	.704
	Hotelling's Trace	2.375	20.183[a]	2.000	17.000	.000	.704
	Roy's Largest Root	2.375	20.183[a]	2.000	17.000	.000	.704
time * support	Pillai's Trace	.365	4.878[a]	2.000	17.000	.021	.365
	Wilks' Lambda	.635	4.878[a]	2.000	17.000	.021	.365
	Hotelling's Trace	.574	4.878[a]	2.000	17.000	.021	.365
	Roy's Largest Root	.574	4.878[a]	2.000	17.000	.021	.365

a. Exact statistic

b. Design: Intercept + support
   Within Subjects Design: time

Mauchly's Test of Sphericity[b]

Measure: MEASURE_1

Within Subjects Effect	Mauchly's W	Approx. Chi-Square	df	Sig.	Epsilon[a] Greenhouse-Geisser	Huynh-Feldt	Lower-bound
time	.545	10.310	2	.006	.687	.767	.500

Tests the null hypothesis that the error covariance matrix of the orthonormalized transformed dependent variables is proportional to an identity matrix.

a. May be used to adjust the degrees of freedom for the averaged tests of significance. Corrected tests are displayed in the Tests of Within-Subjects Effects table.

b. Design: Intercept + support
   Within Subjects Design: time

(continued)

Tests of Within-Subjects Effects

Measure: MEASURE_1

Source		Type III Sum of Squares	df	Mean Square	F	Sig.	Partial Eta Squared
time	Sphericity Assumed	159.033	2	79.517	12.078	.000	.402
	Greenhouse-Geisser	159.033	1.375	115.676	12.078	.001	.402
	Huynh-Feldt	159.033	1.534	103.699	12.078	.000	.402
	Lower-bound	159.033	1.000	159.033	12.078	.003	.402
time * support	Sphericity Assumed	108.633	2	54.317	8.251	.001	.314
	Greenhouse-Geisser	108.633	1.375	79.016	8.251	.004	.314
	Huynh-Feldt	108.633	1.534	70.836	8.251	.003	.314
	Lower-bound	108.633	1.000	108.633	8.251	.010	.314
Error(time)	Sphericity Assumed	237.000	36	6.583			
	Greenhouse-Geisser	237.000	24.747	9.577			
	Huynh-Feldt	237.000	27.605	8.585			
	Lower-bound	237.000	18.000	13.167			

The *p*–values for the tests of **time** and **time** x **support**. Use either the *Greenhouse–Geisser* or *Sphericity Assumed* values (in this example both **time** and **time** x **support** are significant using either criteria since *p* < .05 for each test).

Tests of Within-Subjects Contrasts

Measure: MEASURE_1

Source	time	Type III Sum of Squares	df	Mean Square	F	Sig.	Partial Eta Squared
time	Linear	93.025	1	93.025	8.463	.009	.320
	Quadratic	66.008	1	66.008	30.349	.000	.628
time * support	Linear	105.625	1	105.625	9.610	.006	.348
	Quadratic	3.008	1	3.008	1.383	.255	.071
Error(time)	Linear	197.850	18	10.992			
	Quadratic	39.150	18	2.175			

Tests of Between-Subjects Effects

Measure: MEASURE_1
Transformed Variable: Average

Source	Type III Sum of Squares	df	Mean Square	F	Sig.	Partial Eta Squared
Intercept	97526.017	1	97526.017	2852.101	.000	.994
support	212.817	1	212.817	6.224	.023	.257
Error	615.500	18	34.194			

Support is significant since *p* < .05.

Estimated Marginal Means

1. support

Measure: MEASURE_1

support	Mean	Std. Error	95% Confidence Interval	
			Lower Bound	Upper Bound
mentor	38.433	1.068	36.190	40.676
no mentor	42.200	1.068	39.957	44.443

2. time

Measure: MEASURE_1

time	Mean	Std. Error	95% Confidence Interval	
			Lower Bound	Upper Bound
1	41.100	.682	39.667	42.533
2	41.800	.814	40.090	43.510
3	38.050	1.114	35.710	40.390

3. support * time

Measure: MEASURE_1

support	time	Mean	Std. Error	95% Confidence Interval	
				Lower Bound	Upper Bound
mentor	1	41.000	.965	38.973	43.027
	2	39.600	1.151	37.182	42.018
	3	34.700	1.575	31.391	38.009
no mentor	1	41.200	.965	39.173	43.227
	2	44.000	1.151	41.582	46.418
	3	41.400	1.575	38.091	44.709

Profile Plots

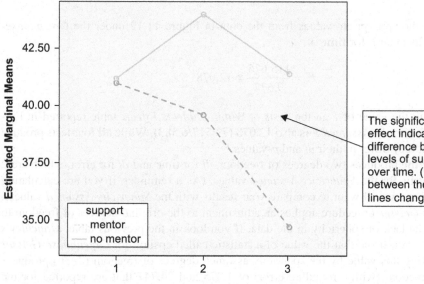

The significant interaction effect indicates that the difference between the levels of support changed over time. (i.e., the *distance* between the top and bottom lines changed over time).

Figure 11.12 **Output for the one-between–one-within ANOVA.**

As was discussed in Chapter 10, if the sphericity assumption is not met, the ANOVA F test (reported as *Sphericity Assumed* in the *Tests of Within Subjects Effects* table) is inaccurate, yielding results that lead to rejecting a true null hypothesis more often than is warranted. As a result of the inaccuracy of the F test when the assumption of sphericity is violated, several alternative F tests that adjust for the lack of sphericity have been proposed. There are three such "adjustment procedures" in the *Tests of Within-Subjects Effects* table: *Greenhouse-Geisser*, *Huynh-Feldt*, and *Lower-bound*. For reasons discussed in Chapter 10, we will evaluate the *Greenhouse-Geisser F* in the output. While the *Greenhouse-Geisser* adjustment provides a more accurate result when the assumption of sphericity has been violated, because it is tedious to calculate by hand, its solution is usually only considered when conducting analyses by computer. Therefore, those who are using SPSS to confirm results of hand calculations will want to use the *Sphericity Assumed* values.

Test of Within-Subjects Effects

The next table, *Tests of Within-Subjects Effects*, provides the answer to two of our research questions, that is, whether or not the stress scores differ for the three time occasions and whether or not there is an interaction between **time** and **support**.

As was the case with the one-way ANOVA discussed in Chapter 8, the F test is a ratio of two variances, with each variance represented as a mean square (*MS*) in the output.

$$F = \frac{MS\,Effect}{MS\,Error}$$

In the one-between–one-within ANOVA, the tests that include the within subjects factor (i.e., **time** and **time × support**) have an error term that is different from the test of the between subjects factor (i.e., **support**). In the *Tests of Within-Subjects Effects* table, **time** and **time × support** share the same error term, *MS Error(time)*. For **time**, the F ratio is:

$$F = \frac{MS\,Time}{MS\,Error\,(Time)}$$

Substituting the appropriate values from the data in Figure 11.12 under the *Greenhouse-Geisser* row results in an F for **time** of:

$$F = \frac{115.676}{9.577} = 12.078$$

which agrees with the value of F in the *Tests of Within-Subjects Effects* table reported in Figure 11.12. [The *Sphericity Assumed F* is also 12.078 (79.517/6.583). While all four tests produce the same F value, they differ in their df and p-values.]

The test of **time** produces two degrees of freedom, df for time and df for error, which are 2 and 36, respectively, for the *Sphericity Assumed* values. (As a reminder, if you are calculating the F values by hand you'll want to compare your results with the *Sphericity Assumed* values). The *Greenhouse-Geisser* procedure applies an adjustment to the original degrees of freedom to compensate for the lack of sphericity in the data. If you look in the previous table, *Mauchley's Test of Sphericity*, you'll see that the value of a statistic called epsilon for *Greenhouse-Geisser* is .687. Multiplying this value by the sphericity assumed degrees of freedom (2, 36) produces the degrees of freedom (within rounding error) of 1.375 and 24.747 that are reported for the *Greenhouse-Geisser* test.

The reported p-value found under the column "*Sig.*" for *Greenhouse-Geisser* for **time** is .001. Since the p-value is less than .05, the null hypothesis that the means of the three time occasions are equal is rejected, and it is concluded that at least one of the time occasions is different from the others.

Moving to the test of **time × support**, the *Greenhouse-Geisser F* is 8.251 (79.016/9.577) with a p-value of .004. Since the p-value is less than .05, the null hypothesis is rejected, and it is concluded that there is a significant **time × support** interaction (a write-up of the results will be provided later in the chapter).

Tests of Within-Subjects Contrasts

The next table, *Tests of Within-Subjects Contrasts*, can be used for conducting certain follow-up tests for within subjects main effects and interactions. This table will not be discussed for the one-between–one-within ANOVA, as we will be using an alternative method for conducting follow-up tests, which will be discussed shortly.

Tests of Between-Subjects Effects

The *Tests of Between-Subjects Effects* table reports the results of the test of the between subjects factor, **support**. The F for **support** is 6.224 (*MS support/MS error* = 212.817/34.194) with a corresponding p-value of .023.[6] Since the p-value is less than .05, the null hypothesis that the mean stress levels are equal for mentored and nonmentored teachers is rejected (a write-up of the results for **support** will be provided later in the chapter).

Estimated Marginal Means

The *Estimated Marginal Means* tables present the means for the levels of each of the factors and for the interaction. The first table, *support*, presents the means for the mentored and nonmentored groups. Since **support** was significant, we'll inspect the means to determine which group had lower stress scores. The marginal means for support shows that those who had a mentor (mean = 38.43) had lower mean stress levels than those who did not have a mentor (mean = 42.20).

The next table, *time*, shows the means for the levels of **time**. Since there are three levels to **time**, we cannot definitively conclude which of the three time occasions are significantly different without further testing (recall the nonspecific nature of the alternative hypothesis with three or more groups). (Due to space considerations, follow-up tests will not be conducted here; however, instructions for conducting follow-up tests for the within subjects factor are provided on the summary page prior to the chapter exercises.)

The last table, *support*time*, shows the means for the six conditions in (3 time × 2 support) the study. To interpret the significant interaction effect, we'll focus our attention on the *Profile Plots* table, which presents the means of the six conditions in graphical form.

Profile Plots

The *Profile Plots* graph displays a plot of the means of the six conditions in the study. As we specified earlier in SPSS, **time** is on the horizontal axis and the levels of **support** are represented as separate lines (in the plot, 1, 2, and 3 correspond to **before, week4,** and **week8,** respectively, for **time**). Inspecting the means, prior to the start of the program, the mentored and nonmentored groups had mean stress levels that were nearly identical (41.00 vs. 41.20), while at both four and eight weeks mentored teachers reported lower stress levels than nonmentored teachers (39.60 vs. 44.00 at four weeks and 34.70 vs. 41.40 at eight weeks). The significant interaction effect indicates that the lines are significantly nonparallel, confirming that the difference between the mentored and nonmentored groups changed over time.

Testing of the Interaction Effect: Simple Effects Analyses

While the interaction effect indicates that the lines are significantly nonparallel, it does not indicate *which* points are significantly different from one another.[7] To determine which points are significantly different, simple effects testing will be conducted. Simple effects tests are used to examine differences for one factor *at a single level* of the other factor. In the current example, several different simple effects tests could be conducted, including testing support (mentored vs. nonmentored teachers) at each level of time (i.e., testing across the lines in the *Profile Plot*), as well as testing time (**before, week4,** and **week8**) at each level of support (i.e., testing within each line in the *Profile Plot*).

To illustrate simple effects testing for the one-between–one-within ANOVA, we'll test whether mentored versus nonmentored teachers differed significantly in their scores before the program began, at four weeks, and at eight weeks (referred to as 1, 2, and 3 in the interaction plot). This entails conducting three separate independent-samples t tests, one for each level of time.

Since the *t* tests are follow-up tests, they will each be conducted at alpha level of .016 (.05/3) to ensure that the total alpha for the three tests combined does not exceed .05 (see Chapter 10 for more details on adjusting alpha for follow-up tests).

Testing mentored versus nonmentored teachers at each level of time would imply the following three null hypotheses:

$$H_0: \mu_{\text{mentored\_before}} = \mu_{\text{not mentored\_before}}$$

$$H_0: \mu_{\text{mentored\_4 weeks}} = \mu_{\text{not mentored\_4 weeks}}$$

$$H_0: \mu_{\text{mentored\_8 weeks}} = \mu_{\text{not mentored\_8 weeks}}$$

The commands for running the independent samples *t* tests are provided next (see Chapter 7 for more details on the independent samples *t* test).

1. From the menu bar select **Analyze > Compare Means > Independent-Samples T Test . . .**
2. Move **support** to the *Grouping Variable* box.
3. Click *Define Groups*. Assign a *1* to Group 1 and a *2* to Group 2.
4. With the *Ctrl* key held down, select **before**, **week4**, and **week8** and click the right-arrow button (➡) to move them to the *Test Variable(s)* box (see Figure 11.13).
5. Click *OK*.

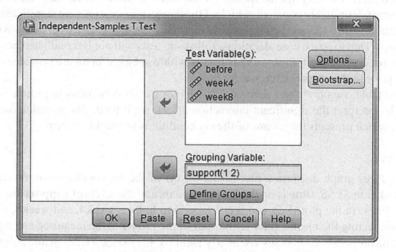

Figure 11.13 The *Independent-Samples T Test* dialog box.

Results of the Simple Effects Analyses—Testing Support at Each Level of Time

The results of the independent-samples *t* tests are shown in Figure 11.14. The *Independent Samples Test* table shows that support is significant at both four weeks ($p = .015$) and eight weeks ($p = .008$) but not at before ($p = .885$) (recall that each test was evaluated at an alpha level of .016). The means in the *Group Statistics* table indicate that at both four and eight weeks those who were mentored reported significantly less stress than those who were not mentored. These results will be incorporated into the overall write-up of the results provided at the conclusion of the chapter.

Other tests of simple effects could have been conducted, such as testing for differences across **time** for each support group. For example, we could test stress levels across **time** for those who had a mentor, which would imply a one-way within subjects ANOVA. If the ANOVA was significant, then as was illustrated in Chapter 10, all pairwise comparisons of **time** could be tested using dependent samples *t* tests (i.e., 1 vs. 2, 1 vs. 3, and 2 vs. 3). While these tests will not be illustrated here due to space considerations, a test of mentored teachers over time will be addressed in Exercise 3 at the conclusion of this chapter (with the solution provided in Appendix C).

T–Test

Group Statistics

	support	N	Mean	Std. Deviation	Std. Error Mean
before	mentor	10	41.0000	3.29983	1.04350
	no mentor	10	41.2000	2.78089	.87939
week4	mentor	10	39.6000	4.08792	1.29271
	no mentor	10	44.0000	3.12694	.98883
week8	mentor	10	34.7000	6.00093	1.89766
	no mentor	10	41.4000	3.68782	1.16619

Independent Samples Test

		Levene's Test for Equality of Variances		t-test for Equality of Means						95% Confidence Interval of the Difference	
		F	Sig.	t	df	Sig. (2-tailed)	Mean Difference	Std. Error Difference		Lower	Upper
before	Equal variances assumed	.483	.496	−.147	18	.885	−.20000	1.36463		−3.06699	2.66699
	Equal variances not assumed			−.147	17.498	.885	−.20000	1.36463		−3.07290	2.67290
week4	Equal variances assumed	1.984	.176	−2.703	18	.015	−4.40000	1.62754		−7.81934	−.98066
	Equal variances not assumed			−2.703	16.846	.015	−4.40000	1.62754		−7.83621	−.96379
week8	Equal variances assumed	2.693	.118	−3.008	18	.008	−6.70000	2.22736		−11.37950	−2.02050
	Equal variances not assumed			−3.008	14.949	.009	−6.70000	2.22736		−11.44890	−1.95110

> With an adjusted alpha of .016, **week4** and **week8** are significant, with *p*–values < .016 (**before** is not significant, since its *p*–value is > .016).

Figure 11.14 **The output of the independent-samples *t* tests (the tests of simple effects following the significant interaction).**

Effect Sizes

The measure of effect size commonly used with the one-between–one-within ANOVA is partial eta-square (η^2). To calculate partial eta-square for the effect of interest, the sums of squares (*SS*) from the appropriate table (either the *Tests of Within-Subjects Effects* or the *Tests of Between-Subjects Effects* table) are used. The formula for partial eta-square is:

$$\text{partial } \eta^2 = \frac{SS_{Effect}}{SS_{Effect} + SS_{Error}}$$

The values SS_{Effect} for and SS_{Error} refer to the *Type III Sum of Squares* in the ANOVA table in Figure 11.12. (For **time** and **time × support**, SS_{error} is expressed as $SS_{Error(time)}$.) For **time**, inserting the appropriate values into the above formula produces a partial eta-square of:

$$\text{partial } \eta^2 = \frac{159.033}{159.033 + 237.000} = .402$$

which agrees with the value reported in the *Tests of Within-Subjects Effects* table.

The larger the value of partial eta-square, the more variance the effect explains in the dependent variable. Conventional effect size measures for small, medium, and large effect sizes for partial eta-square have not been provided.

Expression of the Results in APA Format

In writing the results for the one-between–one-within ANOVA, the conclusion of the hypothesis test, the degrees of freedom (*df*), the *F* value, the *p*-value, and the effect size are reported for each of the tests along with the means and standard deviations for the groups (the means and standard deviations may be reported in a separate table if desired). A sample write-up in APA format is presented next.

Written Results

A 2 × 3 one-between–one-within ANOVA on teaching stress was conducted with support (mentored, not mentored) as the between subjects factor and time (before, four weeks, and eight weeks) as the within subjects factor. The results showed a significant main effect for support, $F(1, 18) = 6.22$, $p < .05$, partial $\eta^2 = .26$, and a significant main effect for time, *Greenhouse-Geisser* adjusted $F(1.38, 24.75) = 12.08$, $p < .05$, partial $\eta^2 = .40$. For support, mentored teachers reported significantly less stress than nonmentored teachers. There was also a significant support × time interaction, *Greenhouse-Geisser* adjusted $F(1.38, 24.75) = 8.25$, $p < .05$, partial $\eta^2 = .31$. Simple effects analyses were conducted for support at each level of time, with each test conducted at an alpha level of .016. The results of the simple effects tests indicated that mentored teachers reported significantly less stress than nonmentored teachers at four weeks, $t(18) = -2.70$, $p < .016$, and at eight weeks, $t(18) = -3.01$, $p < .016$. There was not a significant difference between mentored and nonmentored teachers before beginning teaching, $t(18) = -.15$, $p > .016$. Means and standard deviations for mentored and nonmentored teachers at before, four weeks, and eight weeks are reported in Figure 11.15.

	Mentored		Not mentored	
Time	*M*	*SD*	*M*	*SD*
Before	41.00	3.30	41.20	2.78
4 weeks	39.60	4.09	44.00	3.13
8 weeks	34.70	6.00	41.40	3.69

Figure 11.15 **Means and standard deviations for mentored and non-mentored teachers before the academic year began, at four weeks, and at eight weeks.**

Assumptions of the One-between–One-within Subjects ANOVA

1. *The observations are independent between the participants.*
    Violating this assumption can seriously compromise the accuracy of the one-between–one-within subjects ANOVA. If there is reason to believe the independence assumption has been violated, the one-between–one-within subjects ANOVA should not be used.
2. *Normality.*
    This assumption means that (1) the dependent variable should be normally distributed in the population for each level of the within subjects factor and (2) the mean score for the subjects (averaged across the levels of the within subjects factor) should be normally distributed for each level of the between subjects variable. See Chapter 8 for the consequences on violating the normality assumption.
3. *Homogeneity of variance.*
    This assumption means that the variances should be equal in the population for each level of the between subjects factor (the variances are calculated on the scores for the participants averaged across the levels of the within subjects factor). See Chapter 8 for consequences of violating this assumption.

4. *Sphericity.*

The sphericity assumption requires that the variances of the difference scores are equal for all pairs of levels of the within subjects factor in the population. Since violating the assumption of sphericity can compromise the accuracy of the ANOVA test, using an alternative procedure that adjusts for the presence of sphericity (e.g., *Greenhouse-Geisser*) is recommended. See Chapter 10 for more details on the sphericity assumption.

5. *Homogeneity of variance-covariance matrices.*

This assumption means that the corresponding variances and covariances are equal for the different levels of the between subjects factor (a covariance is a measure of the shared variability between two variables). In the current example, with three levels to the within subjects factor, this assumption means that the three corresponding variances (var_{before}, var_{week4}, var_{week8}) and the three covariances ($cov_{(before, week4)}$, $cov_{(before, week8)}$, $cov_{(week4, week8)}$) are equal for the two groups. With equal or approximately equal sample sizes, small to moderate violations of the equal variance-covariance matrix assumption are generally tolerable. If the inequality in both the sample sizes and the variance-covariance matrices between the groups is moderate to large, the one-between–one-within subjects ANOVA should not be used.

Summary of Steps for Conducting a One-between–One-within ANOVA in SPSS

I. **Data Entry and Analysis**
   1. Create one variable for the between subjects factor and a separate variable for each *level* of the within subjects factor.
   2. Create value labels for the between subjects variable. In the *Value Labels* dialog box, enter the numeric values and labels as appropriate. Click *OK*.
   3. Enter the data.
   4. Select **Analyze > General Linear Model > Repeated Measures . . .**
   5. In the *Repeated Measures Define Factor(s)* dialog box, enter a name for the within subjects factor in the *Within Subject Factor Name* text box and the number of levels in the *Number of Levels* box. Click *Add*. Click *Define*.
   6. In the *Repeated Measures* dialog box, move the between subjects factor to the *Between-Subjects Factor(s)* box. Move the levels of the within subjects factor to the *Within-Subjects Variables* box.
   7. Click *Options*. Move each of the factors and the interaction term to the *Display Means for* box. Under *Display*, click *Descriptive statistics* and *Estimates of effect size*. Click *Continue*.
   8. Click *OK*.

II. **Interpretation of the Results**
   1. In the *Tests of Within-Subjects Effects* table, interpret the results of the tests of the within subjects factor and the interaction by reading either the *Greenhouse-Geisser* or the *Sphericity Assumed p*-values (use the sphericity assumed values if comparing results to hand calculations). Interpret the results of the between subjects factor by examining the *p*-value in the *Tests of Between-Subjects Effects* table.
      - If the between subjects factor is significant, examine the marginal means if there are two levels to the factor. For three or more levels, run Tukey's test (by clicking *Post Hoc* and selecting *Tukey*) and interpret the results accordingly (see Chapter 8 for more details on Tukey's test). If the within subjects factor is significant, examine the marginal means if there are two levels to the factor. If there are three or more levels, conduct dependent samples *t* tests as appropriate. If the interaction is significant, describe the nature of the interaction or conduct simple effect tests (if desired) using an experiment-wise alpha of .05.
      - If none of the tests for the one-between–one-within ANOVA are significant, stop. Write the results stating that the tests of the main effects and the interaction are not significant.

Exercises

1. A clinical psychologist compared the effectiveness of cognitive-behavioral and psychoanalytic therapy over time. Twenty people who were seeking therapy agreed to participate in the study, with 10 of the participants receiving cognitive-behavioral therapy and 10 receiving psychoanalytic therapy. The participants were administered a general measure of well-being before therapy began, at eight weeks and again at 16 weeks. The well-being measure ranged from 10 to 50, with higher scores indicating higher levels of well-being. The data are provided in Figure 11.16.

Therapy	Before	Week8	Week16	Therapy	Before	Week8	Week16
1	19	18	22	2	23	23	17
1	18	18	21	2	19	19	20
1	21	22	24	2	16	17	15
1	22	23	28	2	18	19	19
1	24	24	26	2	23	25	24
1	18	21	27	2	24	25	23
1	19	23	25	2	19	20	18
1	19	20	23	2	22	24	22
1	17	18	16	2	20	20	19
1	23	24	28	2	22	22	23

Figure 11.16 The data for Exercise 1. For therapy, 1 = "cognitive-behavioral" and 2 = "psychoanalytic."

Enter the data in SPSS and perform the appropriate analyses to answer the questions below. Name the variables therapy, before, week8, and week16, respectively.

a. State the null and alternative hypothesis for each test of interest.
b. State a research question for each test of interest.
c. Test for main effects and the interaction (use $\alpha = .05$ for each test). Which tests, if any, are significant? Which tests, if any, are not significant?
d. Report the effect size for each of the tests. Which of the tests has the largest effect?
e. Write the results of the study using APA format as appropriate.

2. Conduct simple effects tests of the interaction effect in Exercise 1. Test to see if there are differences between the two therapies at each of the three time occasions (i.e., perform a separate test of the two therapy groups at before, week 8, and week 16). Evaluate each test at an appropriate alpha level so that the overall alpha for the three tests does not exceed .05.

3. In the problem addressed in the chapter, simple effects analyses were conducted by testing mentored versus nonmentored teachers at each level of time. Another possible analysis is to test whether there is a difference in stress scores for those who were mentored over the three time occasions. Perform this test in SPSS and answer each of the questions below. The data are provided in the file *teaching stress.sav* in the Chapter 11 folder online at www.routledge.com/cw/yockey. Open the file in SPSS and perform the appropriate analyses to answer the questions below (those who are mentored are assigned a value of "1" for **support**). (*Hint*: To perform the test, either the *Select Cases* or *Split File* procedure is required. See Appendix A for more information on these procedures.)

a. State the null and alternative hypothesis for the test of interest.
b. State a research question for the test of interest.
c. Is there a significant difference in stress scores across the three time occasions for mentored teachers? Test at $\alpha = .05$.
d. If time is significant, perform follow-up tests as appropriate. Evaluate each test at an appropriate level so that the overall alpha for the set of follow-up tests does not exceed .05. Which tests, if any, are significant? Which tests, if any, are not significant?
e. Write the results of the study using APA format as appropriate.

Notes

1. While within subjects factors most commonly consist of the same people measured on multiple occasions, they can also consist of related people each measured once (e.g., siblings).
2. Since the alternative hypothesis is nonspecific, if **time** is significant, further testing will be required to assess where the differences are. Compare this to the hypothesis for **support** which has only two groups: If **support** is significant, the means for the two groups only need to be examined to determine which group has less stress (i.e., further testing is not required).
3. To this point we have not created a name for the within subjects factor in SPSS (we've created names for the *levels* of the within subjects factor—**before, week4, week8**).
4. The *Multivariate Tests* table tests the within subjects factor **(time)** and any interaction that includes the within subjects factor. Between subjects factors (by themselves) are not tested in this table.
5. When there are only two levels to a within subjects factor, the assumption of sphericity is not required.
6. There are not different adjustment procedures for **support** since the sphericity assumption does not apply to between subjects factors.
7. For example, mentored vs. nonmentored teachers may be significantly different only at time 3, or they may be significantly different at both time 2 and time 3.

The Pearson *r* Correlation Coefficient

The Pearson *r* correlation coefficient measures the degree of the linear relationship between two variables. The degree of the relationship is expressed by the letter *r*; *r* can be positive (higher scores on one variable are associated with higher scores on the other variable), negative (higher scores on one variable are associated with lower scores on the other variable), or zero (no relationship between the scores on the two variables). The values of the correlation coefficient can range from –1.0 (a perfect negative relationship) to 1.0 (a perfect positive relationship). An example where the Pearson *r* correlation coefficient may be used is presented next.

Example

For a research project, a student wanted to examine whether there was a relationship between meaning in life and psychological well-being. Thirty students who agreed to participate in the study were administered a meaning in life scale and a measure of psychological well-being. The scores on the meaning in life scale ranged from 10 to 70 (with higher scores indicating greater meaning in life), and the well-being scale ranged from 5 to 35 (with higher scores indicating greater well-being).

Objective and Data Requirements of the Pearson *r* Correlation Coefficient

The Pearson *r* Correlation Coefficient

Objective	Data Requirements	Example
To measure the degree of the linear relationship between two variables.	Two continuous variables[1]	Variable 1: Meaning in life Variable 2: Well-being

Null and Alternative Hypotheses

The null hypothesis states that there is no relationship between the two variables in the population. The population symbol for the correlation coefficient is given by the Greek letter ρ (pronounced "rō"):

$$H_0: \rho = 0$$

The alternative hypothesis states that there is a relationship between the two variables in the population:

$$H_1: \rho \neq 0$$

Evaluation of the Null Hypothesis

The Pearson *r* correlation coefficient provides a test of the null hypothesis that there is no relationship between meaning in life and psychological well-being. If the test produces results that seem unlikely if the null hypothesis is true (results that occur less than 5% of the time), then the null hypothesis is rejected. If the test produces results that seem fairly likely if the null hypothesis is true (results that occur greater than 5% of the time), then the null hypothesis is not rejected.

Research Question

The fundamental question of interest in a research study can also be expressed in the form of a research question, such as:

"Is there a relationship between meaning in life and psychological well-being?"

The Data

The data for the 30 participants are presented in Figure 12.1.

Participant	Meaning in Life	Well-being	Participant	Meaning in Life	Well-being
1	35	19	16	70	31
2	65	27	17	25	12
3	14	19	18	55	20
4	35	35	19	61	31
5	65	34	20	53	25
6	33	34	21	60	32
7	54	35	22	35	12
8	20	28	23	35	28
9	25	12	24	50	20
10	58	21	25	39	24
11	30	18	26	68	34
12	37	25	27	56	28
13	51	19	28	19	12
14	50	25	29	56	35
15	30	29	30	60	35

Figure 12.1   **The data for the correlation coefficient example. (*Note:* The participant variable is included for illustration but will not be entered into SPSS.)**

Data Entry and Analysis in SPSS

Steps 1 and 2 below describe how to enter the data in SPSS. The data file is also available online at www.routledge.com/cw/yockey under the name *meaning.sav* in the Chapter 12 folder. If you prefer to open the file from the web site, skip to Step 3.

Step 1: Create the Variables

1. Start SPSS.
2. Click the *Variable View* tab.

In the *Variable View* window, two variables will be created, one for meaning in life and one for psychological well-being. The variables will be named **meaning** and **wellbeing**, respectively.

3. Enter the variable names **meaning** and **wellbeing**, respectively, in the first two rows of the *Variable View* window. Under *Measure*, classify both variables as scale (see Figure 12.2 for details on page 158).

Step 2: Enter the Data

1. Click the *Data View* tab. The variables **meaning** and **wellbeing** appear in the first two columns of the *Data View* window.

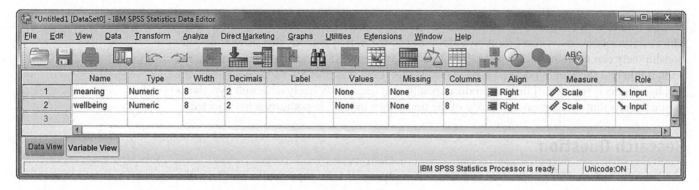

Figure 12.2 The *Variable View* window with the variables meaning and wellbeing entered.

2. Consulting Figure 12.1, enter the scores for each of the participants on the two variables of interest. For the first participant, enter the scores *35* and *19* for the variables **meaning** and **wellbeing**, respectively. Using this approach, enter the data for all 30 participants. The completed data set is shown in Figure 12.3.

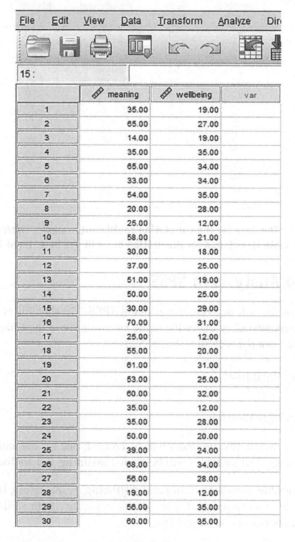

Figure 12.3 The data file for the Pearson *r* correlation coefficient example.

Step 3: Analyze the Data

1. From the menu bar, select **Analyze > Correlate > Bivariate . . .** (see Figure 12.4).

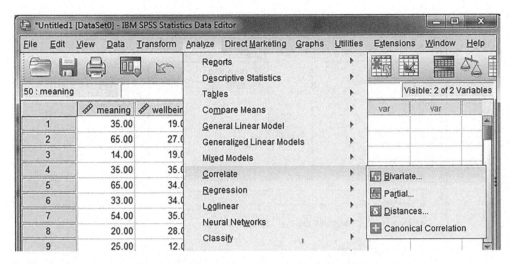

Figure 12.4   **Menu commands for the Pearson *r* correlation coefficient.**

A *Bivariate Correlations* dialog box appears with the variables **meaning** and **wellbeing** on the left-hand side of the dialog box (see Figure 12.5).

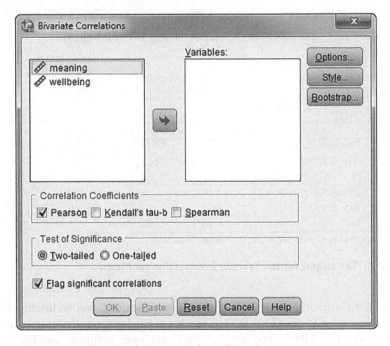

Figure 12.5   **The *Bivariate Correlations* dialog box.**

2. With the *Ctrl* key held down, select the variables, **meaning** and **wellbeing**, and click the right-arrow button (➡) to move them to the *Variables* box (see Figure 12.6 on page 160).
3. Click *OK*.

The correlation procedure runs in SPSS and the results are presented in the *Viewer* window.

Step 4: Interpret the Results

The output of the *Correlations* procedure is displayed in Figure 12.7 on page 160.

Correlations

SPSS produces a single table of output, labeled *Correlations*, which contains the answer to our research question, that is, whether or not there is a relationship between the variables **meaning** and **wellbeing**.

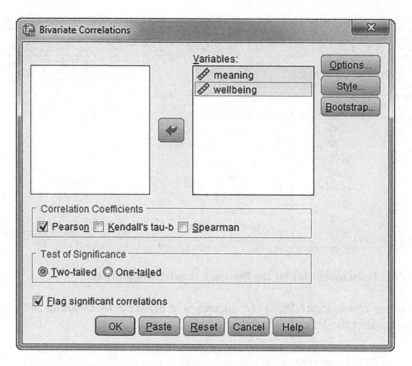

Figure 12.6 **The *Bivariate Correlations* dialog box (continued).**

Correlations

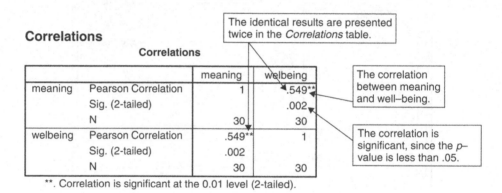

Correlations

		meaning	welbeing
meaning	Pearson Correlation	1	.549**
	Sig. (2-tailed)		.002
	N	30	30
welbeing	Pearson Correlation	.549**	1
	Sig. (2-tailed)	.002	
	N	30	30

** . Correlation is significant at the 0.01 level (2-tailed).

Figure 12.7 **The output for the Pearson *r* correlation coefficient.**

Notice in the *Correlations* table that the variables **meaning** and **wellbeing** are presented twice, once in the rows and once in the columns (this is a redundancy that occurs in all *Correlations* tables produced by SPSS). The value of the correlation coefficient and the *p*-value of the test of the null hypothesis can be found by locating where **meaning** and **wellbeing** intersect. The *Correlations* table indicates that the correlation between **meaning** and **wellbeing** is .549 with a corresponding *p*-value of .002 based on 30 participants. Since the *p*-value of .002 is less than .05, the null hypothesis is rejected, and it is concluded that there is a positive relationship between **meaning** and **wellbeing** in the population (the two asterisks to the right of the correlation coefficient indicate that the correlation is statistically significant at the .01 level, since .002 is less than .01). The remaining two cells show a correlation of 1, a perfect positive correlation. This shouldn't be a surprise however, since these values correspond to the correlation of a variable with itself (**meaning** with **meaning** and **wellbeing** with **wellbeing**), which is always equal to 1.

Effect Sizes

Unlike the other statistical procedures we have considered thus far, the correlation coefficient itself is a commonly used measure of effect size. Cohen (1988) gave estimates of values of *r* of ±.1, ±.3, and ±.5 as corresponding to small, medium, and large effect sizes, respectively.

Based on Cohen's guidelines, the correlation of .549 corresponds to a large effect size in practice, suggesting a fairly strong positive relationship between meaning in life and psychological well-being.

Expression of the Results in APA Format

While SPSS presents the sample size (N) in the *Correlations* table, the degrees of freedom are not provided, although they are typically presented in the written results. The formula for the degrees of freedom (df) is:

$$df = (N - 2)$$

where N corresponds to the total sample size (number of participants) in the study. With 30 people in the study, the degrees of freedom are equal to 28.

In writing the results, the conclusion of the hypothesis test, the value of r, the degrees of freedom (df), and the p-value are reported. An example of a brief write-up in APA format is presented next.

Written Results

There is a significant positive relationship between meaning in life and psychological well-being, $r(28) = .55, p < .05$.

When calculating a correlation coefficient, it is often of interest to produce a scatterplot to check for a linear (straight-line) relationship between the two variables and to check for outliers. The commands for producing scatterplots are provided in Chapter 3. (For more information on checking for linearity and outliers, consulting an introductory statistics textbook is recommended.)

Assumptions of the Pearson Correlation Coefficient

1. *Independence of observations between the participants.*
   This assumption means that the scores for each of the participants should be independent of all other participants' scores (an example of violating the independence assumption would be if two participants worked together on the well-being measure). If the independence assumption has been violated, the correlation coefficient should not be used.
2. *Bivariate normality.*
   This assumption means that each of the variables should be normally distributed in the population and that for any value of one variable, the scores on the other variable should be normally distributed. For moderate to large sample sizes, most types of nonnormal data tend to have relatively little impact on the accuracy of the test of the correlation coefficient.

Summary of Steps for Conducting a Pearson Correlation Coefficient in SPSS

I. **Data Entry and Analysis**
   1. Create two variables in SPSS.
   2. Enter the data.
   3. Select **Analyze > Correlate > Bivariate . . .**
   4. Move the two variables to the *Variables* box.
   5. Click *OK*.

II. **Interpretation of the Results**
   1. Check the *p*-value in the *Correlations* table.
      - If $p \leq .05$, the null hypothesis is rejected. Write the results indicating that there is a significant (positive or negative) relationship between the two variables.
      - If $p > .05$, the null hypothesis is not rejected. Write the results indicating that there is not a significant relationship between the two variables.

Exercises

1. A student was interested in examining whether there was a relationship between the amount of time studying (in minutes) and the grade received on an exam (on a 0 to 100 scale). The amount of time spent studying (**examprep**) and the final grade on the exam (**grade**) for 25 students is reported in Figure 12.8.

examprep (in minutes)	grade
450	90
65	50
120	75
240	82
100	55
490	85
200	79
400	83
55	60
40	48
280	74
180	96
365	85
200	63
290	77
200	82
105	80
460	89
300	55
450	92
365	95
80	55
185	75
180	81
300	87

Figure 12.8 **The data for the 25 participants.**

Enter the data in SPSS, and perform the appropriate analyses to answer the questions below. Name the variables **examprep** and **grade**.
   a. State the null and alternative hypotheses.
   b. State a research question for the data.
   c. Calculate the correlation coefficient between the two variables in SPSS. What is the value of the correlation?
   d. Is the correlation significant? Test at $\alpha = .05$.
   e. What is the effect size for the study? Would you characterize the effect size as small, medium, or large?
   f. Write the results of the study using APA format as appropriate.
2. A researcher was interested in investigating whether there was a relationship between marital satisfaction and level of empathic understanding (i.e., the level of empathy one has). One spouse was selected from each of 25 married couples and was administered both a marital satisfaction scale and an empathy scale. The marital satisfaction scale ranged from 15 to 60, and the empathy scale ranged from 10 to 50 (higher scores on

the scales indicate greater degrees of marital satisfaction and empathy, respectively). The data are located in the file *Chapter 12_Exercise 2.sav* in the Chapter 12 folder online at www.routledge.com/cw/yockey (the variables are named **maritalsatisfaction** and **empathy**). Open the file in SPSS, and perform the appropriate analyses to answer the questions below.

    a.   State the null and alternative hypotheses.

    b.   State a research question for the data.

    c.   Calculate the correlation coefficient between the two variables in SPSS. What is the value of the correlation?

    d.   Is the correlation significant? Test at $\alpha = .05$.

    e.   What is the effect size for the study? Would you characterize the effect size as small, medium, or large?

    f.   Write the results of the study using APA format as appropriate.

3.   A researcher investigated whether there was a relationship between the time spent being read to as a child (at age 3) and later performance on a second-grade English skills exam. The parental report of the amount of time spent reading to their child (on a 1 to 10 scale) and the scores on an English skills exam (on a 10 to 50 scale) were recorded for 30 students (higher scores indicate being read to more at age 3 and better performance on the exam in second grade, respectively). The data are located in the file *Chapter 12_Exercise 3.sav* in the Chapter 12 folder online at www.routledge.com/cw/yockey (the variables are named **readingtime** and **examscores**). Open the file in SPSS, and perform the appropriate analyses to answer the questions below.

    a.   State the null and alternative hypotheses.

    b.   State a research question for the data.

    c.   Calculate the correlation coefficient between the two variables in SPSS. What is the value of the correlation?

    d.   Is the correlation significant? Test at $\alpha = .05$.

    e.   What is the effect size for the study? Would you characterize the effect size as small, medium, or large?

    f.   Write the results of the study using APA format as appropriate.

Note

1.   While most correlations are calculated on two continuous variables, the Pearson correlation coefficient can also be calculated on one dichotomous and one continuous variable (called a point-biserial correlation), or on two dichotomous variables (called a phi coefficient).

Simple Linear Regression

Simple linear regression is used when the objective is to predict scores on one variable using scores on another variable.[1] In regression, the variable that is being predicted is known as the dependent or criterion variable, and the variable that is used to predict scores is known as the independent or predictor variable. An example in which linear regression is used is presented next.

Example

For a research project a student wanted to examine whether or not social support (the degree to which one can turn to others for support) is predictive of psychological well-being in college students. Twenty-five students who agreed to participate in the study were administered measures of social support and psychological well-being. The range of possible responses for social support is from 8 to 40 and for well-being is from 10 to 70, with higher scores indicating higher levels of social support and well-being, respectively.

Objective and Data Requirements of Simple Regression

Simple Linear Regression

Objective	Data Requirements	Example
To predict scores on a dependent variable using scores from an independent variable.	Dependent variable • Continuous Independent variable • Continuous[2]	Dependent variable • Well-being Independent variable • Social support

Null and Alternative Hypotheses

The null hypothesis states that social support does not predict well-being. To evaluate the null hypothesis, a regression equation is created (the equation will be introduced later), and a regression coefficient, known as a beta weight, is tested to see whether it is significantly different from zero. A beta weight significantly different from zero indicates that the independent variable is a significant predictor of the dependent variable. The population symbol for the regression coefficient is given by the Greek letter β, or beta.

The null hypothesis states that the beta weight is equal to zero:

$H_0: \beta_{SSI} = 0$ (The beta weight for social support is equal to zero; social support does not predict well-being.)

The alternative hypothesis states that the beta weight does not equal zero:

$H_1: \beta_{SSI} \neq 0$ (The beta weight for social support is not equal to zero; social support predicts well-being.)

Evaluation of the Null Hypothesis

The linear regression procedure in SPSS provides a test of the null hypothesis that social support does not predict well-being. If the test produces results that seem unlikely if the null hypothesis is true (results that occur less than 5% of the time), then the null hypothesis is rejected. If the test produces results that seem fairly likely if the null hypothesis is true (results that occur greater than 5% of the time), then the null hypothesis is not rejected.

Research Question

The fundamental question of interest in a research study can also be expressed in the form of a research question, such as:

"Does social support predict psychological well-being in college students?"

The Data

The social support and well-being scores for the 25 participants are presented in Figure 13.1.

Participant	Social Support	Well-being	Participant	Social Support	Well-being
1	20	32	14	35	66
2	38	65	15	32	25
3	35	60	16	34	52
4	30	56	17	35	70
5	12	25	18	28	51
6	31	25	19	17	32
7	18	65	20	24	42
8	28	56	21	31	25
9	14	23	22	16	61
10	24	42	23	32	52
11	34	60	24	19	26
12	28	51	25	25	41
13	32	58			

Figure 13.1   **The data for the multiple regression example. (*Note*: The participant variable is included for illustration but will not be entered into SPSS.)**

Data Entry and Analysis in SPSS

Steps 1 and 2 below describe how to enter the data in SPSS. The data file is also available online at www.routledge.com/cw/yockey under the name *well being.sav* in the Chapter 13 folder. If you prefer to open the file from the web site, skip to Step 3.

Step 1: Create the Variables

1. Start SPSS.
2. Click the *Variable View* tab.

In SPSS, two variables will be created, one for social support and one for well-being. The variables will be named **support** and **wellbeing,** respectively.

3. Enter the variable names **support** and **wellbeing** in the first two rows of the *Variable View* window. Under *Measure*, classify both variables as scale (see Figure 13.2 on page 166 for details).

Step 2: Enter the Data

1. Click the *Data View* tab. The variables **support** and **wellbeing** appear in the first two columns of the *Data View* window.

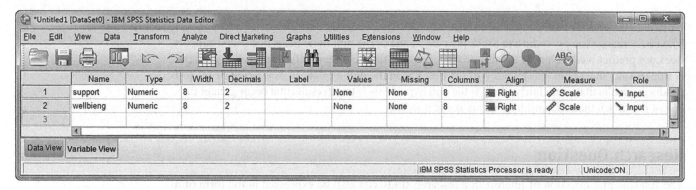

Figure 13.2 The *Variable View* window with the variables support and wellbeing entered.

2. Consulting Figure 13.1, enter the scores for each of the participants on the two variables of interest. For the first participant, enter the scores *20* and *32* on the variables
support and **wellbeing,** respectively. Using this approach, enter the data for all 25
participants. The completed data file is shown in Figure 13.3.

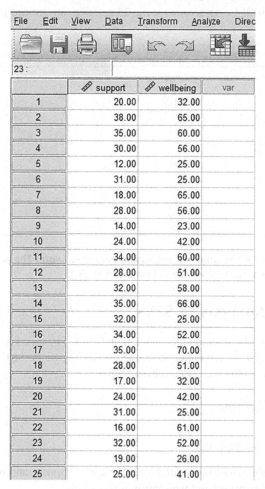

Figure 13.3 The completed data file for the
linear regression example.

Step 3: Analyze the Data

1. From the menu bar, select **Analyze > Regression > Linear . . .** (see Figure 13.4).

A *Linear Regression* dialog box appears with the variables **support** and **wellbeing** on the
left-hand side of the dialog box (see Figure 13.5).

2. Select the variable, **wellbeing,** and click the upper right-arrow button (⬆) to move it
into the *Dependent* box.

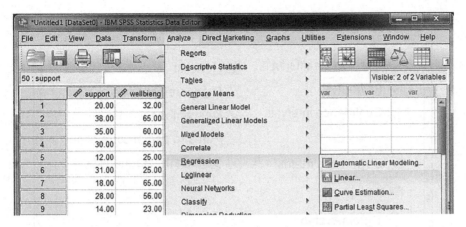

Figure 13.4   **Menu commands for the linear regression procedure.**

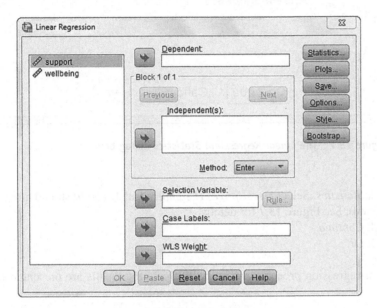

Figure 13.5   **The *Linear Regression* dialog box.**

3. Select the variable, **support,** and click the second right-arrow button from the top (➡)
    to move it into the *Independent(s)* box (see Figure 13.6).

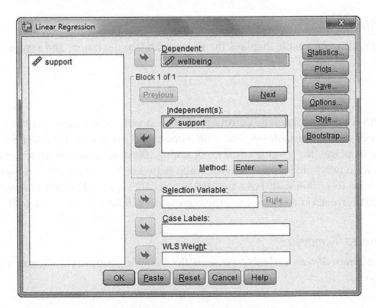

Figure 13.6   **The *Linear Regression* dialog box (continued).**

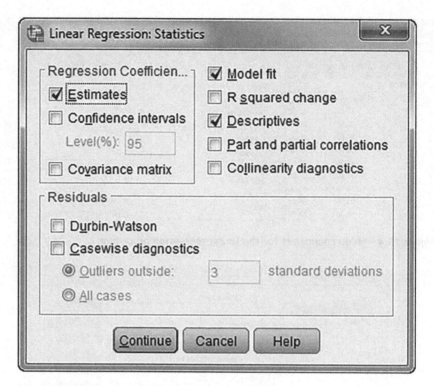

Figure 13.7   **The *Linear Regression: Statistics* dialog box.**

4. Click *Statistics*. Select *Descriptives* (*Estimates* and *Model fit* should already be selected). See Figure 13.7 for details.
5. Click *Continue*.
6. Click *OK*.

The linear regression procedure runs in SPSS and the results are presented in the *Viewer* window.

Step 4: Interpret the Results

The output of the linear regression procedure is displayed in Figure 13.8.

Descriptive Statistics

The *Descriptive Statistics* table displays the mean, standard deviation, and sample size for each of the variables.

Correlations

The *Correlations* table displays the correlation between well-being and social support. The correlation between the two variables is .490 with a one-tailed *p*-value of .0064 (SPSS rounds down to three decimal places for a value of .006; doubling .0064 produces, within rounding error, a value of .013 for a two-tailed test). The correlation between the two variables is significant using either a one-tailed test (.006 < .05) or a two-tailed test (.013 < .05). In simple linear regression, if the (two-tailed) correlation is significant, the regression will be significant as well.

Variables Entered/Removed

The *Variables Entered/Removed* table presents the variable (**support**) that was used to predict well-being scores.

Regression

Descriptive Statistics

	Mean	Std. Deviation	N
wellbeing	46.4400	15.70318	25
support	26.8800	7.52950	25

Correlations

		wellbeing	support
Pearson Correlation	wellbeing	1.000	.490
	support	.490	1.000
Sig. (1-tailed)	wellbeing	.	.006
	support	.006	.
N	wellbeing	25	25
	support	25	25

The Pearson correlation coefficient between well–being and social support.

Variables Entered/Removed[b]

Model	Variables Entered	Variables Removed	Method
1	support[a]	.	Enter

a. All requested variables entered.
b. Dependent Variable: wellbeing

Model Summary

Model	R	R Square	Adjusted R Square	Std. Error of the Estimate
1	.490[a]	.240	.207	13.98053

a. Predictors: (Constant), support

The R^2 value of .24 indicates that social support accounted for 24% of the variance in well–being scores.

ANOVA[b]

Model		Sum of Squares	df	Mean Square	F	Sig.
1	Regression	1422.692	1	1422.692	7.279	.013[a]
	Residual	4495.468	23	195.455		
	Total	5918.160	24			

a. Predictors: (Constant), support
b. Dependent Variable: wellbeing

The *ANOVA* and *Coefficients* tables provide a test of the same null hypothesis in simple regression, that is, whether support is a significant predictor of well–being (notice the identical p–values for the two tests). Social support is a significant predictor of well–being, since the p–value is less than .05.

Coefficients[a]

Model		Unstandardized Coefficients		Standardized Coefficients	t	Sig.
		B	Std. Error	Beta		
1	(Constant)	18.954	10.565		1.794	.086
	support	1.023	.379	.490	2.698	.013

a. Dependent Variable: wellbeing

Figure 13.8 **The output for the linear regression procedure.**

Model Summary

The *Model Summary* table displays *R, R²* (*R* Square), Adjusted *R²*, and the standard error of the estimate. The first three of these values measure the degree to which well-being was predicted from social support, and the last value measures the degree to which well-being was *not* predicted from social support. Each of these values is discussed next.

The first value, *R*, is the multiple correlation coefficient, and, in simple regression, is equal to the absolute value of the Pearson correlation between social support and well-being (*R* ranges from 0 to 1). The second value, R^2, is the square of *R* (.490² = .24) and, when multiplied by 100%, is interpreted as the percentage of total variance in the dependent variable that is accounted for by the independent variable. In the current example, social support accounted for 24% (.24 × 100%) of the variance in well-being scores. Adjusted R^2 modifies the value of R^2 in an attempt to better estimate the true population value (R^2 calculated on the sample tends to overestimate the population value.) Finally, the standard error of the estimate indicates the degree to which the independent variable was *unable* to predict scores on the dependent variable. The value of 13.98 indicates that, when using social support scores to predict well-being, the regression equation was "off" in predicting well-being scores by about 13.98 points on average.

ANOVA

The next table, *ANOVA*, tests whether social support was a significant predictor of well-being. This test is conducted using an analysis of variance (ANOVA), which was discussed in Chapter 8. In simple regression, a *p*-value less than .05 in the *ANOVA* table indicates that the independent variable is a significant predictor of the dependent variable. Since the *p*-value of .013 is less than .05, social support is a significant predictor of well-being.

Coefficients

The last table, *Coefficients*, provides the necessary values to construct a regression equation and to test the null hypothesis of whether social support is a significant predictor of well-being. (Since the *ANOVA* table already indicated that social support was a significant predictor of well-being, the test of the predictor in the *Coefficients* table is redundant in simple regression.)[3]

The regression equation will be discussed first, followed by the test of social support.

In linear regression, an equation is created in the form of:

$$\hat{Y} = a + bX$$

Where

$\hat{Y}$ = the predicted score on the dependent variable. In our example, $\hat{Y}$ corresponds to the predicted well-being scores.
a = the *Y*-intercept; the value of $\hat{Y}$ when $X = 0$.
b = the slope of the regression line.
X = the scores on the independent variable for each of the participants. In our example, *X* corresponds to the social support scores.

The values in the regression equation, *a* (the *Y*-intercept), and *b* (the slope), are found in the *Coefficients* table in the *Unstandardized Coefficients* column labeled "*B*." In the *Coefficients* table, the value of the *Y*-intercept is 18.954 and the value of the slope is 1.023. Substituting these values into the regression equation formula produces the following equation for predicting well-being scores:

$$\hat{Y}_{\text{well-being}} = 18.954 + 1.023(\text{social support})$$

This is the regression equation based on the 25 college students. For a given score on social support, a predicted well-being score can be found. For example, the first two participants had social support scores of 20 and 38, respectively. Inserting these scores into the above equation produces the following predicted well-being scores:

Predicted well-being score for participant 1

$$\hat{Y}_{\text{well-being}} = 18.954 + 1.023(20)$$

$$\hat{Y}_{\text{well-being}} = 39.41$$

Predicted well-being score for participant 2

$$\hat{Y}_{\text{well-being}} = 18.954 + 1.023(38)$$

$$\hat{Y}_{\text{well-being}} = 57.83$$

A predicted score can be found for each of the individuals in the data set.[4] The predicted scores will almost always have some error (they will not match the actual scores exactly); the higher the value of R, the closer the predicted values will tend to be to the actual values, with an R of 1 resulting in perfect prediction for all individuals.

Testing Social Support for Significance

A test of social support is also provided in the *Coefficients* table. In the last two columns of the table, the t and p-values for the test of social support are presented. The test of social support produced a t of 2.698 with a corresponding p-value of .013. Because the p-value of .013 is less than .05, the null hypothesis that the beta weight is equal to zero is rejected, and it is concluded that social support is a significant predictor of psychological well-being. Notice that the p-value for social support in the *Coefficients* table (.013) is identical to the p-value provided in the ANOVA table (.013). These p-values are the same because, as was indicated earlier, in simple regression they test the same null hypothesis, that is, whether or not social support is a significant predictor of psychological well-being.

While the values from the *Unstandardized Coefficients* columns were used in finding predicted scores, the *Standardized Coefficients* value will be presented in the write-up of the results. The standardized coefficient is referred to as a beta weight, and it is equal to the value of the regression coefficient if the predictor and the criterion variable were in z-score form (i.e., if both variables were standardized with a mean of zero and a standard deviation of 1).[5] The value of beta in the standardized coefficients column is equal to .490, which is identical to the Pearson correlation coefficient between the two variables that was reported in the *Correlations* table (beta will always be equal to the Pearson correlation in simple regression).

While the test of the constant is usually not of interest in simple regression, it tests whether the Y-intercept is significantly different from zero. In this case, the value of 18.954 is not significantly different from zero since the p-value for the test (.086) is greater than .05.

Effect Sizes

The measure of effect size commonly used for simple regression is given by R^2. Cohen (1988) expressed R^2 values in simple regression of .01, .09, and .24 as corresponding to small, medium, and large effect sizes, respectively. In our example, an $R^2 = .24$ indicates that 24% of the variance in well-being scores can be accounted for by knowing social support scores, representing a large effect.

Expression of the Results in APA Format

In the write-up of the results, the standardized regression coefficient, the result of the test of the predictor (social support), and the value of R^2 will be provided. A sample write-up of the results is presented next.

Written Results

A regression analysis was conducted with well-being as the criterion variable and social support as the predictor. Social support was a significant predictor of well-being, $\beta = .49$, $t(23) = 2.70$, $p < .05$, and accounted for 24% ($R^2 = .24$) of the variance in well-being scores.

   (*Note*: The degrees of freedom (*df*) for *t* are equal to $N - 2$ in simple regression, where N is equal to the number of *pairs* of scores in the study. In our example $N = 25$; therefore $df = 23$.)

Assumptions in Simple Regression

1. *Independence of observations between the participants.*
   The independence assumption means that the scores for each participant should be independent of all other participants' scores (an example of violating the independence assumption would be if two different participants worked on the well-being measure together). Violating this assumption can seriously compromise the accuracy of the statistical tests performed using the regression procedure. If there is reason to believe the independence assumption has been violated, linear regression should not be used.

2. *Bivariate normality.*
   This assumption means that each of the variables should be normally distributed in the population, and that for any value of one variable, the scores on the other variable should also be normally distributed. For moderate to large sample sizes, most types of nonnormal data tend to have relatively little impact on the accuracy of the regression procedure.

3. *Homoscedasticity.*
   Homoscedasticity means that the variances on the dependent variable are equal in the population for all levels of the independent variable. Mild to moderate violations of this assumption are generally tolerable in simple regression.

Summary of Steps for Conducting a Simple Linear Regression Analysis in SPSS

  I. **Data Entry and Analysis**

     1. Create two variables in SPSS, one for the independent variable and one for the dependent variable.
     2. Enter the data.
     3. Select **Analyze > Regression > Linear . . .**
     4. Move the independent and dependent variables to their respective boxes.
     5. Click *Statistics*. Click *Descriptives* (*Estimates* and *Model fit* should already be selected). Click *Continue*.
     6. Click *OK*.

  II. **Interpretation of the Results**

     1. In the chapter description, all the tables (*Descriptive Statistics*, *Correlations*, *Variables Entered/Removed*, *Model Summary*, *ANOVA*, and *Coefficients*) were described. In this summary, only information from the *Model Summary* and *Coefficients* tables will be described.
   - Note the value of R^2 in the *Model Summary* table.
   - Examine the *p*-value for the predictor in the *Coefficients* table (or in the *ANOVA* table, as these tests are equivalent in simple regression).

- If the predictor is significant ($p \leq .05$), the null hypothesis is rejected. Write the results indicating that the independent variable is a significant predictor of the dependent variable.
- If the predictor is not significant ($p > .05$), the null hypothesis is not rejected. Write the results indicating that the independent variable is not a significant predictor of the dependent variable.

Exercises

1. A researcher investigated whether a father's level of optimism was predictive of his son's optimism as a young adult. Twenty fathers and sons who agreed to participate in the study were each administered a scale measuring their current level of optimism (the scale ranged from 10 to 50, with higher scores indicating greater optimism). The data are provided in Figure 13.9.

Father	Son
40	45
30	35
25	20
29	35
20	22
25	35
46	48
49	39
46	49
23	38
46	35
26	28
16	19
29	45
46	31
49	41
37	31
31	36
42	45
43	48

Figure 13.9 **The optimism scores of 20 fathers and sons.**

Enter the data in SPSS and perform the appropriate analyses to answer the questions below. Name the variables **father** and **son,** respectively.
a. State the null and alternative hypotheses.
b. State a research question for the data.
c. Is the predictor significant? Test using $\alpha = .05$.
d. What is the effect size? Would you characterize the effect size as small, medium, or large?
e. Write a regression equation for the data.
f. Write the results of the study using APA format as appropriate.

2. An employee for a school district wanted to know whether a seventh-grade math skills entrance exam was predictive of performance (as measured by the final grade) in seventh-grade mathematics. The entrance exam scores and the final course grade in seventh-grade mathematics for 30 students were obtained. The possible range of scores on the entrance exam are from 20 to 100 and the final grade in mathematics is from 0 to 100 (higher scores indicate better performance on both measures). The data are in the file *Chapter 13_Exercise 2.sav* in the Chapter 13 folder online at www.routledge.com/cw/yockey (the variables are named

mathexam and **grade**). Open the file in SPSS and perform the appropriate analyses to answer the questions below.

  a.   State the null and alternative hypotheses.
  b.   State a research question for the data.
  c.   Is the predictor significant? Test using $\alpha = .05$.
  d.   What is the effect size? Would you characterize the effect size as small, medium, or large?
  e.   Write a regression equation for the data.
  f.   Write the results of the study using APA format as appropriate.

3. An industrial psychologist wanted to investigate whether agreeableness (being likable, friendly, and getting along with others) was predictive of success at work. Twenty-five employees were selected and were administered a scale measuring agreeableness (the scale ranged from 7 to 35, with higher scores indicating greater agreeableness). Following the administration of the scale, the supervisor's level of satisfaction with the employee was obtained (satisfaction scores ranged from 0 to 10, with higher scores indicating greater satisfaction). The data are in the file *Chapter 13_Exercise 3. sav* in the Chapter 13 folder online at www.routledge.com/cw/yockey (the variables are named **agreeableness** and **satisfaction**). Open the file in SPSS and perform the appropriate analyses to answer the questions below.

  a.   State the null and alternative hypotheses.
  b.   State a research question for the data.
  c.   Is the predictor significant? Test using $\alpha = .05$.
  d.   What is the effect size? Would you characterize the effect size as small, medium, or large?
  e.   Write a regression equation for the data.
  f.   Write the results of the study using APA format as appropriate.

Notes

1. Linear regression is related to correlation (correlation was discussed in Chapter 12); in fact, a significant correlation between two variables is required in order for one variable to be a significant predictor of the other in linear regression. However, the objectives of the two procedures are somewhat different. Where correlation describes the relationship between two variables, in simple linear regression the goal is to assess whether one variable is a significant predictor of another variable.
2. While continuous predictors are typically used in simple regression, a predictor variable can be categorical if it consists of only two values (i.e., it is dichotomous). If the categorical variable consists of more than two categories, special coding of the variable is required and multiple regression should be used.
3. While the *ANOVA* and *Coefficients* tables provide the same test in simple regression, they are not identical in multiple regression, as is illustrated in Chapter 14.
4. The predicted scores can be solved for in SPSS by clicking the *Save* button in the *Linear Regression* dialog box (shown in Figure 13.6) and then clicking *Unstandardized* in the *Predicted Values* section of the dialog box. The predicted scores will then be placed in the data file to the right of the variable **wellbeing.**
5. When the regression coefficients are standardized, the *Y*-intercept is equal to zero and is dropped from the *Coefficients* table (which is why there is no value reported for *Constant* in the *Standardized Coefficients* column).

Multiple Linear Regression

Multiple linear regression is used when the objective is to predict scores on one variable using scores from *two or more* different variables.[1] In multiple regression, the variable that is being predicted is known as the dependent or criterion variable, and the variables that are used to predict the dependent variable are known as the independent or predictor variables. An example in which multiple linear regression may be used is presented next.

Example

For a project in a research methods class, a student wanted to investigate whether connectedness, optimism, and academic success were predictive of meaning in life in college students. Thirty students who agreed to participate in the study were administered the four measures, which are described in Figure 14.1 on page 176.

Objective and Data Requirements of Multiple Regression

Multiple Linear Regression

Objective	Data Requirements	Example
To predict the scores on a dependent variable using scores on two or more independent variables.	Dependent variable • Continuous Independent variables • Continuous or categorical[2]	Dependent variable • Meaning in life Independent variables • Optimism • Connectedness • Academic success

Null and Alternative Hypotheses

In multiple regression, there are separate null and alternative hypotheses for each predictor (independent) variable. A regression equation is created (the equation will be introduced later), and the regression weight for each predictor (known as a beta weight) is tested to see whether it is significantly different from zero. A beta weight significantly different from zero indicates that the independent variable is a significant predictor of the dependent variable. The population symbol for the regression coefficient is given by the Greek letter, β, or beta.

The null hypothesis for each of the predictors is that the beta weight is equal to zero:

$$H_0: \beta_{\text{connect}} = 0 \quad \text{(H.1)} \quad \text{(The beta weight of connect is equal to zero; connect does not predict meaning in life.)}$$

Scale	What it measures	Scale range
Meaning in life (meaning)	The degree of meaning one currently finds in life.	10–70; higher scores indicate greater meaning in life.
Connectedness (connect)	How connected one feels to others; the degree to which one may turn to others for support.	8–40; higher scores indicate greater perceived support from others.
Optimism (optimism)	How optimistic one is about their life.	10–50; higher scores indicate greater optimism.
Academic success (success)	The degree to which a person has achieved academic success in their life.	5–25; higher scores indicate greater academic success.

Figure 14.1 **Description of the measures used in the multiple regression example.**

$H_0: \beta_{\text{optimism}} = 0$ (H.2)   (The beta weight of optimism is equal to zero; optimism does not predict meaning in life.)

$H_0: \beta_{\text{success}} = 0$ (H.3)   (The beta weight of success is equal to zero; success does not predict meaning in life.)

The alternative hypothesis for each of the predictors is that the beta weight is not equal to zero:

$H_1: \beta_{\text{connect}} \neq 0$ (The beta weight of connect is not equal to zero; connect predicts meaning in life.)

$H_1: \beta_{\text{optimism}} \neq 0$ (The beta weight of optimism is not equal to zero; optimism predicts meaning in life.)

$H_1: \beta_{\text{success}} \neq 0$ (The beta weight of success is not equal to zero; success predicts meaning in life.)

In addition to testing the individual predictors for significance, another hypothesis in multiple regression is whether the regression equation, with all the predictors included, significantly predicts the dependent variable. If the regression equation is significant, the predictors (taken together) account for a significant amount of variance in meaning in life scores (i.e., they predict meaning in life). A measure of the amount of variance accounted for is given by R^2 (which ranges from 0 to 1), with an $R^2 = 0$ indicating that no variance in meaning in life scores is accounted for by the predictors, and an $R^2 = 1$ indicating that all of the variance in meaning in life scores is accounted for by the predictors (in practice R^2 typically falls somewhere between 0 and 1).

The null hypothesis states that the predictors (taken as a whole) do not account for any variance in meaning in life scores in the population (i.e., they do not predict meaning in life):

$$H_0: R^2 = 0 \tag{H.4}$$

The alternative hypothesis states that the predictors (taken as a whole) account for variance in meaning in life scores in the population (i.e., they predict meaning in life):

$$H_1: R^2 > 0$$

Evaluation of the Null Hypothesis

The multiple regression procedure in SPSS provides tests of the null hypotheses that each of the predictors individually (hypotheses H.1, H.2, and H.3) and combined (hypothesis H.4) do not predict meaning in life. If, for a given test of interest, the test produces results that seem unlikely if the null hypothesis is true (results that occur less than 5% of the time), the null hypothesis is rejected. If the test produces results that seem fairly likely if the null hypothesis is true (results that occur greater than 5% of the time), the null hypothesis is not rejected.

Research Questions

The fundamental questions of interest in a research study can also be expressed in the form of research questions, such as:

Individual predictors (hypotheses H.1, H.2, and H.3)

> "Does connectedness predict meaning in life?"
> "Does optimism predict meaning in life?"
> "Does academic success predict meaning in life?"

All predictors simultaneously (hypothesis H.4)

> "When taken together, do connectedness, optimism, and academic success predict meaning in life?"

The Data

The meaning in life (**meaning**), connectedness (**connect**), optimism (**optimism**), and academic success (**success**) scores for the 30 participants are presented in Figure 14.2.

Participant	Meaning	Connect	Optimism	Success	Participant	Meaning	Connect	Optimism	Success
1	34	25	14	12	16	54	36	29	18
2	62	41	35	20	17	68	37	42	22
3	54	38	40	18	18	53	29	46	15
4	59	36	35	17	19	33	20	23	14
5	28	18	32	15	20	45	21	27	11
6	31	28	15	18	21	25	29	32	7
7	64	25	35	22	22	61	38	39	22
8	57	22	45	24	23	53	21	30	17
9	26	19	32	21	24	22	21	18	11
10	44	27	23	12	25	40	25	30	16
11	62	31	47	17	26	50	25	41	18
12	54	25	50	20	27	32	16	17	12
13	59	24	35	14	28	55	30	34	21
14	68	28	31	16	29	35	19	22	7
15	36	31	17	19	30	52	21	42	13

Figure 14.2   **The data for the multiple regression example. (*Note*: The participant variable is included for illustration but will not be entered into SPSS.)**

Data Entry and Analysis in SPSS

Steps 1 and 2 below describe how to enter the data in SPSS. The data file is also available online at www.routledge.com/cw/yockey under the name *meaning in life.sav* in the Chapter 14 folder. If you prefer to open the file from the web site, skip to Step 3.

Step 1: Create the Variables

1. Start SPSS.
2. Click the *Variable View* tab.

In SPSS, four variables will be created, one for the criterion variable (meaning in life) and one for each of the predictors (connectedness, optimism, and success). The variables will be named **meaning, connect, optimism,** and **success,** respectively.

3. Enter the variable names **meaning, connect, optimism,** and **success,** respectively, in the first four rows of the *Variable View* window. Under *Measure*, classify all four variables as scale (see Figure 14.3 on page 178 for details).

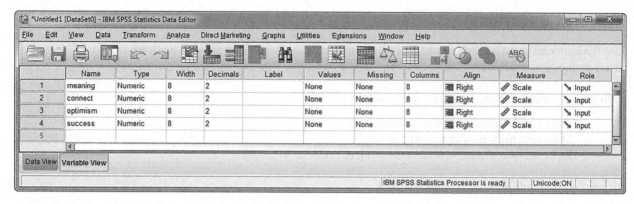

Figure 14.3 The *Variable View* window with the variables meaning, connect, optimism, and success entered.

Step 2: Enter the Data

1. Click the *Data View* tab. The variables **meaning, connect, optimism,** and **success** appear in the first four columns of the *Data View* window.
2. Consulting Figure 14.2, enter the scores for each of the participants on the four variables of interest. For the first participant, enter the scores *34, 25, 14,* and *12,* on the variables **meaning, connect, optimism,** and **success,** respectively. Using this approach, enter the data for all 30 participants. The completed data set is presented in Figure 14.4.

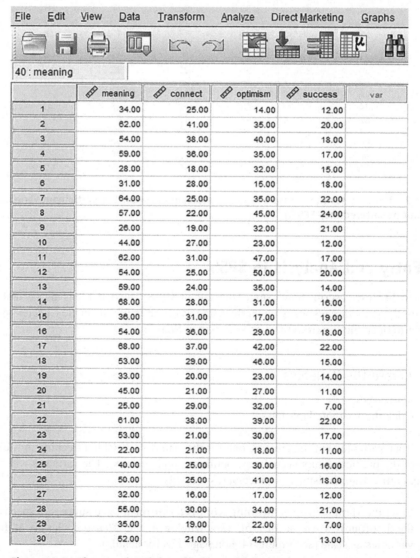

Figure 14.4 The completed data file for multiple regression example.

Step 3: Analyze the Data

1. From the menu bar, select **Analyze > Regression > Linear . . .** (see Figure 14.5).

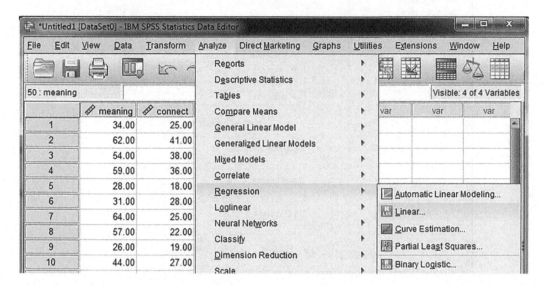

Figure 14.5   **Menu commands for the multiple regression procedure.**

A *Linear Regression* dialog box appears with the variables **meaning, connect, optimism,** and **success** in the left-hand side of the dialog box (see Figure 14.6).

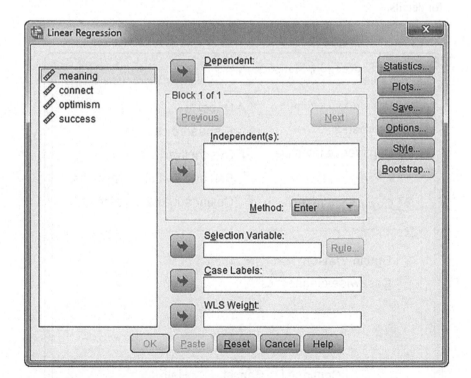

Figure 14.6   **The *Linear Regression* dialog box.**

2. Select the dependent variable, **meaning,** and click the upper right-arrow button (➡) to move it into the *Dependent* box.
3. With the *Ctrl* key held down, select the independent variables **connect, optimism,** and **success** and click the second right-arrow button (➡) from the top to move them into the *Independent(s)* box. See Figure 14.7 on page 180 for details.

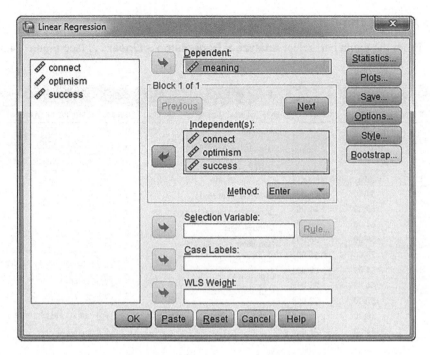

Figure 14.7 The *Linear Regression* dialog box (continued).

4. Click the *Statistics* button. The *Linear Regression: Statistics* dialog box opens. Select *Descriptives* (*Estimates* and *Model fit* should already be selected). See Figure 14.8 for details.

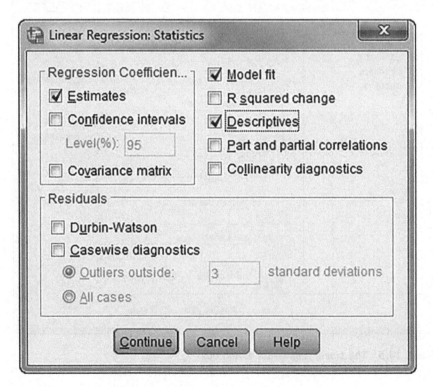

Figure 14.8 The *Linear Regression: Statistics* dialog box.

5. Click *Continue*.
6. Click *OK*.

The multiple regression procedure runs in SPSS and the results are presented in the *Viewer* window.

Step 4: Interpret the Results

The output of the multiple linear regression procedure is displayed in Figure 14.9.

Descriptive Statistics

The *Descriptive Statistics* table displays the mean, standard deviation, and sample size for each of the variables.

Correlations

The *Correlations* table displays the bivariate correlations (i.e., the correlation between two variables) for all the variables included in the study (for a review of correlation, see Chapter 12). Ideally, each of the predictors will correlate moderately to highly with the criterion variable (higher correlation tends to lead to better prediction), and the predictors will not correlate too highly with each other (low correlations among the predictors allows them to make relatively unique contributions in predicting the dependent variable).[3] The *Correlations* table shows that all correlations between the predictors and the criterion are significant (all have p-values $< .05$), with the highest correlation between **meaning** and **optimism** (.66), and the lowest correlation between **meaning** and **success** (.56). The predictors are moderately correlated with each other, with values ranging from .31 to .47.

Regression
Descriptive Statistics

	Mean	Std. Deviation	N
meaning	47.2000	13.90212	30
connect	26.8667	6.76570	30
optimism	31.9333	10.02044	30
success	16.3000	4.38768	30

The correlation between the predictors and the criterion variable (meaning in life).

Correlations

		meaning	connect	optimism	success
Pearson Correlation	meaning	1.000	.561	.663	.555
	connect	.561	1.000	.307	.425
	optimism	.663	.307	1.000	.474
	success	.555	.425	.474	1.000
Sig. (1-tailed)	meaning	.	.001	.000	.001
	connect	.001	.	.050	.010
	optimism	.000	.050	.	.004
	success	.001	.010	.004	.
N	meaning	30	30	30	30
	connect	30	30	30	30
	optimism	30	30	30	30
	success	30	30	30	30

(continued)

Variables Entered/Removed[b]

Model	Variables Entered	Variables Removed	Method
1	success, connect, optimism[a]	.	Enter

a. All requested variables entered.
b. Dependent Variable: meaning

Model Summary

Model	R	R Square	Adjusted R Square	Std. Error of the Estimate
1	.778[a]	.606	.560	9.22060

a. Predictors: (Constant), success, connect, optimism

> The predictors account for 61% of the variance in meaning in life scores.

ANOVA[b]

Model		Sum of Squares	df	Mean Square	F	Sig.
1	Regression	3394.295	3	1131.432	13.308	.000[a]
	Residual	2210.505	26	85.019		
	Total	5604.800	29			

a. Predictors: (Constant), success, connect, optimism
b. Dependent Variable: meaning

> Since the *p*–value is less than .05, the overall regression model (with all predictors included) is significant. The predictors collectively account for a significant amount of variance in meaning in life scores.

Coefficients[a]

Model		Unstandardized Coefficients		Standardized Coefficients		
		B	Std. Error	Beta	t	Sig.
1	(Constant)	−1.971	8.281		−.238	.814
	connect	.691	.282	.336	2.449	.021
	optimism	.653	.196	.470	3.334	.003
	success	.599	.470	.189	1.274	.214

a. Dependent Variable: meaning

> Both **connect** and **optimism** are significant, since their *p*–values are less than .05. They both account for a significant amount of *unique* variance in meaning scores.

Figure 14.9 **The output for the multiple linear regression procedure.**

Variables Entered/Removed

The *Variables Entered/Removed* table summarizes the variables that were used to predict meaning in life. Notice that all of the predictors (**success, connect,** and **optimism**) are displayed in the *Variables Entered* box. A note below the table reads "all requested variables entered," which indicates that all predictors were included simultaneously in the regression model. Alternative procedures exist that allow for a subset of the predictors to enter the regression model first, followed by other predictors second, and so on. One of the more popular of these procedures is hierarchical regression, which allows predictors to be entered in an order specified by the user. With hierarchical regression, one or more predictors have the "first shot" at predicting the criterion variable, one or more other predictors have the "second shot," and so on.[4]

Model Summary

The *Model Summary* table displays R, R^2 (R Square), Adjusted R^2, and the standard error of the estimate. The first three of these values measure the degree to which meaning in life was predicted from the three independent variables, while the last value measures the degree to which meaning in life was *not* predicted from the three variables. Each of these values is discussed below.

The first value, R, is known as the multiple correlation coefficient, and it is equal to the absolute value of the correlation between the original meaning in life scores and the predicted meaning in life scores from the regression analysis (R ranges from 0 to 1). The second value, R^2, is the square of R ($.7782 \approx .61$) and, when multiplied by 100%, is interpreted as the percentage of total variance in the dependent variable that is accounted for by the independent variables. In the current example, the variables **connect, optimism,** and **success** account for 61% ($.61 \times 100\%$) of the variance in meaning in life scores. Adjusted R^2 modifies the value of R^2 in an attempt to better estimate the true population value (R^2 calculated on the sample tends to overestimate the population value). Finally, the standard error of the estimate indicates the degree to which the independent variables were *unable* to predict scores on the dependent variable. The value of 9.2206 indicates that, when using the variables **connect, optimism,** and **success** to predict meaning in life, the regression equation was "off" in predicting meaning in life scores by about 9.22 points on average.

ANOVA—Testing the Overall Regression for Significance

The next table, *ANOVA*, tests whether the regression model, with all of the predictors included, significantly predicts meaning in life (which is analogous to a test of whether R^2 is significantly greater than zero). This test is conducted using an analysis of variance (ANOVA), which was discussed in Chapter 8. In the *ANOVA* table, a p-value less than or equal to .05 indicates that the regression model, with all the predictors included, significantly predicts meaning in life scores. Since the reported p-value of .000 (which should be read as "less than .001") is less than .05, the null hypothesis that $R^2 = 0$ is rejected, and it is concluded that the regression model (with the three predictors included) significantly predicts meaning in life.

Coefficients—Testing the Individual Predictors for Significance

The last table, *Coefficients*, provides the necessary values to construct a regression equation and test each of the predictors for significance.

The regression equation will be discussed first, followed by the test of whether **connect, optimism,** and **success** are significant predictors of meaning in life.

In multiple regression, an equation is created in the form of:

$$\hat{Y} = a + b_1 X_1 + b_2 X_2 + b_3 X_3$$

Where:

$\hat{Y}$ = the predicted score on the dependent variable. In our example, $\hat{Y}$ corresponds to the predicted meaning in life scores.

a = the Y-intercept; the value of $\hat{Y}$ when all Xs = 0.

b_i = the regression coefficient for the ith predictor. In this example, i takes on the values of 1, 2, or 3 for the first (**connect**), second (**optimism**), and third (**success**) predictors, respectively.

X_i = the *score* on the ith predictor (independent variable) for the participants. In this example, i takes on the values of 1, 2, and 3 for the first, second, and third predictors, respectively.

The regression equation can be extended for as many predictors as are included in the regression model. For example, if a fourth predictor was included, $+b_4 X_4$ would be added to the above equation.

The values in the regression equation, a (the Y-intercept; called "constant" in SPSS) and b_1, b_2, and b_3 (the regression coefficients for each of the predictors), are found in the *Coefficients* table in the *Unstandardized Coefficients* column heading labeled "B." In the *Coefficients* table, the value of the Y-intercept is -1.971 and the coefficients of **connect, optimism,** and **success** are .691, .653, and .599, respectively. Substituting these values into the regression equation formula produces the following equation for predicting meaning in life scores:

$$\hat{Y}_{\text{meaning in life}} = -1.971 + .691(\text{connect}) + .653(\text{optimism}) + .599(\text{success})$$

This is the regression equation based on the scores of the 30 college students. Given an individual's score on the three predictors, a predicted meaning in life score can be found. For example, the first participant had **connect, optimism,** and **success** scores of 25, 14, and 12, respectively. Inserting these scores into the equation yields a predicted meaning in life score of:

$$\hat{Y}_{\text{Meaning in life}} = -1.971 + .691(25) + .653(14) + .599(12)$$

$$\hat{Y}_{\text{Meaning in life}} = 31.634$$

A predicted score can be found using this method for each individual in the data set.[5] The predicted scores will almost always have some error (they will not match the actual scores exactly); the higher the value of R, the more closely the predicted values will be to the actual values, with an R of 1 resulting in perfect prediction (the predicted scores would match the actual scores exactly).

Interpreting the Direction of the Regression Coefficients

The fact that the regression weights for each of the predictors are positive (.691, .653, and .599) means, for example, that a one-point increase in **connect** (e.g., moving from 25 to 26) would result in a .691 point predicted *increase* in meaning in life scores, assuming all other predictors were held constant. A negative regression weight has the opposite interpretation, that is, a one-point increase in the predictor would result in a *decrease* in the predicted score by the value of the regression weight, assuming all other predictors were held constant.

Testing Each of the Predictors for Significance

A test of each of the predictors may be found in the *Coefficients* table. The last two columns of the table present t and p-values for each of the predictors. In the *Coefficients* table, both **connect** ($t = 2.449$, $p = .021$) and **optimism** ($t = 3.334$, $p = .003$) are significant, since their p-values are less than .05. **Success**, on other hand, is not significant, since its p-value of .214 is greater than .05.

Notice the column labeled *Standardized Coefficients* in the *Coefficients* table. While the unstandardized coefficients were used in finding predicted scores, the standardized coefficients will be presented in the write-up of the results. The standardized coefficients are referred to as beta weights and are equal to the value of the regression coefficients if the predictors and the criterion were in z-score form (i.e., if they were standardized with a mean of zero and a standard deviation of 1).[6]

While in most cases the constant is not of interest in multiple regression, the test of the constant reported in the *Coefficients* table is a test of whether the Y-intercept is significantly different from zero. In this case, the value of -1.971 is not significantly different from zero since the p-value for the test (.814) is greater than .05.

Effect Sizes

Measures of effect size in regression are given by R^2. Cohen (1988) expressed R^2 values of .02, .13, and .26 as corresponding to small, medium, and large effect sizes, respectively. In the above example, an R^2 of .61 would be considered to be a very large effect in practice, indicating that the predictors accounted for 61% of the variance in meaning in life scores.

Expression of the Results in APA Format

In the write-up of the results for multiple regression, both the test of the regression model with all the predictors included (including R^2 and the results of the ANOVA test) and the test of the individual predictors (including beta, the t value and the p-value) will be provided. A sample write-up is presented next.

Written Results

A multiple regression was conducted predicting meaning in life from the variables connectedness, optimism, and academic success. Overall, the regression was significant, $F(3, 26) = 13.31$, $p < .05$, $R^2 = .61$. Of the predictors investigated, both connectedness ($\beta = .34$, $t(26) = 2.45$, $p < .05$) and optimism ($\beta = .47$, $t(26) = 3.33$, $p < .05$) were significant. Academic success was not a significant predictor of meaning in life, $\beta = .19$, $t(26) = 1.27$, $p > .05$.

(*Note:* The degrees of freedom for each of the t tests in multiple regression are equal to $N - p - 1$, where p = the number of predictors and N = the number of participants in the study.)

Assumptions in Multiple Regression

1. *Independence of observations between the participants.*
    Independence of observations means that the scores for each of the participants are independent of one another (the participants shouldn't influence each other in completing the measures). Violating this assumption can seriously compromise the accuracy of the statistical tests performed using the multiple regression procedure. If there is reason to believe the independence assumption has been violated, the multiple regression procedure should not be used.
2. *The variables are distributed multivariate normal in the population.*
    This assumption means that each variable should be both normally distributed on its own and for all possible combinations of the other variables (e.g., the success scores should be normally distributed for all possible score combinations on meaning, connect, and optimism). For moderate to large sample sizes, most types of nonnormal data tend to have relatively little impact on the accuracy of the multiple regression procedure.
3. *Homoscedasticity.*
    Homoscedasticity means that the variances on the dependent variable are equal in the population for all possible combinations of levels of the independent variables. Mild to moderate violations of this assumption are generally tolerable in multiple regression.[7]

Summary of Steps for Conducting a Multiple Regression Analysis in SPSS

I. Data Entry and Analysis
1. Create a separate variable in SPSS for each predictor and for the criterion.
2. Enter the data.
3. Select **Analyze > Regression > Linear . . .**
4. Move the independent variables and the dependent variable to their respective boxes.
5. Click *Statistics*. Select *Descriptives* (*Estimates* and *Model fit* should already be selected). Click *Continue*.
6. Click *OK*.

II. Interpretation of the Results
1. In the chapter description, all the tables (*Descriptive Statistics*, *Correlations*, *Variables Entered/Removed*, *Model Summary*, *ANOVA*, and *Coefficients*) were described. In this summary, only information from the *Model Summary*, *ANOVA*, and *Coefficients* tables will be described.
    a. Note the value of R^2 in the *Model Summary* table. In the *ANOVA* table, if $p \leq .05$, the null hypothesis that $R^2 = 0$ is rejected, indicating that the regression model (with all the predictors included) accounts for a significant amount of variance in the dependent variable.
    b. In the *Coefficients* table, examine the p-value for each of the predictors.
        *   If one or more of the predictors is significant ($p \leq .05$), the null hypothesis that the beta weight is zero for the predictor(s) of interest is rejected.

Write the results indicating the variable(s) that significantly predict(s) the criterion variable. Indicate any nonsignificant predictors as well.

- If none of the predictors are significant ($p > .05$ for each of the predictors in the *Coefficients* table), the null hypothesis that the beta weight is zero for each of the predictors is not rejected. Write the results indicating that the predictor variables do not significantly predict the criterion variable.

Exercises

1. An industrial psychologist examined predictors of job satisfaction among 30 employees of different companies. The predictors investigated included the importance of work (**importance**), the opportunity for advancement in the company (**advance**), and the ability to express ideas to the boss (**express**). The criterion variable is job satisfaction (**satisfaction**). Higher scores on each of the variables indicate higher levels of the characteristic of interest (e.g., higher scores on satisfaction indicate greater satisfaction with one's job). The data are provided in Figure 14.10.

Satisfaction	Importance	Advance	Express
35	20	12	18
48	24	22	20
22	10	17	12
38	8	25	12
33	20	10	17
45	15	30	15
30	12	20	19
38	22	9	17
45	21	18	23
23	12	14	11
13	8	16	15
41	21	29	17
33	15	24	17
40	21	23	17
48	19	21	25
45	18	13	22
23	10	22	18
45	15	10	20
27	22	21	21
12	12	21	8
12	6	18	17
41	22	31	15
29	17	25	15
42	19	21	19
30	20	27	15
39	24	19	18
42	22	19	21
46	19	15	17
25	8	21	19
41	17	12	23

Figure 14.10 **The data for Exercise 1.**

Enter the data in SPSS and perform the appropriate analyses to answer the questions below. Name the variables **satisfaction, importance, advance,** and **express,** respectively.

a. State the null and alternative hypotheses for the individual predictors.

b. State the null and alternative hypothesis for the overall regression model.

c. Write a research question for each of the predictors and for the overall regression model.

d. What is R^2 for the model? Is the overall model significant?

e. Which, if any, of the predictors are significant? Which, if any, predictors are not significant?

    f.   What is the effect size for the overall regression model? Would you characterize the effect size as small, medium, or large?

    g.   Write a regression equation for the data.

    h.   Write the results using APA format as appropriate.

2.   A researcher was interested in predicting happiness from the variables forgiveness and social support. Twenty-five people who agreed to participate in the study were administered the three measures of interest, which are described in Figure 14.11.

Measure	What It Measures	Scale Range
Happiness (**happiness**)	The level of happiness one currently finds in life.	7–35; higher scores indicate greater happiness.
Forgiveness (**forgiveness**)	The degree to which one can forgive others.	10–50; higher scores indicate a greater willingness to forgive.
Social Support (**support**)	The degree to which one feels they can turn to others for support.	5–25; higher scores indicate a stronger support network.

Figure 14.11 **The variables for Exercise 2.**

    The data are provided in the file *Chapter 14_Exercise 2.sav* in the Chapter 14 folder online at www.routledge.com/cw/yockey. Open the file in SPSS and perform the appropriate analyses to answer the questions below.

    a.   State the null and alternative hypotheses for the individual predictors.

    b.   State the null and alternative hypothesis for the overall regression model.

    c.   Write a research question for each of the predictors and for the overall regression model.

    d.   What is R^2 for the model? Is the overall model significant?

    e.   Which, if any, of the predictors are significant? Which, if any, predictors are not significant?

    f.   What is the effect size for the overall regression model? Would you characterize the effect size as small, medium, or large?

    g.   Write a regression equation for the data.

    h.   Write the results using APA format as appropriate.

3.   A researcher was interested in predicting fear of death from the variables well-being and meaning in life. Fifty people who agreed to participate in the study were administered scales measuring each of the three variables, which are described in Figure 14.12.

Measure	What It Measures	Scale Range
Fear of death (**feardeath**)	The degree of fear one has toward death.	8–48; higher scores indicate greater fear of death.
Well-being (**wellbeing**)	The level of well-being one currently has in life.	5–40; higher scores indicate greater well-being.
Meaning in life (**meaning**)	The degree of meaning one currently finds in life.	30–70; higher scores indicate more meaning in life.

Figure 14.12 **The variables for Exercise 3.**

    The data are provided in the file *Chapter 14_Exercise 3.sav* in the Chapter 14 folder online at www.routledge.com/cw/yockey. Open the data file in SPSS and perform the appropriate analyses to answer the questions below.

    a.   State the null and alternative hypotheses for the individual predictors.

    b.   State the null and alternative hypothesis for the overall regression model.

    c.   Write a research question for each of the predictors and for the overall regression model.

    d.   What is R^2 for the model? Is the overall model significant?

    e.   Which, if any, of the predictors are significant? Which, if any, predictors are not significant?

    f.   What is the effect size for the overall regression model? Would you characterize the effect size as small, medium, or large?

    g.   Write a regression equation for the data.

    h.   Write the results using APA format as appropriate.

Notes

1. Multiple regression is a fairly complex topic and only an introduction is presented here. Stevens (2002) is a good resource for more information on the topic.

2. Categorical variables with two levels (e.g., gender) may be entered directly into SPSS as a single predictor; categorical variables with three or more levels must be recoded into multiple predictors (with the number of predictors equal to the number of categories − 1) prior to entering them into the regression equation. See Cohen, Cohen, West, and Aiken (2002) for more information on coding categorical predictors with three or more levels.

3. High correlations among the predictors can lead to a problem known as multicollinearity, which can result in unstable estimates for the predictors in the regression equation. See Stevens (2002) for more details on multicollinearity.

4. In hierarchical regression one or more predictors enter the model and a first regression is run, then one or more *new* predictors enter the model and a second regression is run, and so on. A primary objective of hierarchical regression is to see if the predictor(s) added in a later run account for a significant amount of variance above and beyond the predictor(s) added earlier.

5. SPSS can solve for these scores by clicking the *Save* button in the *Linear Regression* dialog box (shown in Figure 14.6) and then clicking on *Unstandardized in the Predicted Values* section of the dialog box. The predicted scores will then be placed in a new variable to the right of **success** in the data file.

6. When the regression coefficients are standardized, the *Y*-intercept is equal to zero and is dropped from the *Coefficients* table (which is why there is no value reported for *Constant* in the *Standardized Coefficients* column).

7. If one or more categorical predictors are included in the model, and the inequality in the sample sizes is moderate to large, then the presence of homoscedasticity can compromise the accuracy of the multiple regression procedure.

The Chi-Square Goodness of Fit Test

The chi-square goodness of fit procedure tests whether the proportion (or frequency) of cases that fall within each category of a variable are consistent with the proportions (or frequencies) specified under the null hypothesis. An example in which the chi-square goodness of fit test may be used is presented next.

Example

A student interested in social psychology wanted to investigate whether perceived responsibility varied as a function of group size (i.e., are people held more or less responsible for an action based on the size of the group they are in?). Ninety college students participated in the study, where they were described three scenarios in which a woman was in need of help, with the scenarios differing only by the number of people available nearby to help the woman. In the three scenarios, the group sizes consisted of one person, five people, and 25 people. In all three scenarios, the participants were told no one helped the woman. When the scenarios were described, the participants were asked to consider *a single person* in each of the groups and to indicate in which of the three scenarios the individual was most responsible for failing to help the woman (they were instructed to choose only one of the three scenarios).

Objective and Data Requirements of the Chi-Square Goodness of Fit Test

The Chi-Square Goodness of Fit Test

Objective	Data Requirements	Example
To test whether the proportions (or frequencies) in the sample differ significantly from the proportions (or frequencies) specified under the null hypothesis.	One categorical variable with two or more categories. Each participant provides a *frequency* (by falling in one of the categories).	Categorical Variable • Group size (1, 5, 25)

Null and Alternative Hypotheses

The null hypothesis states that perceived responsibility does *not* vary as a function of group size, which would imply an equal proportion of cases (or number of people) in each of the three categories:

H_0: Perceived responsibility does not vary by group size (the proportion or number of people who choose each category is equal in the population).

The alternative hypothesis states that perceived responsibility varies by group size, which would imply an unequal proportion of cases (or number of people) in the three categories:

H_1: Perceived responsibility varies by group size (the proportion or number of people who choose each category is not equal in the population).

Evaluation of the Null Hypothesis

The chi-square goodness of fit tests whether the proportions in each of the categories are equal to those specified in the null hypothesis. If the test produces results that seem unlikely if the null hypothesis is true (results that occur less than 5% of the time), then the null hypothesis is rejected. If the test produces results that seem fairly likely if the null hypothesis is true (results that occur greater than 5% of the time), then the null hypothesis is not rejected.

Research Question

The fundamental question of interest in a research study can also be expressed in the form of a research question, such as:

"Does perceived responsibility vary by group size?"

The Data

The data for the 90 participants are presented in Figure 15.1. Of the 90 participants, 42 chose the one-person category as the most responsible, 30 chose the five-person category, and 18 chose the 25-person category as the most responsible. These data are often referred to as *observed frequencies*, since they were "observed" in the study.

One person (alone)	5 person	25 person
42	30	18

Figure 15.1 **The number of participants who chose the one-person, five-person, and 25-person categories as most responsible (i.e., the observed frequencies).**

The chi-square goodness of fit test compares the frequencies observed in the study (those shown in Figure 15.1) to the frequencies that are expected under the null hypothesis (called the *expected frequencies*). To determine the expected frequencies, first we'll need to find the proportion of people expected to choose each of the categories if the null hypothesis is true. Since the null hypothesis states that perceived responsibility does *not* vary for the different group sizes, we would expect an equal proportion of people to select each category. With three categories, one-third of the participants should select each category, as is shown in Figure 15.2 below.

One person (alone)	5 person	25 person
1/3	1/3	1/3

Figure 15.2 **The proportion of participants expected to choose each category if the null hypothesis is true.**

Once the proportions are determined for each of the categories, they are converted into expected frequencies by multiplying each proportion by the total sample size (N) in the study.

The formula for generating the expected frequency for each of the categories is provided as follows:

Expected frequency for a category = (proportion of cases expected in that category) × (N)

Applying this formula to each of the categories produces the following expected frequencies:

Expected frequency in "1-person" category = (1/3) × 90 = 30.
Expected frequency in "5-person" category = (1/3) × 90 = 30.
Expected frequency in "25-person" category = (1/3) × 90 = 30.

The expected frequencies for the three categories are summarized in Figure 15.3.

One person (alone)	5 person	25 person
30	30	30

Figure 15.3 **The number of people expected to fall within each category if the null hypothesis is true (the expected frequencies).**

The chi-square goodness of fit test compares the observed frequencies in Figure 15.1 to the expected frequencies in Figure 15.3. In general, the greater the discrepancy between the observed and expected frequencies, the more likely the null hypothesis will be rejected.[1]

Before entering the data into SPSS, we'll discuss two different methods of data entry for the chi-square procedure. The two methods differ in how the data file is structured and will be referred to as the *weight cases* and the *individual observations* methods of data entry. These methods are described next.

Weight Cases Method

With the weight cases method of data entry, the number of rows required in the *Data View* window is equal to the number of *categories* for the variable of interest (in this example there would be three rows of data for the three different group size categories). Two variables are required in SPSS: one for the different categories and one for the number of people falling within each category (i.e., the frequencies). The weight cases method is typically used when the frequencies are already tallied for each of the categories (as the data are in this example; see Figure 15.1 for more details).

Individual Observations Method

With the individual observations method of data entry, the number of rows required in the *Data View* window is equal to the number of *people* in the study (in this example there would 90 rows of data for the 90 participants). Only one variable is required in SPSS, with a participant receiving a given value (e.g., 1, 2, or 3) for falling in a particular category. This approach is most useful when the frequencies have not already been tallied in each of the categories but instead are entered directly, such as from an instrument or a survey form.

The features of the weight cases and individual observations methods of data entry are summarized in Figure 15.4.

Method	Number of variables required in SPSS	Number of rows of data required in the *Data View* window	When to use
Weight cases	Two — one for the different categories and one for the frequencies	Equal to the number of *categories* of the variable (in our example, 3)	When the data are provided in summarized form (e.g., see Figure 15.1)
Individual observations	One — for the different categories	Equal to the number of *participants* in the study (in our example, 90)	When the data have not already been summarized (e.g., entering data from surveys)

Figure 15.4 **Features of the weight cases and individual observations methods of data entry for the chi-square goodness of fit procedure.**

Since the data are already tallied for each of the categories (as is shown in Figure 15.1), we'll use the weight cases method of data entry, which will require two variables to be entered in SPSS. (For those who prefer to use the individual observations method of data entry, a description of how to structure the data file using this method is provided in Figure 15.7 and an example may be found in Exercise 2 in the end-of-chapter exercises.)

Data Entry and Analysis in SPSS

Steps 1 and 2 describe how to enter the data in SPSS. The data file is also available online at www.routledge.com/cw/yockey under the name *no help.sav* in the Chapter 15 folder. If you prefer to open the file from the web site, skip to Step 3.

Step 1: Create the Variables

1. Start SPSS.
2. Click the *Variable View* tab.

In SPSS, two variables will be created, one for the different group size categories (i.e., 1, 5, and 25) and one for the frequencies (i.e., the number of people who chose each group size as most responsible). The variables will be named **groupsize** and **frequency**, respectively.

3. Enter the name **groupsize** and **frequency** in the first two rows of the *Variable View* window. Under *Measure*, classify **groupsize** as nominal and **frequency** as scale (see Figure 15.5).

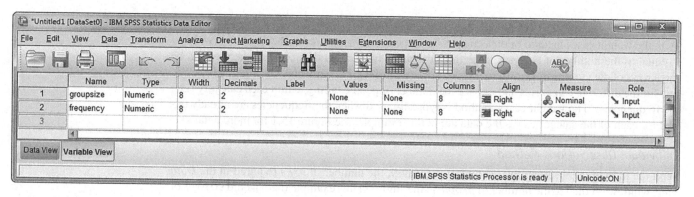

Figure 15.5 The *Variable View* window with the variables groupsize and frequency entered.

Next, we'll create value labels for the different categories in our study. We'll assign the one-person category a 1, the five-person category a 2, and the 25-person category a 3.

4. Using the process described in Chapter 1, create value labels for the variable **groupsize**. For **groupsize**, 1 = "1 person," 2 = "5 person," and 3 = "25 person."

Step 2: Enter the Data

1. Click the *Data View* tab. The variables **groupsize** and **frequency** appear in the first two columns of the *Data View* window.

Since we're using the weight cases method of data entry, we'll need to create a separate row in the data file for each of the three conditions in our study. The structuring of the data file using the weight cases method is illustrated in Figure 15.6.

Inspecting Figure 15.6, we'll enter three rows of data in SPSS, with each row corresponding to a different category in our study.

To enter the data

1. In the first row of the *Data View* window, enter a *1* and *42* for the variables **groupsize** and **frequency**, respectively. In row 2, enter a *2* and *30* for **groupsize** and **frequency**, respectively, and in row 3, enter a *3* and *18*. The completed data set is presented in Figure 15.7.

Groupsize	Frequency
1	42
2	30
3	18

Figure 15.6 **The values for groupsize and frequency using the weight cases method of data entry. For groupsize, *1* corresponds to the one-person category, *2* corresponds to the five-person category, and *3* corresponds to the 25-person category.**

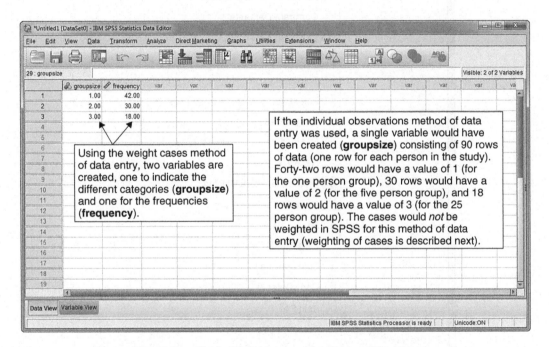

Figure 15.7 **The completed data file for the chi-square goodness of fit example.**

Step 3: Analyze the Data

Prior to running the chi-square analysis, we'll first need to weight the cases for **frequency**.[2] Weighting the cases indicates that the values for a given variable represent *the total number of observations* as opposed to a single score. For example, when **frequency** is weighted, this indicates in SPSS that the value of 42 in the first category corresponds to 42 *people*, not a score of 42.

*To weight the cases for **frequency***

1. From the menu bar, select **Data > Weight Cases . . .** (see Figure 15.8 on page 194).
2. The *Weight Cases* dialog box opens. Select *Weight cases by* and select the variable, **frequency**. Click the right-arrow button (➤) to move **frequency** into the *Frequency Variable* box (see Figure 15.9 on page 194 for details).
3. Click *OK*. This indicates that the frequency values (42, 30, and 18) correspond to *the total number of people* in each category, not a single score.[3]

With the cases weighted for **frequency**, we can now perform the chi-square goodness of fit test in SPSS.

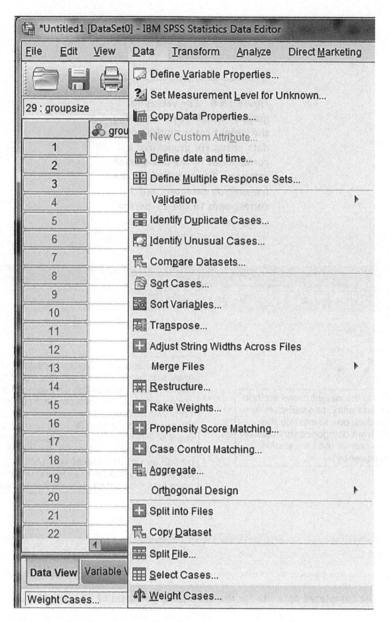

Figure 15.8   **Menu commands for the *Weight Cases* procedure.**

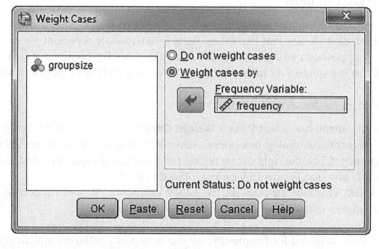

Figure 15.9   **The *Weight Cases* dialog box.**

1. From the menu bar, select **Analyze > Nonparametric Tests > Legacy Dialogs >
    Chi-square . . .** (see Figure 15.10).

A *Chi-Square* dialog box appears with the variables **groupsize** and **frequency** in the left-hand
side of the box (see Figure 15.11).

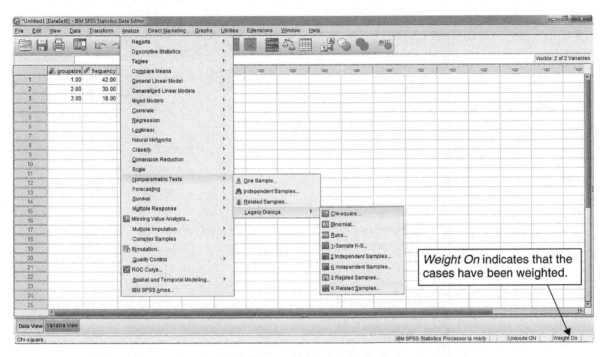

Figure 15.10   **Menu commands for the chi-square goodness of fit procedure.**

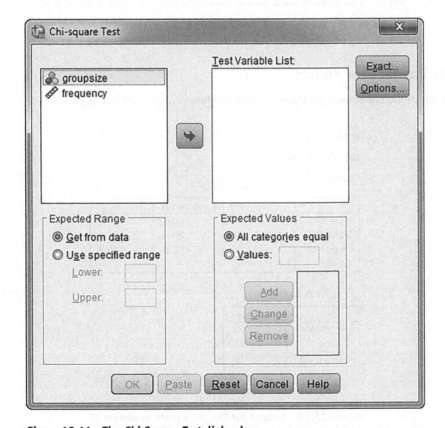

Figure 15.11   **The *Chi-Square Test* dialog box.**

2. Select the variable, **groupsize**, and click the right-arrow button (⬆) to move it into the *Test Variable List* box (see Figure 15.12). (*Note*: **Frequency** should remain on the left-hand side of the dialog box.)
3. Click *OK*.

The chi-square goodness of fit test runs and the results are presented in the *Viewer* window.

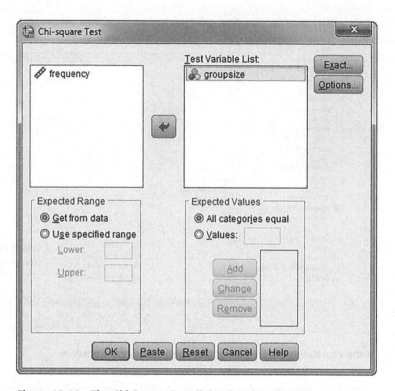

Figure 15.12 **The *Chi-Square Test* dialog box (continued).**

Step 4: Interpret the Results

The output of the chi-square goodness of fit procedure is displayed in Figure 15.13.

NPar Tests

Chi–Square Test

Frequencies

groupsize

	Observed N	Expected N	Residual
1 person	42	30.0	12.0
5 person	30	30.0	.0
25 person	18	30.0	−12.0
Total	90		

Test Statistics

	groupsize
Chi-Square[a]	9.600
df	2
Asymp. Sig.	.008

a. 0 cells (.0%) have expected frequencies less than 5. The minimum expected cell frequency is 30.0.

Figure 15.13 **Output for the chi-square goodness of fit test procedure.**

Groupsize

The first table, labeled *groupsize*, reports the observed frequencies (*Observed N*), the expected frequencies (*Expected N*), and the residual, or the difference between the observed and expected frequencies for the one-person, five-person, and 25-person categories. In the table, observed frequencies of 42, 30, and 18 are reported for the one-person, five-person, and 25-person categories, respectively. An expected frequency of 30 is reported for each of the three categories, which confirms our calculations for the expected frequencies shown earlier. Notice that in the residual column there is a difference of 12 between the observed and expected frequencies for the one-person and 25-person categories (for the one-person category *Observed N > Expected N*, while for the 25-person category *Expected N > Observed N*). Whether the difference between the observed and expected frequencies is large enough to be statistically significant will be considered next.

Test Statistics

The next table, *Test Statistics*, provides the answer to our research question, that is, whether perceived responsibility varies as a function of group size. The chi-square goodness of fit test produces a chi-square statistic, which is given by:

$$\chi^2 = \sum \frac{(\text{observed frequency} - \text{expected frequency})^2}{\text{expected frequency}}$$

where the observed and expected frequencies correspond to the *Observed N* and the *Expected N*, respectively, in the *groupsize* table. Inserting the observed and expected frequencies from the *groupsize* table produces a chi-square (χ^2) value of:

$$\chi^2 = \frac{(42-30)^2}{30} + \frac{(30-30)^2}{30} + \frac{(18-30)^2}{30}$$

$$\chi^2 = 9.60$$

which is equal to the *Chi-Square* value in the *Test Statistics* table. The chi-square test has 2 degrees of freedom (*df* = the number of categories – 1), and a *p*-value (reported as *Asymp. Sig.*) of .008. Because the *p*-value is less than .05, the null hypothesis that the frequencies are equal across the three categories is rejected, indicating that perceived responsibility varies by group size.

Since the results are significant, we'll examine the difference between the observed and expected frequencies in the *groupsize* table to determine which of the categories the participants viewed as being most (and least) responsible for not helping. For the one-person category, the observed frequency was 42 while the expected frequency was 30, indicating that 12 more people chose the one-person category than expected. For the five-person category, there was no difference between the observed and expected frequencies (30 observed vs. 30 expected), while for the 25-person category, 12 fewer people chose the category than expected (18 observed vs. 30 expected). In summary, people chose the one-person category more than expected and the 25-person category less than expected (with no difference between the observed and expected categories for the five-person category). This suggests that people perceive a greater responsibility to help others when a person is alone as compared to being in a large group.

Expression of the Results in APA Format

In writing the results, the conclusion of the hypothesis test, the degrees of freedom, the sample size, the chi-square value, and the *p*-value are reported. For significant results, the relationship between the observed and expected frequencies should also be described. An example of a brief write-up in APA format is presented next.

Written Results

The perceived responsibility for failing to help a person in need varied as a function of group size, χ^2 (2, *N* = 90) = 9.60, *p* < .05. Participants rated people who are alone as most responsible and those who are in large groups (25 people) as least responsible for failing to help a person in need.

The percentage of people who rated the one-person, five-person, and 25-person groups as being the most responsible was 46.7%, 33.3%, and 20.0%, respectively.[4]

(*Note*: The "2" to the right of χ^2 in the above results is for the degrees of freedom. The sample size is also provided in parentheses, because unlike the other procedures covered in this text, the sample size cannot be determined from the degrees of freedom for the chi-square test.)

Assumptions of the Chi-Square Goodness of Fit Test

1. *Observations are independent.*
   The independence assumption means that the observations (i.e., the participants) in each of the cells are independent of each other. An example of violating this assumption would be if a person was counted in two different cells (e.g., each participant was asked to provide the top *two* scenarios where perceived responsibility is greatest). Violating the independence assumption can seriously compromise the accuracy of the chi-square test. If there is reason to believe the independence assumption has been violated, the chi-square goodness of fit test should not be used.

2. *The magnitude of the expected cell frequencies.*
   For tables with four cells (categories) or less an expected frequency of 5 or more in each cell is recommended. For larger tables, having one or a few cells with expected frequencies less than 5 will most likely not invalidate the results of the chi-square procedure, although the power may suffer if the total sample size is small.

Summary of Steps for Conducting a Chi-Square Goodness of Fit Test in SPSS

Instructions for conducting a chi-square goodness of fit test in SPSS are provided for both the weight cases and individual observations methods of data entry. (As noted previously, the structuring of the data file for the individual observations method is illustrated in Exercise 2 of the end-of-chapter exercises.)

Ia. Data Entry and Analysis—Weight Cases Method
1. Create two variables in SPSS (one for the categorical variable and one for the frequency variable).
2. Create value labels for the categorical variable. In the *Value Labels* dialog box, enter the numeric values and labels as appropriate. Click *OK*.
3. Enter the data. (For the weight cases method of data entry, the number of rows in the data file is equal to the number of *categories* of the variable.)
4. Weight the cases for the frequency variable by selecting **Data > Weight Cases . . .**
5. Select *Weight cases by* and move the frequency variable to the *Frequency Variable* box. Click *OK*.
6. Select **Analyze > Nonparametric Tests > Legacy Dialogs > Chi-Square . . .**
7. Move the categorical variable to the *Test Variable List* box (the frequency variable should remain on the left).
8. Click *OK*.

Ib. Data Entry and Analysis—Individual Observations Method
1. Create one variable in SPSS (for the categories).
2. Create value labels for the variable. In the *Value Labels* dialog box, enter the numeric values and labels as appropriate. Click *OK*.
3. Enter the data. (For the individual observations method of data entry, the number of rows in the data file is equal to the number of *participants* in the study).
4. Select **Analyze > Nonparametric Tests > Legacy Dialogs > Chi-Square . . .**
5. Move the variable to the *Test Variable List* box.
6. Click *OK*.

II. **Interpretation of the Results (the interpretation is the same regardless of which method of data entry is used)**

In the *Test Statistics* table, examine the p-value (shown in SPSS as *Asymp. Sig.*).

- If $p \leq .05$ the null hypothesis is rejected. Write the results indicating the nature of the relationship between the observed and expected frequencies.
- If $p > .05$ the null hypothesis is not rejected. Write the results indicating that there is not a significant difference between the observed and expected frequencies (e.g., there is not a preference for any of the categories).

Exercises

1. A researcher was interested in investigating the influence of eye size on attraction. Photos of two different people (who were determined by experts to be of similar attractiveness and eye size) were used in the study. The photos were manipulated prior to the study so that one of the two people in the photos had moderately larger eyes (the photos were counterbalanced so that one person had larger eyes for half of the participants and the other person had larger eyes for the other half of the participants). Eighty people viewed both photos, indicating which of the two they found more attractive. The data are presented in Figure 15.14.

Large eyes	Small eyes
60	20

Figure 15.14 **The number of participants who chose each photo as most attractive.**

Enter the data into SPSS and perform the appropriate analyses to answer the questions below. Name the variables **eyesize** and **frequency** (be sure to weight the cases prior to analyzing the data). For **eyesize**, code large eyes a "1" and small eyes a "2."

a. State the null and alternative hypotheses.
b. State a research question for the data.
c. Is there a preference for one of the photos? Test using $\alpha = .05$.
d. Write the results using APA format as appropriate.

2. A market researcher investigated whether people perceive a difference in the picture quality of LED and LCD televisions. Shoppers at a local warehouse store were shown a movie trailer on both an LED and LCD television and were asked to indicate which of the two televisions had the better picture quality. The choices of the 65 shoppers included in the study are provided in Figure 15.15.

LED	LCD
35	30

Figure 15.15 **The number of people who chose LED and LCD televisions as having the best picture quality.**

The data are provided in the file *Chapter 15_Exercise 2.sav* in the Chapter 15 folder online at www.routledge.com/cw/yockey (the variable is named **tv** with LED televisions coded a "1" and LCD televisions coded a "2"). The data file has been entered using the individual observations method (i.e., there is no need to weight the cases for this example). Open the data in SPSS and perform the appropriate analyses to answer the questions below (instructions for analyzing the

data using the individual observations method are provided in the "Summary of Steps" section prior to the chapter exercises).
a. State the null and alternative hypotheses.
b. State a research question for the data.
c. Is there a difference in the perceived picture quality of LED and LCD televisions? Test using $\alpha = .05$.
d. Write the results of the study using APA format as appropriate.

3. A marketing firm conducted a study to assess consumer preferences of differently priced coffees. The leading brand in each category of $3-, $6-, and $10-priced coffee (for 12 oz. of ground coffee) was selected. One hundred and fifty people tasted the three coffee brands (without knowing the cost or brand of each) and indicated which coffee they preferred. The preferences of the 150 participants are shown in Figure 15.16.

$3 brand	$6 brand	$10 brand
30	62	58

Figure 15.16 **The number of people who chose the $3-, $6-, and $10-coffee brands as the best tasting.**

The data are provided in the file *Chapter 15_Exercise 3.sav* in the Chapter 15 folder online at www.routledge.com/cw/yockey. (In the file, the variables are named **cost** and **frequency** with the $3 brand coded a "1," the $6 brand coded a "2," and the $10 brand coded a "3" for **cost**.) Open the data in SPSS and perform the appropriate analyses to answer the questions below (for this problem, be sure to weight the cases prior to analyzing the data).
a. State the null and alternative hypotheses.
b. State a research question for the data.
c. Is there a preference for one (or more) of the coffees? Test using $\alpha = .05$.
d. Write the results of the study using APA format as appropriate.

Notes

1. Strictly speaking, the value of the chi-square statistic is also affected by the absolute size of the expected frequencies.
2. When using the weight cases method of data entry, if the cases are not weighted prior to running the chi-square, the results will be incorrect.
3. It is important to note that the cases remain weighted until either the weight cases option is turned off (by clicking *Do not weight cases* in the *Weight Cases* dialog box and clicking *OK*) or until SPSS is closed. If additional analyses are performed other than the chi-square test, failing to turn the weight cases option off can lead to incorrect analyses and/or error messages.
4. The percentage of people in each of the categories may be calculated in SPSS by running the *Frequencies* procedure on **groupsize** (assuming the cases are weighted). See Chapter 2 for more information on using the *Frequencies* procedure in SPSS.

The Chi-Square Test of Independence

The chi-square test of independence provides a test of whether there is a relationship between two categorical variables, with each variable consisting of two or more categories. An example in which the chi-square test of independence may be used is presented next.

Example

A researcher wanted to investigate whether there was a relationship between personality type (introvert, extrovert) and choice of recreational activity (going to an amusement park, taking a one-day retreat). Each of the 100 participants who agreed to participate in the study were administered a personality measure and, based on their scores on that measure, were classified as either an introvert or extrovert. Each participant was then asked to indicate which day-long recreational activity they would prefer: going to an amusement park or on a retreat. The personality type and choice of recreational activity for each of the participants is provided in Figure 16.1.

		Preferred recreational activity		
		Amusement park	Retreat	Total
Personality type	Introvert	12	28	40
	Extrovert	43	17	60
	Total	55	45	100

Figure 16.1 **Classification table of the 100 study participants.**

In Figure 16.1, personality type is presented in the rows of the table and the preferred recreational activity is presented in the columns. Of the 100 people who participated in the study, 40 were classified as introverts and 60 were classified as extroverts. Of the 40 introverts, 12 preferred the amusement park and 28 preferred the retreat. Of the 60 extroverts, 43 preferred the amusement park and 17 preferred the retreat. The categorical variables in the study are personality type and preferred recreational activity, and the data to be analyzed are in the form of counts or frequencies. The current example is referred to as a 2 × 2 (read "two by two") chi-square with two levels each for personality and recreational activity, resulting in a total of four cells.

Objective and Data Requirements of the Chi-Square Test of Independence

Chi-Square Test of Independence

Objective	Data Requirements	Example
To determine if a relationship exists between two categorical variables.	Frequencies or counts	Frequencies (the number of people in each cell)
	Two categorical variables with two or more categories each	Categorical variables • Personality type (introvert, extrovert) • Recreational activity (amusement park, retreat)

Null and Alternative Hypotheses

The null and alternative hypotheses for the chi-square test of independence are as follows:

H_0: There is not a relationship between personality type and choice of recreational activity.

H_1: There is a relationship between personality type and choice of recreational activity.

Evaluation of the Null Hypothesis

The chi-square test of independence provides a test of the null hypothesis that there is no relationship between personality type and choice of recreational activity. If the test produces results that seem unlikely if the null hypothesis is true (results that occur less than 5% of the time), then the null hypothesis is rejected. If the test produces results that seem fairly likely if the null hypothesis is true (results that occur more than 5% of the time), then the null hypothesis is not rejected.

Research Question

The fundamental question of interest in a research study can also be expressed in the form of a research question, such as:

"Is there a relationship between personality type and preferred recreational activity?"

Data Entry and Analysis in SPSS

Steps 1 and 2 below describe how to enter the data in SPSS. The data file is also available online at www.routledge.com/cw/yockey under the name *choice.sav* in the Chapter 16 folder. If you prefer to open the file from the web site, skip to Step 3.

Step 1: Create the Variables

1. Start SPSS.
2. Click the *Variable View* tab.

In SPSS, three variables will be created, one for the different personality types, one for the preferred activity, and one for the frequencies. The variables will be named **personality**, **activity**, and **frequency**, respectively.

3. Enter the variable names **personality**, **activity**, and **frequency**, respectively, in the first three rows of the *Variable View* window. Under *Measure*, classify **personality** and **activity** as nominal and **frequency** as scale (see Figure 16.2).

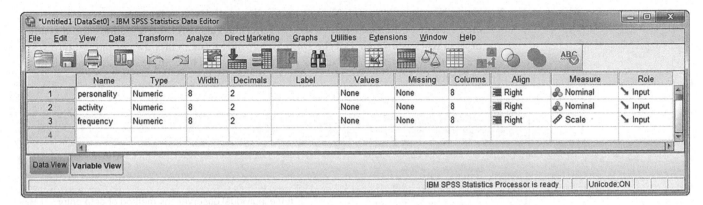

Figure 16.2 The *Variable View* window with the variables personality, activity, and frequency entered.

4. Using the process described in Chapter 1, create value labels for the categorical variables **personality** and **activity**. For **personality**, 1 = "introvert" and 2 = "extrovert." For **activity**, 1 = "amusement park" and 2 = "retreat."

Step 2: Enter the Data

Next, we'll enter the data into SPSS. There are two different methods for entering data into SPSS for the chi-square test of independence: the *weight cases* method and the *individual observations* method (see Chapter 15 for a description of these two methods). As was noted in Chapter 15, the weight cases method is used when the data are provided with the frequencies already tallied in the cells. Since the frequencies are tallied in the cells in our example (see Figure 16.1), we'll use the weight cases method for entering the data. (A description of how to structure the data file using the individual observations method is provided in Figure 16.4.)

In our example, recall that introverts and extroverts can choose either the amusement park or the retreat, resulting in four different conditions in the study (introvert/amusement park, introvert/retreat, extrovert/amusement park, extrovert/retreat). Since we're using the weight cases method of data entry, we'll need to create a separate *row* in the *Data View* window for each of these four conditions. The proper structuring of the data file using the weight cases method is illustrated in Figure 16.3.

Personality	Activity	Frequency
1	1	12
1	2	28
2	1	43
2	2	17

Figure 16.3 The four conditions in the study design. For personality, introverts are assigned a "1" and extroverts are assigned a "2." For activity, amusement park is assigned a "1" and retreat is assigned a "2."

To enter the data

1. Click the *Data View* tab. The variables **personality**, **activity**, and **frequency** appear in the first three columns of the *Data View* window.

Inspecting Figure 16.3, the first condition corresponds to introverts (coded a "1") who chose the amusement park (also coded a "1"), of which there were 12 people total. Therefore, these values will be entered in the first row of the *Data View* window.

2. Enter the values *1*, *1*, and *12*, for **personality**, **activity**, and **frequency**, respectively, in the first row of the *Data View* window. Enter the values for the remaining three conditions in rows 2 through 4 of the *Data View* window (i.e., enter a *1*, *2*, and *28* in row 2, a *2*, *1*, and *43* in row 3, and a *2*, *2*, and *17* in row 4). The completed data file is shown in Figure 16.4.

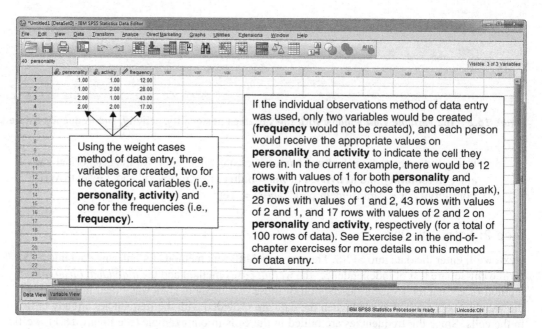

Figure 16.4 **The completed data file for the chi-square test of independence example.**

Step 3: Analyze the Data

Prior to running the chi-square test, we'll first need to weight the cases for **frequency**. Weighting the cases indicates that the values for a given variable represent the *total number of observations* as opposed to a single score. For example, when **frequency** is weighted, a value of 12 for **frequency** will be interpreted as 12 *people*, not a score of 12.

*To weight the cases for **frequency***
1. From the menu bar, select **Data > Weight Cases . . .** (see Figure 16.5).
2. The *Weight Cases* dialog box opens. Select *Weight cases by* and select the variable, **frequency**. Click the right-arrow button (➤) to move **frequency** into the *Frequency Variable* box (see Figure 16.6).
3. Click *OK*. This indicates that the frequency values (12, 28, 43, and 17) correspond to *the total number of people* in each cell, not a single score.[1]

With the cases weighted for **frequency**, now we can perform the chi-square test of independence in SPSS.

To perform the chi-square test of independence
1. From the menu bar, select **Analyze > Descriptive Statistics > Crosstabs . . .** (see Figure 16.7 on page 206).

The *Crosstabs* dialog box opens with the variables **personality**, **activity**, and **frequency** in the left-hand side of the box (see Figure 16.8 on page 206 for details).

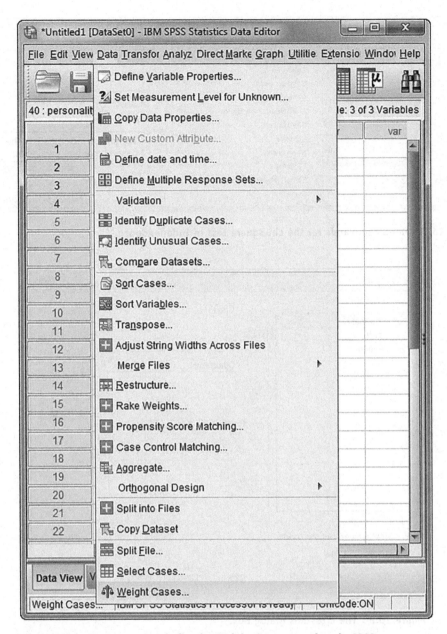

Figure 16.5 **Menu commands for the *Weight Cases* procedure in SPSS.**

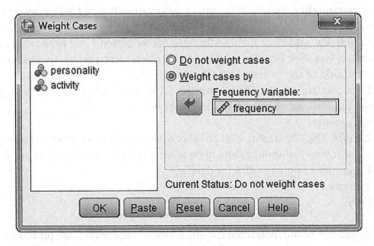

Figure 16.6 **The *Weight Cases* dialog box.**

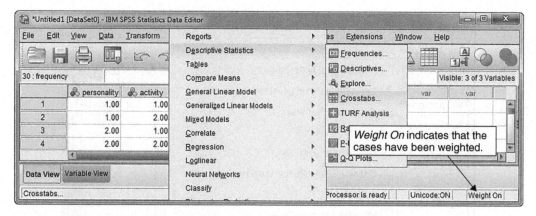

Figure 16.7   Menu commands for the chi-square test of independence.

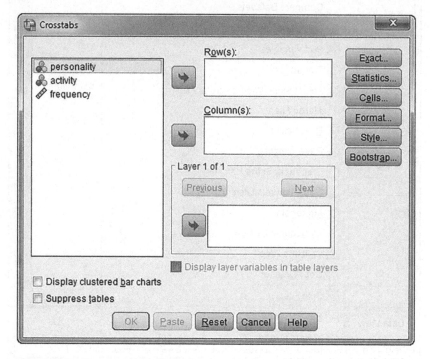

Figure 16.8   The *Crosstabs* dialog box.

2. Select **personality,** and click the upper right-arrow button (⬇) to move it into the *Row(s)* box.
3. Select **activity,** and click the middle right-arrow button (⬇) to move it into the *Column(s)* box. See Figure 16.9 for details. (*Note*: **Frequency** should remain on the left-hand side of the *Crosstabs* dialog box.)
4. Click the *Statistics* button. The *Crosstabs: Statistics* dialog box opens. Select *Chi-square* and *Phi and Cramer's V* (see Figure 16.10).
5. Click *Continue.*
6. Click *Cells.* The *Crosstabs: Cell Display* dialog box opens. Under *Counts* select *Expected* (*Observed* should already be selected) and under *Percentages* select *Row.* See Figure 16.11 on page 208 for details.
7. Click *Continue.*
8. Click *OK.*

The chi-square test of independence runs in SPSS and the results are presented in the *Viewer* window.

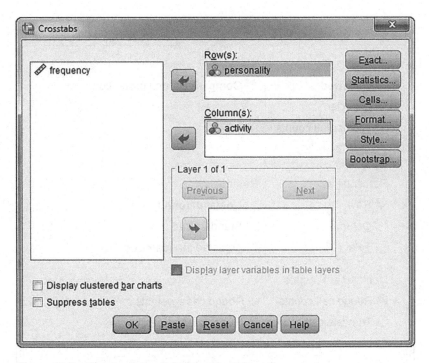

Figure 16.9 **The *Crosstabs* dialog box (continued).**

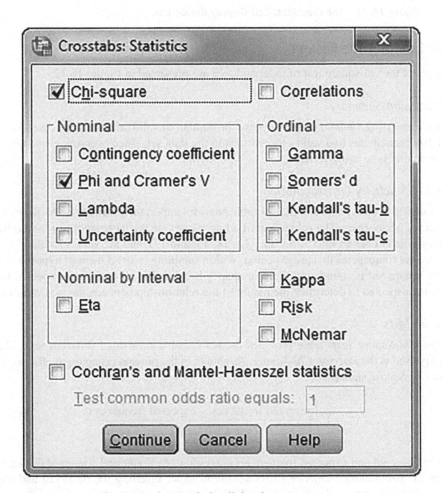

Figure 16.10 **The *Crosstabs: Statistics* dialog box.**

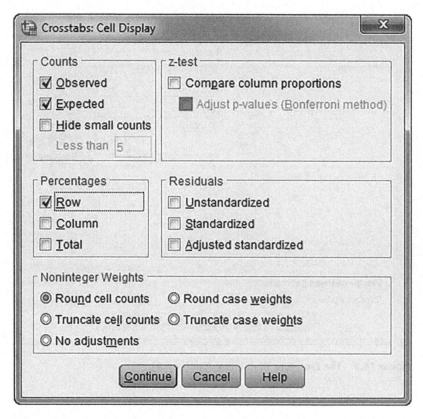

Figure 16.11   **The *Crosstabs: Cell Display* dialog box.**

Step 4: Interpret the Results

The results of the chi-square test of independence are presented in Figure 16.12.

Case Processing Summary

The *Case Processing Summary* table displays the number of valid (and missing) cases for the data set. All 100 participants had valid observations in the data set, since everyone was classified on both personality type and activity.

Personality * activity Crosstabulation

The *personality * activity Crosstabulation* table provides important information about the observed and expected frequencies. The values identified as "*Count*" in the table are the observed frequencies we originally entered into SPSS (i.e., 12, 28, 43, and 17), and the values labeled "*Expected Count*" are the frequencies that are expected (within sampling error) if the null hypothesis is true. If the chi-square test is significant, the discrepancy between the observed and expected frequencies will be inspected to determine the nature of the relationship between the two variables.

Chi-Square Tests

While the *Chi-Square Tests* table provides the results of a number of different tests, the most commonly used is the *Pearson Chi-Square*. As shown in the previous chapter, the formula for the *Pearson Chi-Square* statistic is:

$$\chi^2 = \sum \frac{(\text{observed frequency} - \text{expected frequency})^2}{\text{expected frequency}}$$

where the observed and expected frequencies correspond to *Count* and *Expected Count*, respectively, in the *personality * activity Crosstabulation* table. Inserting the observed and expected frequencies into the chi-square formula produces a chi-square value of:

Crosstabs

Case Processing Summary

	Cases					
	Valid		Missing		Total	
	N	Percent	N	Percent	N	Percent
personality *activity	100	100.0%	0	.0%	100	100.0%

personality * activity Crosstabulation

			activity		Total
			amusement park	retreat	
personality	introvert	Count	12	28	40
		Expected Count	22.0	18.0	40.0
		% within personality	30.0%	70.0%	100.0%
	extrovert	Count	43	17	60
		Expected Count	33.0	27.0	60.0
		% within personality	71.7%	28.3%	100.0%
Total		Count	55	45	100
		Expected Count	55.0	45.0	100.0
		% within personality	55.0%	45.0%	100.0%

Chi-Square Tests

	Value	df	Asymp. Sig. (2-sided)	Exact Sig. (2-sided)	Exact Sig. (1-sided)
Pearson Chi-Square	16.835[b]	1	.000		
Continuity Correction[a]	15.194	1	.000		
Likelihood Ratio	17.230	1	.000		
Fisher's Exact Test				.000	.000
Linear-by-Linear Association	16.667	1	.000		
N of Valid Cases	100				

[a.] Computed only for a 2x2 table
[b.] 0 cells (.0%) have expected count less than 5. The minimum expected count is 18.00.

Symmetric Measures

		Value	Approx. Sig.
Nominal by Nominal	Phi	−.410	.000
	Cramer's V	.410	.000
N of Valid Cases		100	

[a.] Not assuming the null hypothesis.
[b.] Using the asymptotic standard error assuming the null hypothesis.

Figure 16.12   **Output for the chi-square test of independence.**

$$\chi^2 = \frac{(12-22)^2}{22} + \frac{(28-18)^2}{18} + \frac{(43-33)^2}{33} + \frac{(17-27)^2}{27}$$
$$\chi^2 = 16.835$$

which corresponds to the value of the *Pearson Chi-Square* reported in the *Chi-Square Tests* table. The chi-square test has 1 degree of freedom [*df* = (the number of categories of personality – 1) × (the number of categories of recreational activity – 1)] and a *p*-value (*Asymp. Sig.*) of .000 (read as "less than .001"). Because the *p*-value is less than .05, the null hypothesis is rejected, and it is concluded that a relationship exists between personality type and activity preference.

Since the test is significant, we'll examine the difference between the observed and expected frequencies (the counts) in the *personality * activity Crosstabulation* table to determine the nature of the relationship between the two variables. Inspecting the first cell in the table (introverts who chose the amusement park), only 12 chose the amusement park while 22 were expected to, indicating that introverts chose the amusement park less frequently than expected. Moving to the retreat column, 28 introverts chose the retreat while only 18 were expected to, indicating that introverts chose the retreat more frequently than expected. For extroverts, the opposite pattern exists: Extroverts chose the amusement park more often than expected (observed count of 43 vs. an expected count of 33) and the retreat less often than expected (observed count of 17 vs. an expected count of 27). The results are summarized in Figure 16.13.

	Amusement park	Retreat	Conclusion
Introvert	Fewer chose than expected (12 observed, 22 expected)	More chose than expected (28 observed, 18 expected)	Introverts preferred the retreat
Extrovert	More chose than expected (43 observed, 33 expected)	Fewer chose than expected (17 observed, 27 expected)	Extroverts preferred the amusement park

Figure 16.13 **Summary of the results for the chi-square test of independence.**

In summary, the results indicated that introverts preferred the retreat while extroverts preferred the amusement park.

Symmetric Measures

The *Symmetric Measures* table will be discussed in the following section on effect sizes.

Effect Sizes

A commonly used measure of effect size for the chi-square test of independence is Cramer's *V*. The formula for Cramer's *V* is:

$$V = \sqrt{\frac{\chi^2}{N(k-1)}}$$

where χ^2 is the value of the *Pearson Chi-Square* provided in the *Chi-Square Tests* table, *N* is the total sample size in the study, and *k* is the number of levels of the variable with the *fewest* categories. (In our example, *k* = 2, since *each* variable has two levels.)

Inserting the appropriate values from Figure 16.12 yields a value of:

$$V = \sqrt{\frac{16.835}{100(2-1)}} = .41$$

which agrees with the value provided in the *Symmetric Measures* table under *Cramer's V*.

Cohen's (1988) conventions for small, medium, and large effect sizes for Cramer's *V* are .10, .30, and .50, respectively (these effect size designations apply only to tables where at least one of the variables has *only* two categories, i.e., 2 × 2, 2 × 3, 2 × 4 tables, etc.). Therefore, the value of .41 corresponds to a medium effect size, indicating a moderate relationship between the two variables.[2]

Expression of the Results in APA Format

In writing the results, the conclusion of the hypothesis test, the degrees of freedom, the sample size, the chi-square value, the *p*-value, and the effect size are reported. For significant results, the relationship between the observed and expected frequencies and the percentage of people falling within each category may also be described. An example of a brief write-up in APA format is presented next.

Written Results

There is a significant relationship between personality type and choice of recreational activity, $\chi^2(1, N = 100) = 16.84$, $p < .05$, Cramer's $V = .41$. Given the choice of attending a retreat or going to an amusement park, introverts preferred to attend the retreat (70% of the introverts chose the retreat) while extroverts preferred the amusement park (72% of the extroverts chose the amusement park).

Assumptions of the Chi–Square Test of Independence

1. *Observations are independent.*
   The independence assumption means that the observations in each of the cells are independent of each other. An example of violating this assumption would be if a person was counted in two different cells (e.g., a person was allowed to select *both* recreational activities). Violating this assumption can seriously compromise the accuracy of the chi-square test. If there is reason to believe the independence assumption has been violated, the chi-square test of independence should not be used.
2. *The magnitude of the expected cell frequencies.*
   For small tables (tables with four cells) an expected frequency of 5 or more in each cell is recommended. For larger tables, having one or a few cells with expected frequencies less than 5 will most likely not invalidate the results of the chi-square procedure, although the power may suffer if the total sample size is small.

Summary of Steps for Conducting a Chi-Square Test of Independence in SPSS

Instructions for conducting a chi-square test of independence in SPSS are provided below for both the weight cases and individual observations methods of data entry. (As noted previously, the structuring of the data file using the individual observations method is illustrated in Exercise 2 of the end-of-chapter exercises.)

Ia. Data Entry and Analysis—Weight Cases Method
1. Create three variables in SPSS (one for each of the categorical variables and one for the frequency variable).
2. Create value labels for each of the categorical variables. In the *Value Labels* dialog box, enter the numeric values and labels as appropriate. Click *OK*.
3. Enter the data. (For the weight cases method of data entry, the number of rows is equal to the multiple of the number of *categories* of the two variables.)
4. Weight the cases for the frequency variable by selecting **Data > Weight Cases . . .**
5. Select *Weight cases by* and move the frequency variable to the *Frequency Variable* box. Click *OK*.
6. Select **Analyze > Descriptive Statistics > Crosstabs . . .**
7. Move one of the categorical variables to the *Row(s)* box and the other to the *Column(s)* box. (The frequency variable should remain in the left-hand side of the dialog box.)
8. Click *Statistics*. Select *Chi-square* and *Phi and Cramer's V*. Click *Continue*.
9. Click *Cells*. Under *Counts* click *Expected* (*Observed* should already be selected) and under *Percentages*, select *Row*. Click *Continue*.
10. Click *OK*.

Ib. Data Entry and Analysis—Individual Observations Method
1. Create two variables in SPSS (one for each categorical variable).
2. Create value labels for each of the categorical variables. In the *Value Labels* dialog box, enter the numeric values and labels as appropriate. Click *OK*.
3. Enter the data. (For the individual observations method of data entry, the number of rows in the data file is equal to the number of *participants* in the study.)
4. Select **Analyze > Descriptive Statistics > Crosstabs . . .**

5. Move one of the categorical variables to the *Row(s)* box and the other to the *Column(s)* box.
6. Click *Statistics*. Select *Chi-square* and *Phi and Cramer's V*. Click *Continue*.
7. Click *Cells*. Under *Counts* select *Expected* (*Observed* should already be selected) and under *Percentages*, select *Row*. Click *Continue*.
8. Click *OK*.

II. **Interpretation of the Results (the interpretation is the same regardless of which method of data entry is used)**

Check the *p*-value (*Asymp. Sig.*) for *Pearson Chi-Square* in the *Chi-Square Tests* table.
- If $p \leq .05$ the null hypothesis is rejected. Write the results indicating the nature of the relationship between the two variables.
- If $p > .05$ the null hypothesis is not rejected. Write the results indicating that there is not a relationship between the two variables.

Exercises

1. A researcher investigated whether there was a relationship between the type of feeding received as a baby (classified as breastfed—yes/no) and weight in first grade (classified as overweight—yes/no). The parental report of the type of feeding provided as a baby and the body mass index (BMI) of 300 first graders was ascertained. Based on the BMI scores, the first graders were classified as either being overweight or not. The data are provided in Figure 16.14.

		Overweight		
		Yes	No	Total
Breastfed	Yes	16	84	100
	No	56	144	200
	Total	72	228	300

Figure 16.14 **Data for the 300 children in the breastfeeding study.**

Enter the data into SPSS and perform the appropriate analyses to answer the questions below. Name the variables **breastfed**, **overweight**, and **frequency** (be sure to weight the cases prior to analyzing the data). For **breastfed** and **overweight**, code yes a "1" and no a "2."
a. State the null and alternative hypotheses.
b. State a research question for the data.
c. Is there a significant relationship between the type of feeding received as a baby and weight in first grade? Test using $\alpha = .05$.
d. What is the effect size? Would you characterize the effect size as small, medium, or large?
e. Write the results using APA format as appropriate.

2. A student wanted to examine whether there was a relationship between gender and movie preference. One hundred and sixty people outside of a movie theater (95 women and 65 men) were asked whether they would prefer watching an action film or a drama (assuming they had to choose between the two types of movies). The choices of the participants are presented in Figure 16.15.

		Film		
		Action	Drama	Total
gender	Females	15	80	95
	Males	35	30	65
	Total	50	110	160

Figure 16.15 **Gender and movie preference of the 160 study participants.**

The data are provided in the file *Chapter 16_Exercise 2.sav* in the Chapter 16 folder online at www.routledge.com/cw/yockey and are entered using the individual observations method. In the file, the variables are named **gender** (with females coded a "1" and males coded a "2") and **film** (with action movies coded a "1" and dramas coded a "2"). Open the file and perform the appropriate analyses in SPSS to answer the questions below (instructions for analyzing the data using the individual observations method are provided in the "summary of steps" section prior to the chapter exercises).

a. State the null and alternative hypotheses.
b. State a research question for the data.
c. Is there a significant relationship between gender and movie preference? Test using α = .05.
d. What is the effect size? Would you characterize the effect size as small, medium, or large?
e. Write the results using APA format as appropriate.

3. A medical researcher was interested in investigating whether there was a relationship between exercise (yes/no) and experiencing a heart attack (yes/no) among the elderly. Four hundred and five elderly individuals were questioned about their exercise habits and whether or not they had ever experienced a heart attack. The responses of the study participants are presented in Figure 16.16.

		Heart attack		
		Yes	No	Total
Exercise	Yes	10	140	150
	No	35	220	255
	Total	45	360	405

Figure 16.16 **Data for the 405 elderly individuals in the exercise study.**

The data are provided in the file *Chapter 16_Exercise 3.sav* in the Chapter 16 folder online at www.routledge.com/cw/yockey (the variables are named **exercise, heartattack,** and **frequency,** with both **exercise** and **heartattack** coded a "1" for yes and a "2" for no). Open the file and perform the appropriate analyses in SPSS to answer the questions below (for this problem, be sure to weight the cases prior to analyzing the data).

a. State the null and alternative hypotheses.
b. State a research question for the data.
c. Is there a significant relationship between exercise and whether or not one has a heart attack? Test using α = .05.
d. What is the effect size? Would you characterize the effect size as small, medium, or large?
e. Write the results using APA format as appropriate.

Notes

1. It is important to note that the cases remain weighted until either the weight cases option is turned off (by selecting *Do not weight cases* in the *Weight Cases* dialog box and clicking *OK*) or until SPSS is closed. If additional analyses are performed other than the chi-square test, failing to turn the weight cases option off can lead to incorrect analyses and/or error messages.
2. For 2 × 2 tables only, Cramer's *V* is also known as the phi coefficient, which is equal to the Pearson *r* correlation coefficient between two dichotomous variables.

Data Transformations and Other Procedures

In the context of data analysis, certain operations often need to be performed on one or more variables prior to analyzing the data. For example, one commonly required operation is to add a number of variables together in SPSS to produce a total score. In this appendix, a number of commonly used procedures in SPSS will be illustrated, including the *Recode*, *Compute*, *Select Cases*, and *Split File* procedures.

To illustrate each of these procedures, the data presented in Figure A.1 will be used (we'll open the data file from your computer shortly). The data consist of values from 10 participants on the following four variables: **gender** (1 = "male," 2 = "female"), **meaning1**, **meaning2**, and **meaning3**. The last three variables are items from a scale measuring meaning in life.

Participant	gender	meaning1	meaning2	meaning3
1	1	4	2	5
2	1	1	4	2
3	1	5	1	5
4	1	3	3	3
5	1	4	2	4
6	2	4	1	5
7	2	5	2	4
8	2	5	1	5
9	2	1	4	1
10	2	5	1	5

Figure A.1 **The sample data. (*Note*: The participant variable is included for illustration but will not be entered into the data file.)**

The items on the meaning in life scale are presented in Figure A.2.

Item	Items on the Meaning in Life Scale	Strongly Disagree	Disagree	Neither Disagree nor Agree	Agree	Strongly Agree
meaning1	I feel good about the direction of my life.	1	2	3	4	5
meaning2	My life has little meaning.	1	2	3	4	5
meaning3	In general, I feel like I'm on track in my life.	1	2	3	4	5

Figure A.2 **Items on the meaning in life scale. For each item, the response options are 1 (strongly disagree), 2 (disagree), 3 (neither disagree nor agree), 4 (agree) and 5 (strongly agree). Each participant was instructed to choose only one response option for each question.**

The Recode Procedure

For the items on the meaning in life scale shown in Figure A.2, the participants read each statement and choose a response—ranging from strongly disagree to strongly agree—that best characterizes their feelings toward the statement. Reading through each of the items, notice that **meaning1** and **meaning3** are written so that a person with a very high degree of meaning in life would most likely answer "strongly agree" to the items (they would circle a "5" for each item), while **meaning2** is written so that this same person would most likely answer "strongly disagree" to the item (they would circle a "1"). **Meaning2** is an example of a *negative* item, where a person high on the characteristic of interest (meaning in life) answers in the *opposite* direction of the scale. Therefore, in this example, a person with a very high degree of meaning in life would most likely answer items **meaning1**, **meaning2**, and **meaning3** with values of 5, 1, and 5, respectively. Typically, when analyzing the responses on the scale, a total score is calculated by adding together the responses on the items. In this example, a person with a very high degree of meaning in life would have a total score of 11 (5 + 1 + 5). However, because the scale is ultimately designed so that higher scores on the scale correspond to higher levels of meaning in life, a person with a very high degree of meaning in life *should* have a score of 15 (5 + 5 + 5). Since **meaning2** is a negative item, however, this isn't the case. To correct for this, a process called reverse coding is conducted where the responses to the negative item on the scale (**meaning2**) are literally reversed, so that a 1 becomes a 5, a 2 becomes a 4, a 3 remains a 3, a 4 becomes a 2, and a 5 becomes a 1. With **meaning2** reverse coded, a person with a high degree of meaning in life would have a total score of 15 (instead of 11), which is consistent with the intent of the scale. With the rationale for reverse coding provided, let's open the data file and recode the negative item **meaning2** in SPSS.

(*Note*: The following instructions assume that the *SPSS Demystified* files have been downloaded from the web site to your computer. If the files are not on your computer, they may be obtained online at www.routledge.com/cw/yockey.)

To open the file from your computer

1.   Locate the *SPSS Demystified* files on your computer. In the *Appendix A* folder, open the file *Appendix A.sav*.

*To recode the item **meaning2** in SPSS*

1.   From the menu bar, select **Transform > Recode into Different Variables** . . . (see Figure A.3).

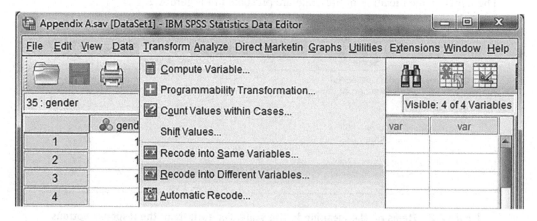

Figure A.3 **Menu commands for the *Recode into Different Variables* procedure.**

2. The *Recode into Different Variables* dialog box opens (see Figure A.4).

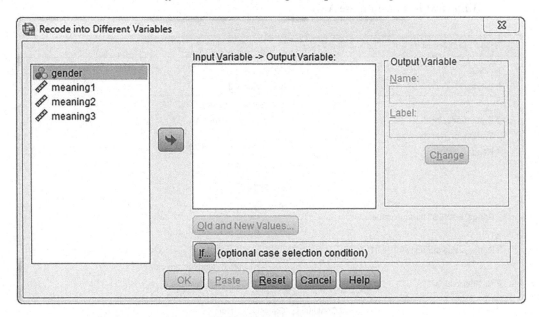

Figure A.4 **The *Recode into Different Variables* dialog box.**

3. Select **meaning2** and click the right-arrow button ( ) to move it to the *Input Variable → Output Variable* box (the box reads *Numeric Variable → Output Variable* once **meaning2** is moved into it). Under *Name*, enter the name **meaning2_recode** (see Figure A.5). This is the name of the new variable that will contain the reverse coded values.

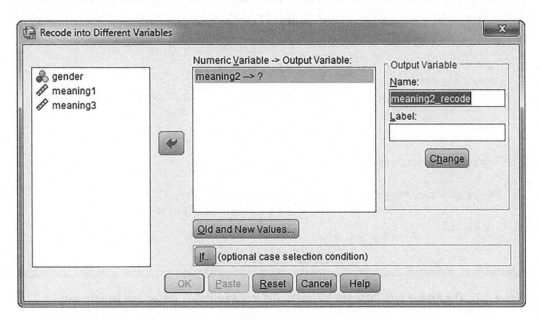

Figure A.5 **The *Recode into Different Variables* dialog box (continued).**

4. Click *Change*. You should see *meaning2 → meaning2_recode* in the *Numeric Variable → Output Variable* box.
5. Click *Old and New Values*. The *Recode into Different Variables: Old and New Values* dialog box opens. This dialog box will be used to recode the values for **meaning2**, so that a 1 becomes a 5, a 2 becomes a 4, and so on.

6. Under *Old Value*, enter a *1* in the *Value* text box. Under *New Value,* enter a *5* in the *Value* text box (see Figure A.6).

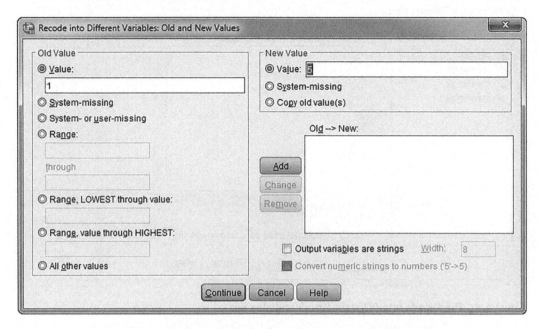

Figure A.6 The *Recode into Different Variables: Old and New Values* dialog box.

7. Click the *Add* button. The *Old → New* box should display 1 → 5 (see Figure A.7).

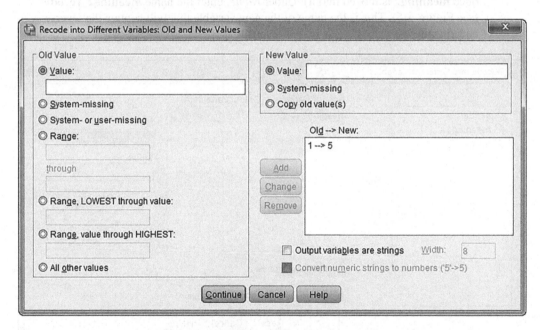

Figure A.7 The *Recode into Different Variables: Old and New Values* dialog box (continued).

8. Enter the remaining values to be recoded (2 → 4, 3 → 3,[1] 4 → 2, 5 → 1), clicking the *Add* button each time an *Old Value* and *New Value* combination has been entered. Once all five pairs of values have been entered, the *Old → New* box should contain the recoded values shown in Figure A.8.[2]
9. Click *Continue*.
10. Click *OK*.

In the SPSS *Data View* window, you should see the new variable **meaning2_recode** in the data file containing the reverse coded items of the variable **meaning2** (see Figure A.9).

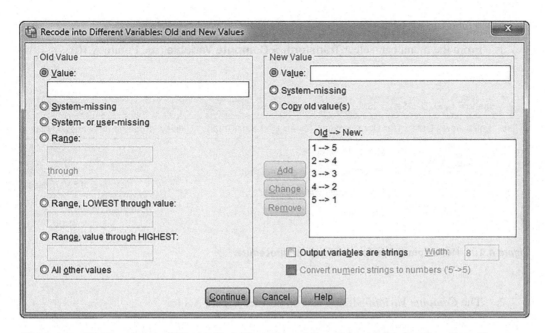

Figure A.8   The *Recode into Different Variables: Old and New Values* dialog box (continued).

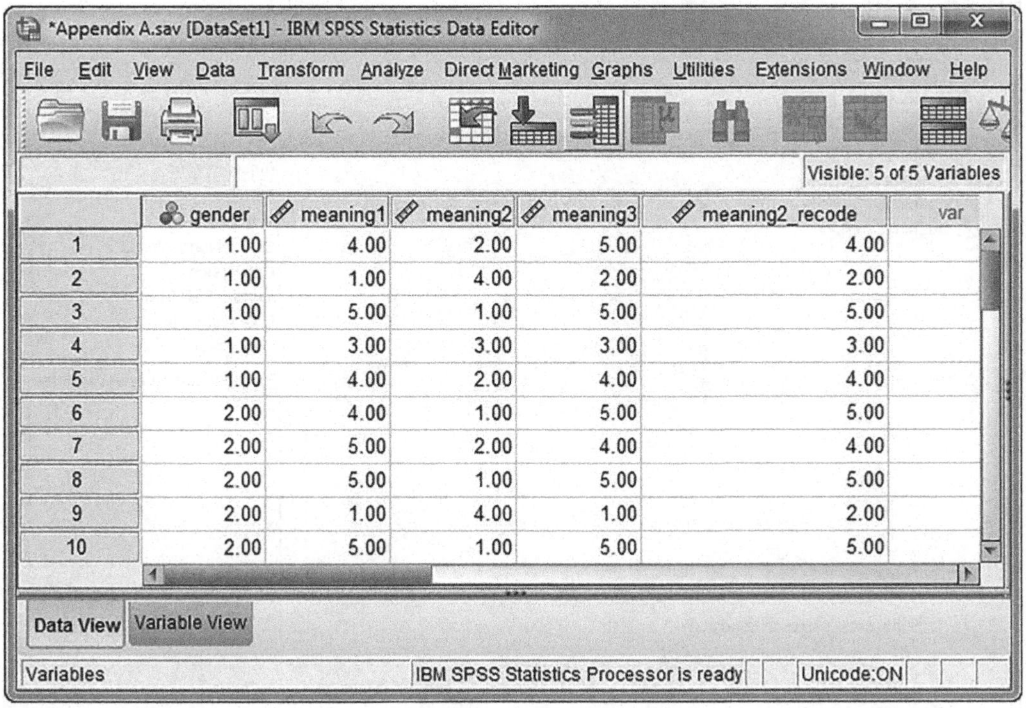

Figure A.9   The *Data Editor* window with the recoded variable meaning2_recode added to the data file.

The Compute Procedure

As was indicated at the beginning of this appendix, a commonly performed operation in SPSS is to add a number of variables together to create a total score. To add variables together in SPSS, the *Compute* procedure is used.

We'll use the *Compute* procedure to add together the items of the meaning in life scale to produce a total score.

To add variables in SPSS

1.   From the menu bar, select **Transform > Compute Variable** (see Figure A.10).

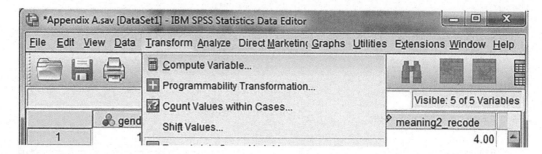

Figure A.10   **Menu commands for the *Compute* procedure.**

2.   The *Compute Variable* dialog box opens (see Figure A.11).

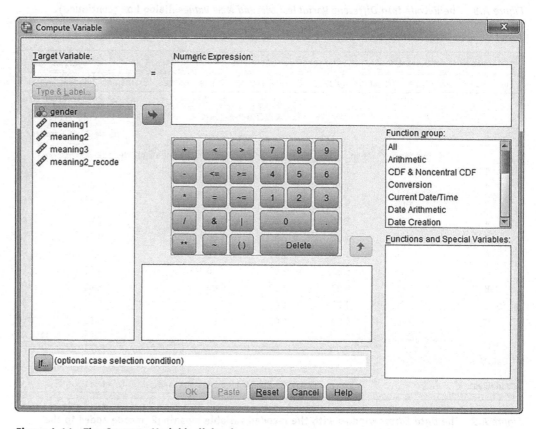

Figure A.11   **The *Compute Variable* dialog box.**

To compute a total score for the meaning in life scale, we'll need to add together the items **meaning1**, **meaning2_recode**, and **meaning3**.[3] To create a new variable in SPSS that is equal to the sum of the three variables, we'll first need to provide a name for the new variable in SPSS that will contain the total score. We'll name the variable **meaning_total**.

1.   In the *Target Variable* box, enter the name **meaning_total**.

To create a total score, we'll move the appropriate variables to the *Numeric Expression* box and add them together using the plus (+) sign.[4]

2. Select the first variable, **meaning1**, and click the right-arrow button (⇥) to move it to the *Numeric Expression* box. Click the plus (+) button below the *Numeric Expression* box (or press the *Shift* and + keys on your keyboard). Move **meaning2_recode** to the *Numeric Expression* box and click the plus (+) button. Finally, move **meaning3** to the *Numeric Expression* box. In the *Numeric Expression* box, the statement should read, *meaning1 + meaning2_recode + meaning3* (see Figure A.12).

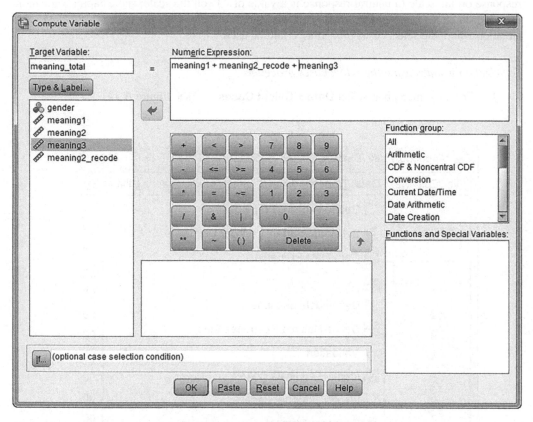

Figure A.12 **The *Compute Variable* dialog box (continued).**

3. Click *OK*. A new variable is created in the *Data View* window named **meaning_total**, which is the sum of variables **meaning1**, **meaning2_recode**, and **meaning3** (see Figure A.13).

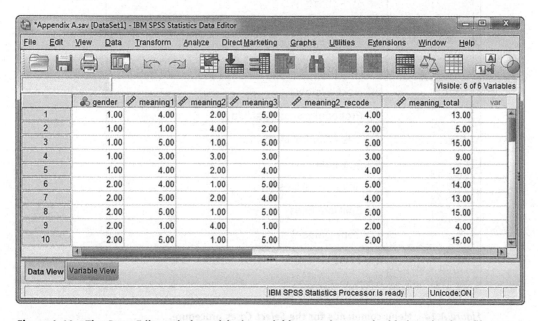

Figure A.13 **The *Data Editor* window with the variable meaning_total added to the data file.**

The Select Cases Procedure

When analyzing data, certain questions of interest may require performing analyses on only *part* of the data file. In this situation, the *Select Cases* procedure may be used.

To illustrate the *Select Cases* procedure, suppose that you wanted to conduct a one-sample *t* test on *males* to see if their responses to **meaning1** were significantly different from a neutral response on the scale (a neutral response is a value of "3" on the scale; see Chapter 5 for more information on the one-sample *t* test). This would require selecting *only* males in the data set, a situation where the select cases procedure could be used.

To select only males using the select cases procedure

1.   From the menu bar, select **Data > Select Cases** . . . (see Figure A.14).

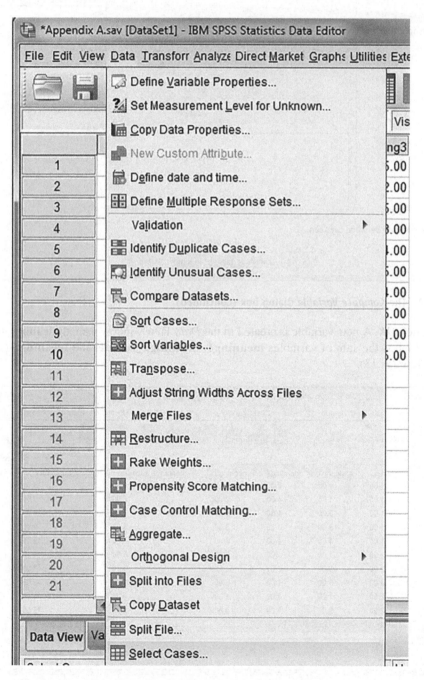

Figure A.14   **Menu commands for the *Select Cases* procedure.**

2. The *Select Cases* dialog box opens (see Figure A.15).

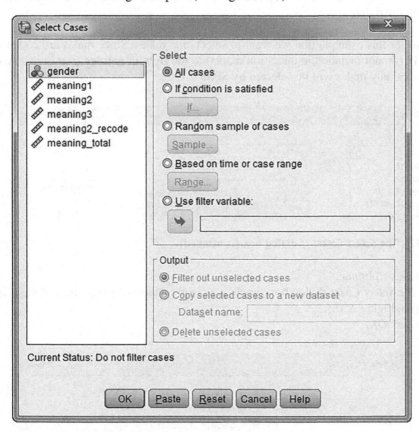

Figure A.15   The *Select Cases* dialog box.

3. Under *Select*, click *If condition is satisfied*.
4. Click the *If* button (located below *If condition is satisfied*). The *Select Cases: If* dialog box opens (see Figure A.16).

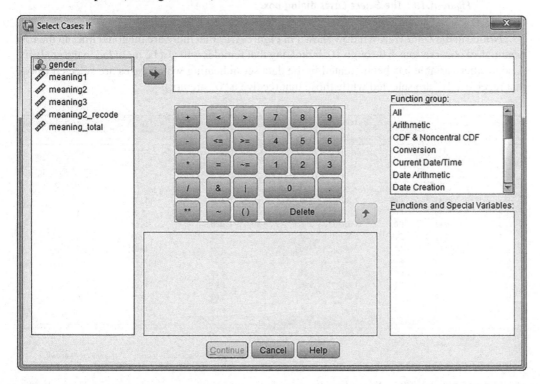

Figure A.16   The *Select Cases: If* dialog box.

5. Select the variable **gender**, and click the right-arrow button (➡) to move it to the box on the right.

Recall for this example that we want to select *only* males. Since males are coded with a 1, enter "= 1" (do not include the quotation marks) to the right of **gender** (see Figure A.17). This indicates that only males will be selected by SPSS.

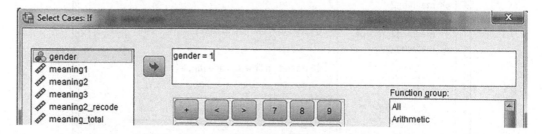

Figure A.17   The *Select Cases: If* dialog box (continued).

6. Click *Continue*.
7. The *Select Cases* dialog box should now read *gender = 1* to the right of the *If* button (see Figure A.18).
8. Click *OK*.

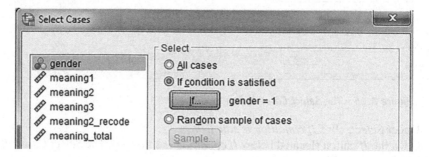

Figure A.18   The *Select Cases* dialog box.

Notice in the *Data View* window shown in Figure A.19 that there are diagonal lines in the row headings of observations 6 through 10, indicating that females will not be included in the analysis. Also, a filter variable has been created in the data set indicating which cases are selected (those that receive a "1" are selected while those that receive a "0" are not).

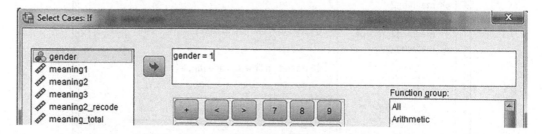

	gender	meaning1	meaning2	meaning3	meaning2_recode	meaning_total	filter_$	var
1	1.00	4.00	2.00	5.00	4.00	13.00	1	
2	1.00	1.00	4.00	2.00	2.00	5.00	1	
3	1.00	5.00	1.00	5.00	5.00	15.00	1	
4	1.00	3.00	3.00	3.00	3.00	9.00	1	
5	1.00	4.00	2.00	4.00	4.00	12.00	1	
6	2.00	4.00	1.00	5.00	5.00	14.00	0	
7	2.00	5.00	2.00	4.00	4.00	13.00	0	
8	2.00	5.00	1.00	5.00	5.00	15.00	0	
9	2.00	1.00	4.00	1.00	2.00	4.00	0	
10	2.00	5.00	1.00	5.00	5.00	15.00	0	

Figure A.19   The data file with males selected.

To answer the initial question that prompted the use of the select cases procedure for this example, a one-sample *t* test was conducted on **meaning1** for males. The results of the one-sample *t* test are provided in Figure A.20.

T–Test

One-Sample Statistics

	N	Mean	Std. Deviation	Std. Error Mean
meaning1	5	3.4000	1.51658	.67823

One-Sample Test

	Test Value = 3					
					95% Confidence Interval of the Difference	
	t	df	Sig. (2-tailed)	Mean Difference	Lower	Upper
meaning1	.590	4	.587	.40000	−1.4831	2.2831

Figure A.20 **The results of the one-sample *t* test on meaning1 for males.**

Notice in the output shown in Figure A.20 that there is no indication that males were selected. The *One-Sample Statistics* table shows an *N* of 5, however, indicating that the test was conducted on only five of the participants in the data file. (As a review of the material covered in Chapter 5, the results indicate that males do not score significantly different from a response of "3" on **meaning1** since the *p*-value of .587 is greater than .05.)[5]

Next we'll illustrate how to use the *Split File* procedure, which is another way to perform analyses on separate parts of a data set in SPSS. Prior to using the *Split File* procedure, however, we'll need to turn off the *Select Cases* procedure so that we have access to the entire data set. If the *Select Cases* procedure is not turned off, all subsequent analyses would be conducted *only* on males.

To turn off the Select Cases procedure

1.   From the menu bar select **Data > Select Cases . . .**
2.   Under *Select*, click the *All Cases* button (see Figure A.21).
3.   Click *OK*.

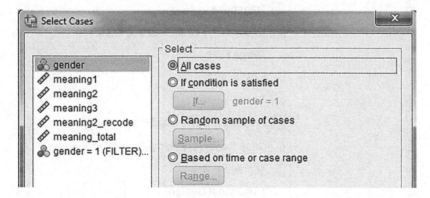

Figure A.21 **The *Select Cases* dialog box.**

In the *Data View* window, all of the cases should now be selected (there should no longer be a line through observations 6–10). While the filter variable still remains in the data file, it is no longer enforced. It may be deleted (if desired) by clicking on the **filter_$** column heading in the *Data View* window and pressing the *Delete* key on the keyboard.

The *Split File* Procedure

Suppose that instead of conducting a one-sample *t* test for males only, you wanted to conduct separate one-sample *t* tests on **meaning1** for males and females. While the *Select Cases* procedure could be used in this situation, it would require performing the analysis twice (once for males and once for females). A more efficient approach would be to use the *Split File* procedure, which automatically performs separate analyses for each group of a variable of interest. The *Split File* procedure is illustrated next.

To perform the Split File procedure

1.   From the menu bar select **Data > Split File** . . . (see Figure A.22).
2.   The *Split File* dialog box opens (see Figure A.23).

There are two different methods for splitting the file: *Compare groups* and *Organize output by groups. Compare groups* reports the results for the groups in the same table, while *Organize*

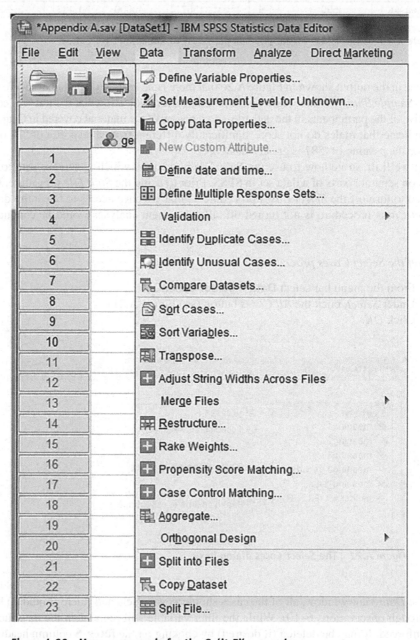

Figure A.22   Menu commands for the *Split File* procedure.

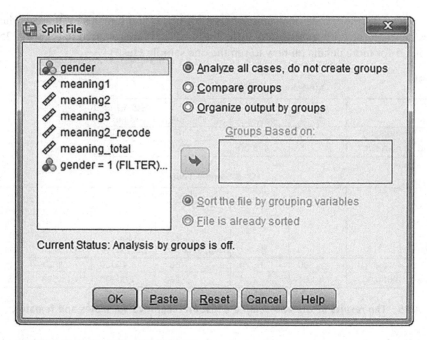

Figure A.23 The *Split File* dialog box.

output by groups reports the results for the groups in separate tables. We'll use the *Compare groups* method.

3.   Select *Compare groups*.
4.   Select **gender**. Click the right-arrow button ( ) to move **gender** to the *Groups Based on* box (see Figure A.24).
5.   Click *OK*.

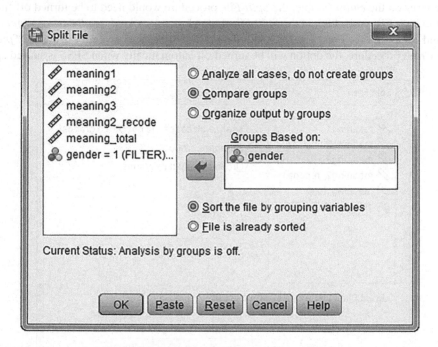

Figure A.24 The *Split File* dialog box (continued).

After clicking *OK* you should see *"Split File On"* displayed in the bottom right-hand corner of the *Data Editor* window.

The results of the separate one-sample *t* tests for males and females evaluating whether the responses on **meaning1** are significantly different from a "3" are reported in Figure A.25. (*Note*: See Chapter 5 for more details on how to run the one sample *t* test.)

T–Test

One-Sample Statistics

gender		N	Mean	Std. Deviation	Std. Error Mean
male	meaning1	5	3.4000	1.51658	.67823
female	meaning1	5	4.0000	1.73205	.77460

One-Sample Test

		Test Value = 3					
						95% Confidence Interval of the Difference	
gender		t	df	Sig. (2-tailed)	Mean Difference	Lower	Upper
male	meaning1	.590	4	.587	.40000	−1.4831	2.2831
female	meaning1	1.291	4	.266	1.00000	−1.1506	3.1506

Figure A.25 **The results of the one-sample *t* test on meaning1 for males and females.**

Using the *Compare groups* option, notice that the output shows the results for males and females together in the *same* tables, with the results for males presented first, followed by the results for females. Alternatively, if the *Organize output by groups* option was selected, the results for males and females would be presented in *separate* tables. (As a review again of the material covered in Chapter 5, is the average response on **meaning1** for either males or females significantly different from a "3"? Neither result is significant, since the *p*-values of .587 and .266 are both greater than .05.)

Turning off the *Split File* Procedure

As was the case with the *Select Cases* procedure discussed earlier, if you wanted to perform subsequent analyses on the *entire* sample, the *Split File* procedure would need to be turned off first. To turn off the *Split File* procedure, in the *Split File* dialog box select *Analyze all cases, do not create groups* and click *OK* (see Figure A.26). (Alternatively, if SPSS is closed after using the *Split File* or *Select Cases* procedure, the option will be turned off automatically when SPSS is started again.)

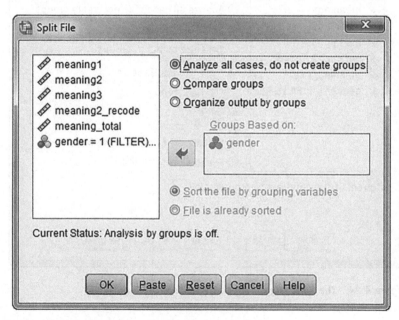

Figure A.26 **Turning off the *Split File* procedure.**

This concludes the discussion of the *Recode*, *Compute*, *Select Cases*, and *Split File* procedures.

Notes

1. While the recode step 3 → 3 may seem unnecessary, if it is omitted, there will be missing values for all 3s in the data set.
2. More than one variable may be recoded in a single SPSS run as long as all the recoded variables have the same scale values (e.g., all variables have the response option 1, 2, 3, 4, and 5). To add additional variables, move each variable to the *Numeric Variable → Output Variable* box (see Figure A.5) and assign an appropriate name for each recoded variable. For example, if a fourth item, **meaning4**, existed and was negative, **meaning4** would be moved to the *Numeric Variable → Output Variable* box and the variable name **meaning4_recode** would be entered in the *Output Variable Name* box. Since the recoded values were already entered for **meaning2_recode**, they would not need to be entered again.
3. Because **meaning2** is a negative item, **meaning2_recode** is used in computing the total score.
4. An alternative method for adding the variables together would be to use the sum function in SPSS. Functions are built-in commands in SPSS that carry out certain operations on variables. Coverage of these functions, however, is beyond the scope of this text.
5. While the *t* test was conducted to illustrate the *Select Cases* procedure, it is unlikely it would have been significant with a sample size of only five participants (due to low power).

B

Solutions to Chapter Exercises

Chapter 1—Introduction to SPSS

1. c.

Case Processing Summary[a]

	Cases					
	Included		Excluded		Total	
	N	Percent	N	Percent	N	Percent
age	7	100.0%	0	.0%	7	100.0%
gender	7	100.0%	0	.0%	7	100.0%
wellbeing	7	100.0%	0	.0%	7	100.0%
activities	7	100.0%	0	.0%	7	100.0%

a. Limited to first 100 cases.

Case Summaries[a]

		age	gender	wellbeing	activities
1		86.00	male	4.00	2.00
2		72.00	female	7.00	6.00
3		59.00	female	6.00	5.00
4		86.00	female	8.00	7.00
5		92.00	female	4.00	1.00
6		68.00	male	2.00	3.00
7		73.00	male	8.00	5.00
Total	N	7	7	7	7

a. Limited to first 100 cases.

d. The value labels (male/female) are output in the *Case Summaries* table. When value labels are created, they are printed in the results by default instead of the numeric values (1, 2) originally entered into SPSS. This is beneficial as it makes reading the results easier and avoids confusing males and females (in the event that it was forgotten which group was assigned a 1 and which group was assigned a 2).

2. b.

Case Processing Summary[a]

	Cases					
	Included		Excluded		Total	
	N	Percent	N	Percent	N	Percent
therapy	12	100.0%	0	.0%	12	100.0%
gender	12	100.0%	0	.0%	12	100.0%
selfesteem	12	100.0%	0	.0%	12	100.0%
angermanage	12	100.0%	0	.0%	12	100.0%

[a.] Limited to first 100 cases.

Case Summaries[a]

	therapy	gender	selfesteem	angermanage
1	nondirective	male	25.00	12.00
2	nondirective	male	30.00	15.00
3	nondirective	male	34.00	13.00
4	nondirective	female	28.00	19.00
5	nondirective	female	39.00	21.00
6	nondirective	female	42.00	15.00
7	directive	male	37.00	9.00
8	directive	male	29.00	19.00
9	directive	male	26.00	22.00
10	directive	female	38.00	17.00
11	directive	female	43.00	11.00
12	directive	female	26.00	21.00
Total N	12	12	12	12

[a.] Limited to first 100 cases.

3. b.

Case Summaries[a]

	gender	number classes	hoursworked
1	male	3.00	20.00
2	male	5.00	10.00
3	female	5.00	20.00
4	female	4.00	14.00
5	female	6.00	6.00
6	male	2.00	.00
7	female	1.00	40.00
8	female	3.00	20.00
9	male	5.00	15.00
10	female	6.00	25.00
Total N	10	10	10

[a.] Limited to first 100 cases.

Chapter 2—Descriptive Statistics

1. a. For gender there are four boys and four girls. For method there are four toe kickers and four heel kickers.

   b.

Statistics

	experience	distance	accuracy
Mean	4.6250	38.8750	5.7500
Std. Deviation	2.61520	7.10005	1.83225

   c.

Report

gender		experience	distance	accuracy
boys	Mean	5.5000	42.5000	6.0000
	Std. Deviation	2.88675	6.45497	2.16025
girls	Mean	3.7500	35.2500	5.5000
	Std. Deviation	2.36291	6.39661	1.73205

Boys have a higher mean on all three variables. Boys also have a larger standard deviation on all three variables.

   d.

Report

method		experience	distance	accuracy
toe kick	Mean	5.0000	44.0000	4.5000
	Std. Deviation	2.16025	4.69042	1.29099
heel kick	Mean	4.2500	33.7500	7.0000
	Std. Deviation	3.30404	5.05800	1.41421

Toe kickers have more experience (5.00) and distance (44.00) in their kicks, while heel kickers have greater accuracy (7.00). Heel kickers have a larger standard deviation on all three variables.

   e.

Report

gender	method		experience	distance	accuracy
boys	toe kick	Mean	5.5000	47.5000	4.5000
		Std. Deviation	.70711	3.53553	.70711
	heel kick	Mean	5.5000	37.5000	7.5000
		Std. Deviation	4.94975	3.53553	2.12132
girls	toe kick	Mean	4.5000	40.5000	4.5000
		Std. Deviation	3.53553	2.12132	2.12132
	heel kick	Mean	3.0000	30.0000	6.5000
		Std. Deviation	1.41421	2.82843	.70711

Girls using the heel kicking method had the lowest mean experience (3.00), while both boys and girls who used the toe kicking method tied for the lowest mean accuracy score (4.50). Boys using the toe kicking method had the highest mean kicking distance of all four conditions (47.50).

2. a. For location, there are 10 people from each region (West Coast, Midwest, and East Coast). There are 15 males and 15 females in the data set.

    b.

Statistics

	taste	clarity
Mean	6.8667	8.1333
Std. Deviation	1.45586	1.16658

    c.

Report

location		taste	clarity
West Coast	Mean	6.9000	7.8000
	Std. Deviation	1.28668	1.03280
Midwest	Mean	7.8000	8.7000
	Std. Deviation	.91894	1.15950
East Coast	Mean	5.9000	7.9000
	Std. Deviation	1.52388	1.19722

The Midwest has the highest mean on both taste (7.80) and clarity (8.70). The East Coast has the largest standard deviation on both taste (1.52) and clarity (1.20).

    d.

Report

gender		taste	clarity
male	Mean	6.6667	8.0667
	Std. Deviation	1.58865	1.27988
female	Mean	7.0667	8.2000
	Std. Deviation	1.33452	1.08233

Females have the highest mean ratings on taste (7.07) and clarity (8.20). Males have the largest standard deviation on both taste (1.59) and clarity (1.28).

    e.

Report

gender	location		taste	clarity
male	West Coast	Mean	6.6000	8.0000
		Std. Deviation	1.14018	1.22474
	Midwest	Mean	8.0000	8.8000
		Std. Deviation	.70711	1.30384
	East Coast	Mean	5.4000	7.4000
		Std. Deviation	1.67332	1.14018
female	West Coast	Mean	7.2000	7.6000
		Std. Deviation	1.48324	.89443
	Midwest	Mean	7.6000	8.6000
		Std. Deviation	1.14018	1.14018
	East Coast	Mean	6.4000	8.4000
		Std. Deviation	1.34164	1.14018

Males on the East Coast have the lowest mean ratings on both taste (5.40) and clarity (7.40). Males in the Midwest have the highest mean ratings on both taste (8.00) and clarity (8.80).

3. a. There are 15 males and 15 females. There are 10 people in each SES group (10 low, 10 middle, and 10 high).

   b.

Statistics

	hourstv	readingscores
Mean	3.1500	28.2667
Std. Deviation	1.37922	12.34262

   c.

Report

gender		hourstv	readingscores
male	Mean	3.3367	25.9333
	Std. Deviation	1.52976	11.90718
female	Mean	2.9633	30.6000
	Std. Deviation	1.23512	12.73241

Males have a higher mean on hourstv (3.34) and females have a higher mean on readingscores (30.60). Males have the largest standard deviation on hourstv (1.53), while females have the largest standard deviation on readingscores (12.73).

   d.

Report

gender	ses		hourstv	readingscores
male	low	Mean	3.3400	18.0000
		Std. Deviation	1.47792	9.87421
	middle	Mean	3.9000	23.8000
		Std. Deviation	1.03983	6.30079
	high	Mean	2.7700	36.0000
		Std. Deviation	2.03150	12.16553
female	low	Mean	3.3400	18.0000
		Std. Deviation	1.47792	9.87421
	middle	Mean	3.6000	36.4000
		Std. Deviation	.51841	11.32696
	high	Mean	1.9500	37.4000
		Std. Deviation	.95851	6.58027

Middle SES males watch the most TV (3.90). High SES females have the highest mean reading scores (37.40).

Chapter 3—Graphical Procedures

1. a.

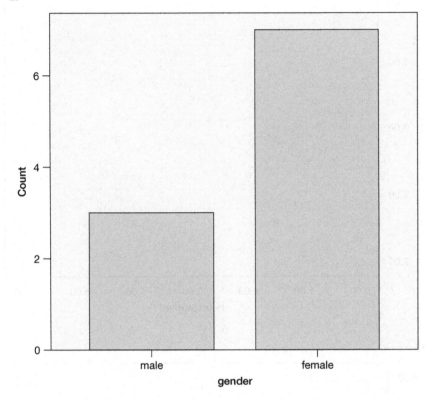

There are three males and seven females.

b.

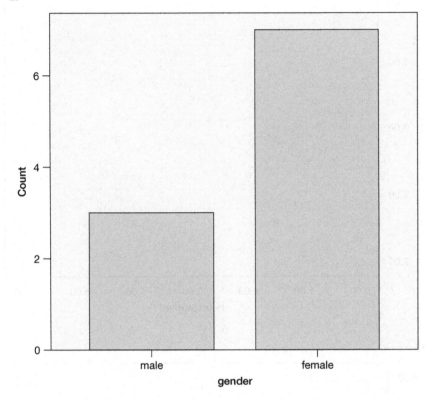

Mean = 3.05
Std. Dev. = 1.848
N = 10

The mean number of hours studied was 3.05.

c.

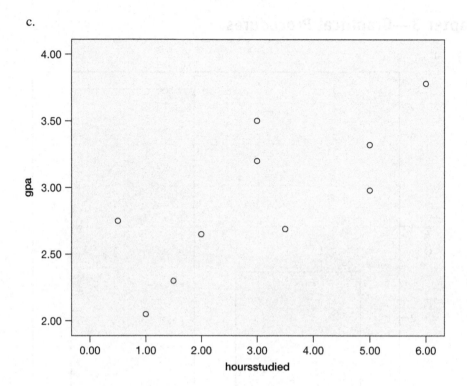

d.

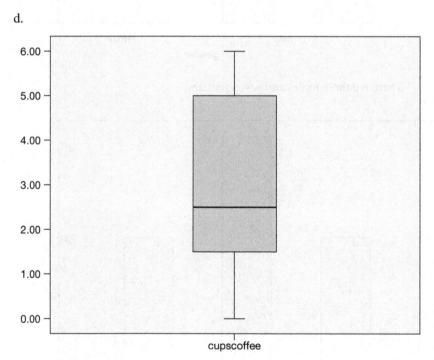

There are no outliers in the boxplot.

2. a.

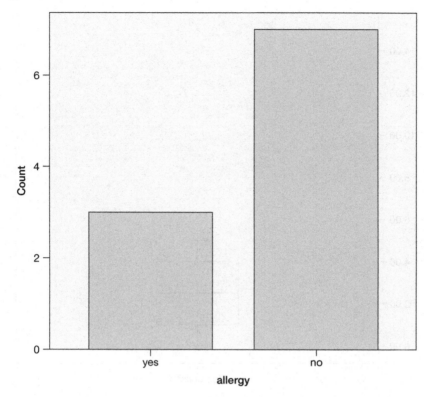

There are three people who have allergies and seven people who do not have allergies.

b.

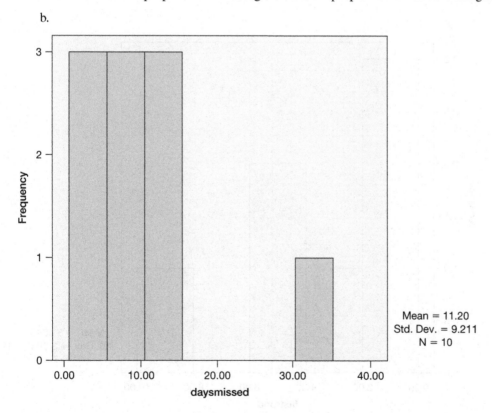

Mean = 11.20
Std. Dev. = 9.211
N = 10

The mean number of days missed per year was 11.20.

c.

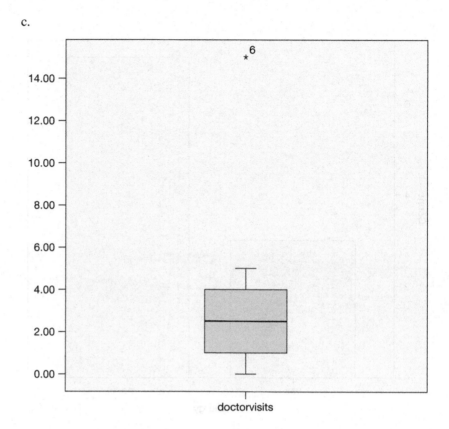

Observation number 6 is an outlier with 15 visits made to the doctor last year.

3.   a.

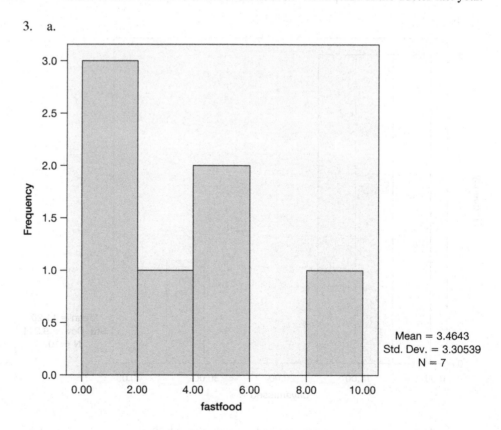

b.

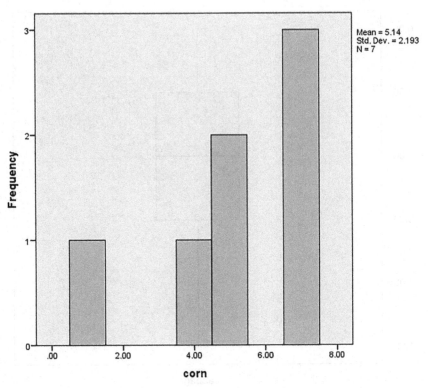

The mean rating for corn is 5.14.

c.

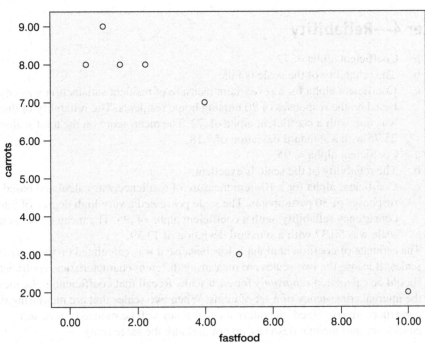

d.

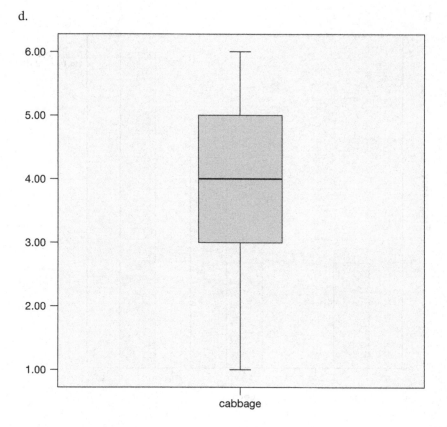

cabbage

There are no outliers in the boxplot.

Chapter 4—Reliability

1. a. Coefficient alpha = .72
    b. The reliability of the scale is fair.
    c. Coefficient alpha for a seven-item measure of resident satisfaction was calculated based on the responses of 20 nursing home residents. The reliability of the scale was fair, with a coefficient alpha of .72. The mean score on the total scale was 25.75 with a standard deviation of 7.18.
2. a. Coefficient alpha = .95
    b. The reliability of the scale is excellent.
    c. Coefficient alpha for a 10-item measure of resilience was calculated based on the responses of 30 participants. The scale possessed a very high degree of internal consistency reliability, with a coefficient alpha of .95. The mean score on the total scale was 50.37 with a standard deviation of 13.59.
3. The estimate of coefficient alpha is low because it was calculated on the *combined* scales. Because the two scales are measuring different characteristics, coefficient alpha should be calculated *separately* for each scale. Recall that coefficient alpha measures the internal consistency of a set of items. When two scales that are measuring different constructs are combined, the internal consistency will be reduced, since self-confidence and manual dexterity do not measure the same thing.

Chapter 5—One-Sample *t* Test

1. a. $H_0: \mu = 50$
        $H_1: \mu \neq 50$
    b. "Do the prognosticators pick winners in football games different from chance levels (50%)?"

c.   No. The prognosticators did not pick winners at different than chance levels ($p = .085$).

d.   Effect size = $(48.0667 - 50)/4.04381 = -0.48$ (or 0.48). Using Cohen's standards, the effect size is small (although it is close to a medium effect).

e.   The prognosticators do not pick winning football teams at a rate different from chance levels ($M = 48.07\%$, $SD = 4.04\%$), $t(14) = -1.85$, $p > .05$, $d = 0.48$.

2.   a. H_0: $\mu = 50$
         H_1: $\mu \neq 50$

b.   "Are the math scores for the fourth graders at the local school district different from the national average (of 50)?"

c.   Yes. The students perform significantly better (higher) on the math exam than the national average ($p = .018$).

d.   Effect size = $(55.44 - 50)/10.73577 = 0.51$. Using Cohen's standards, this represents a medium effect, with the students from the local school district scoring approximately one-half of a standard deviation higher on the exam than the national average.

e.   The students using the new program at the local school district scored significantly higher ($M = 55.44$, $SD = 10.74$) on the standardized math exam than the national average of 50, $t(24) = 2.53$, $p < .05$, $d = 0.51$.

3.   a. H_0: $\mu = 3$
         H_1: $\mu \neq 3$

b.   "Are the students either in favor of or opposed to the candidate?"

c.   No. The students were neither in favor of nor opposed to the candidate ($p = .290$).

d.   Effect size = $(3.16 - 3)/1.05676 = 0.15$. Using Cohen's standards, the effect size is very small.

e.   The students were neither significantly in favor of nor opposed to the candidate, ($M = 3.16$, $SD = 1.06$), $t(49) = 1.07$, $p < .05$, $d = 0.15$.

Chapter 6—Independent-Samples *t* Test

1.   a. H_0: $\mu_{\text{minimally invasive}} = \mu_{\text{traditional}}$
         H_1: $\mu_{\text{minimally invasive}} \neq \mu_{\text{traditional}}$

b.   "Is there a difference in reported pain between minimally invasive and traditional surgical procedures?"

c.   The variances are not significantly different, Levene's $F = .005$, $p < .05$.

d.   Yes ($p = .001$).

e. $d = -3.58\sqrt{\dfrac{15+15}{15*15}} = -1.31$ or 1.31. The effect is very large, with MIS patients reporting pain levels that were 1.31 standard deviations lower on average than patients who had traditional surgery.

f.   There is a significant difference in the reported pain levels between minimally invasive and traditional surgical procedures, $t(28) = -3.58$, $p < .05$, $d = 1.31$. Those who had minimally invasive surgery ($M = 4.73$, $SD = 1.67$) reported significantly less postoperative pain than those who had traditional surgery ($M = 6.87$, $SD = 1.60$).

2.   a. H_0: $\mu_{\text{systematic desensitization}} = \mu_{\text{implosion}}$
         H_1: $\mu_{\text{systematic desensitization}} \neq \mu_{\text{implosion}}$

b.   "Is there a difference in the level of snake fear between those who received systematic desensitization and those who received implosion therapy?"

c.   The variances are not significantly different, Levene's $F = 2.29$, $p > 05$.

d.   Yes ($p = .010$).

e. $d = -2.86\sqrt{\dfrac{10+10}{10*10}} = -1.28$ or 1.28. This is a very large effect size, with fear levels 1.28 standard deviations lower for those who had systematic desensitization.

f. There is a significant difference in the level of reported snake fear between systematic desensitization and implosion therapeutic techniques, $t(18) = -2.86$, $p < .05$, $d = 1.28$. Those who received systematic desensitization ($M = 47.10$, $SD = 6.82$) reported significantly less fear of snakes than those who received implosion therapy ($M = 59.30$, $SD = 11.64$).

3. a. $H_0: \mu_{\text{home with a pet}} = \mu_{\text{home without a pet}}$
$H_1: \mu_{\text{home with a pet}} \neq \mu_{\text{home without a pet}}$

b. "Is there a difference in the resident satisfaction between nursing homes with a pet and those without a pet?"

c. The variances are not significantly different, Levene's $F = .241$, $p > .05$.

d. No ($p = .284$).

e. $d = -1.08\sqrt{\dfrac{30 + 30}{30 * 30}} = -0.28$ or 0.28. This is a small effect.

f. There is a not significant difference in the satisfaction levels between nursing home residents who have access to a pet and those who do not, $t(58) = -1.08$, $p > .05$, $d = 0.28$.

Chapter 7—Dependent-Samples t Test

1. a. $H_0: \mu_{\text{before film}} - \mu_{\text{after film}} = 0$
$H_1: \mu_{\text{before film}} - \mu_{\text{after film}} \neq 0$

b. "Is there a difference in attitudes toward the political candidate after viewing the campaign film as compared to before?"

c. Yes ($p = .001$).

d. $d = (-6/5.73212) = -1.05$ or 1.05. The effect size is 1.05, indicating that attitudes were over one standard deviation higher after viewing the campaign film as compared to before. This is a large effect.

e. The attitudes toward the political candidate were significantly more favorable after viewing the campaign film ($M = 60.13$, $SD = 17.53$) as compared to before ($M = 54.13$, $SD = 15.68$), $t(14) = -4.05$, $p < .05$, $d = 1.05$.

2. a. $H_0: \mu_{\text{stress before relaxation}} - \mu_{\text{stress after relaxation}} = 0$
$H_1: \mu_{\text{stress before relaxation}} - \mu_{\text{stress after relaxation}} \neq 0$

b. "Is there a difference in the stress levels of air traffic controllers before using the relaxation exercises as compared to after?"

c. Yes ($p = .047$).

d. $d = (1.4/3.69156) = 0.38$ The effect size is 0.38, indicating that stress levels were .38 standard deviations lower after using the relaxation exercise as compared to before. This is a small effect.

e. The stress levels of the air traffic controllers were significantly lower after using the relaxation exercise ($M = 34.83$, $SD = 8.78$) as compared to before, ($M = 36.23$, $SD = 9.76$), $t(29) = 2.08$, $p < .05$, $d = 0.38$.

3. a. $H_0: \mu_{\text{before training}} - \mu_{\text{after training}} = 0$
$H_1: \mu_{\text{before training}} - \mu_{\text{after training}} \neq 0$

b. "Is there a difference in accuracy of tennis shots before receiving training from a sports psychologist as compared to after?"

c. Yes ($p = .002$).

d. $d = (-4.2/4.21223) = -1.00$ or 1.00. The effect size is 1.00, indicating that the shots were more accurate by the amount of one standard deviation after receiving the eight weeks of training. This is a large effect.

e. The accuracy scores of the collegiate tennis players were significantly higher after receiving training from the sports psychologist ($M = 89.27$, $SD = 5.78$) as compared to before ($M = 85.07$, $SD = 6.46$), $t(14) = -3.86$, $p < .05$, $d = 1.00$.

Chapter 8—One-Way ANOVA

1. a. H_0: $\mu_{\text{Drug A}} = \mu_{\text{Drug B}} = \mu_{\text{Placebo}}$
        H_1: At least one of the means is different from the others.
    b. "Does the level of pain experienced by people with migraine headaches depend on the type of drug used?"
    c. The variances are not significantly different, $F(2, 18) = 1.27$, $p > .05$.
    d. Yes ($p = .002$).
    e. $\eta^2 = \dfrac{46.205}{93.057} = .50$. This is a large effect.
    f. A and B are less than the placebo. There is not a significant difference between A and B.
    g. The pain levels of migraine sufferers differed by the type of drug used, $F(2, 18) = 8.88$, $p < .05$, $\eta^2 = .50$. Tukey's post hoc procedure revealed that those who took drug A ($M = 4.64$, $SD = 1.61$) and those who took drug B ($M = 4.60$, $SD = 1.87$) had significantly lower reported pain than those who took the placebo ($M = 7.76$, $SD = 1.30$). There was not a significant difference in the pain levels between drug A and drug B.

2. a. H_0: $\mu_{\text{motorcycle}} = \mu_{\text{hybrid car}} = \mu_{\text{nonhybrid car}}$
        H_1: At least one of the means is different from the others.
    b. "Does the level of frustration over gas prices differ for the owners of different types of vehicles?"
    c. The variances are not significantly different, $F(2, 27) = .05$, $p > .05$.
    d. Yes ($p < .001$).
    e. $\eta^2 = \dfrac{101.267}{169.367} = .60$. This is a large effect.
    f. Hybrid owners are less frustrated than motorcycle and nonhybrid car owners. Motorcycle owners are less frustrated than nonhybrid car owners.
    g. The frustration levels differed for the different vehicle owners, $F(2, 27) = 20.08$, $p < .05$, $\eta^2 = .60$. Tukey's post hoc procedure revealed that hybrid vehicle owners ($M = 3.50$, $SD = 1.43$) and motorcycle owners ($M = 5.80$, $SD = 1.69$) reported significantly less frustration than nonhybrid vehicle owners ($M = 8.00$, $SD = 1.63$). Hybrid owners also reported significantly less frustration than motorcycle owners.

3. a. H_0: $\mu_{\text{Company A}} = \mu_{\text{Company B}} = \mu_{\text{Company C}}$
        H_1: At least one of the means is different from the others.
    b. "Does the response time to alarm calls differ by alarm company?"
    c. The variances are not significantly different, $F(2, 42) = .001$, $p > .05$.
    d. No ($p = .974$).
    e. $\eta^2 = \dfrac{132.844}{104933.2} = .001$. The effect size is (essentially) zero.
    f. The ANOVA was not significant. Tukey's test is not required.
    g. The response time to alarm calls was not significantly different for the different alarm companies, $F(2, 42) = .03$, $p > .05$, $\eta^2 = .001$.

Chapter 9—Two-Way ANOVA

1. a. H_0: $\mu_{\text{males}} = \mu_{\text{females}}$; H_1: $\mu_{\text{males}} \neq \mu_{\text{females}}$; H_0: $\mu_{\text{cell phone}} = \mu_{\text{no cell phone}}$;
        H_1: $\mu_{\text{cell phone}} \neq \mu_{\text{no cell phone}}$
        H_0: There is not a gender × cell phone interaction;
        H_1: There is a gender × cell phone interaction.
    b. "Is there a difference in driving performance between males and females?"
        "Is there a difference in driving performance between those who spoke on a cell phone while driving and those who did not?"
        "Is there an interaction between gender and cell phone usage?"

c.   There is not a significant difference in the cell variances,
$F(3, 20) = 2.47, p > .05$.

d.   Gender is not significant ($p = .584$); cell phone is significant ($p < .001$);
gender × cell phone is not significant ($p = .258$).

e.

Test	Partial eta–square
Gender	.02
Cell phone	.76
Gender × cell phone	.06

Cell phone has the largest effect.

f.   A 2 × 2 between-subjects ANOVA was conducted with driving performance as the
dependent variable and gender and cell phone usage as the independent variables.
There was a significant cell phone effect, $F(1, 20) = 61.63, p < .05$, partial $\eta^2 =$
.76, with those speaking on a cell phone having significantly poorer driving performance ($M = 31.58, SD\ 4.42$) than those who did not speak on a cell phone
($M = 44.50, SD = 3.53$). There was not a significant gender effect, $F(1, 20) = .31$,
$p > .05$) partial $\eta^2 = .02$, nor was there a significant interaction effect, $F(1, 20) =$
$1.36, p > .05$, partial $\eta^2 = .06$.

2.   a. $H_0: \mu_{\text{method A}} = \mu_{\text{method B}}; H_1: \mu_{\text{method A}} \neq \mu_{\text{method B}};$
$H_0: \mu_{\text{natural science}} = \mu_{\text{social science}}; H_1: \mu_{\text{natural science}} \neq \mu_{\text{social science}}$
H_0: There is not a method × major interaction; H_1 There is a method × major
interaction.

b.   "Is there a difference in math anxiety between the different teaching methods?"
"Do natural science majors and social science majors differ in math anxiety?"
"Is there an interaction between teaching method and college major?"

c.   There is not a significant difference in the cell variances, $F(3, 36) = 2.26, p > .05$.

d.   Method ($p = .0022$), major ($p = .001$), and the method × major interaction
($p = .008$) are all significant.

e.

Test	Partial eta–square
Method	.24
Major	.27
Method × major	.18

Major has the largest effect.

f.   A 2 × 2 between-subjects ANOVA was conducted with math anxiety as the
dependent variable and teaching method and college major as the independent
variables. There was a significant teaching method effect, $F(1, 36) = 11.35, p <$
.05, partial $\eta^2 = .24$, with those who received instruction under method B having
significantly lower math anxiety ($M = 35.55, SD = 8.44$) than those under method
A ($M = 45.75, SD = 14.29$). There was a significant major effect, $F(1, 36) = 13.20$,
$p < .05$, partial $\eta^2 = .27$, with natural science majors reporting significantly lower
math anxiety ($M = 35.15, SD = 9.20$) than social science majors ($M = 46.15, SD =$
13.48). There was also a significant method × major interaction effect, $F(1, 36) =$
$7.88, p < .05$, partial $\eta^2 = .18$. Under method B, the difference in math anxiety
between natural science majors ($M = 34.30$) and social science majors ($M =$
36.80) was small. Under method A, however, social science majors ($M = 55.50$)
had substantially higher levels of math anxiety than natural science majors
($M = 36.00$).

3.   a.   The 31–50-pound group on the whole grain diet lost the most weight (11.50 pounds).
The 11–30-pound group on the nonwhole grain diet lost the least weight (.40 pounds).

b. For the 11–30-pound group, those on the whole grain diet lost slightly more weight than those on the nonwhole grain diet (they lost two pounds more). For the 31–50-pound group, however, those on the whole grain diet lost substantially more weight than those on the nonwhole grain diet (a difference of 9.40 pounds). The interaction illustrates the combined effect of eating the whole grain diet *and* being 31–50-pounds overweight on weight loss, as this group lost substantially more weight than the other groups. The whole grain diet appears to be particularly effective for those who began the study more overweight (31–50 pounds).

Chapter 10—One-Way within Subjects ANOVA

1. a. H_0: $\mu_{\text{three months}} = \mu_{\text{six months}} = \mu_{\text{nine months}}$
        H_1: At least one of the means is different from the others.
    b. "Does the number of truancies change over time under the truancy prevention program?"
    c. Yes ($p < .001$—*Greenhouse-Geisser*; $p < .001$—sphericity assumed).
    d. Partial $\eta^2 = .52$.
    e. Each test will be conducted at .016 (.05/3).
    f. The truancy rate differed significantly over time, *Greenhouse-Geisser* adjusted $F(1.71, 23.98) = 15.20$, $p < .05$, partial $\eta^2 = .52$. Dependent-samples t tests revealed that students had significantly fewer truancies at nine months ($M = 25.47$, $SD = 8.18$) than at six months ($M = 32.00$, $SD = 7.46$), $t(14) = 3.92$, $p < .016$, and at nine months compared to three months ($M = 33.00$, $SD = 7.08$), $t(14) = 4.75$, $p < .016$. There was not a significant difference in the number of truancies between six months and three months, $t(14) = .87$, $p > .016$.
        (*Note*: If you prefer to use the sphericity assumed values, substitute the *Greenhouse-Geisser df* with 2 and 28 (the sphericity assumed *df*), and delete the phrase "*Greenhouse-Geisser* adjusted.")

2. a. H_0: $\mu_{\text{before therapy}} = \mu_{\text{four weeks}} = \mu_{\text{eight weeks}}$
        H_1: At least one of the means is different from the others.
    b. "Does well-being change over time when receiving psychoanalytic therapy?"
    c. No ($p = .330$—*Greenhouse-Geisser*; $p = .341$—sphericity assumed).
    d. Partial $\eta^2 = .07$.
    e. Follow-up tests are not conducted since the overall ANOVA is not significant.
    f. The general well-being scores of those who received psychoanalytic therapy did not change over time, *Greenhouse-Geisser* adjusted $F(1.50, 20.94) = 1.12$, $p > .05$, partial $\eta^2 = .07$.
        (*Note*: If you prefer to use the sphericity assumed values, substitute the *Greenhouse-Geisser df* with 2 and 28 (the sphericity assumed *df*), and delete the phrase "*Greenhouse-Geisser* adjusted.")

3. a. H_0: $\mu_{\text{free wifi}} = \mu_{\text{pay per wifi}} = \mu_{\text{no wifi}}$
        H_1: At least one of the means is different from the others.
    b. "Does the likelihood of visiting a fast-food restaurant differ for the type of wifi service offered?"
    c. Yes ($p < .001$—*Greenhouse-Geisser*; $p < .001$—sphericity assumed).
    d. Partial $\eta^2 = .70$.
    e. Each test will be conducted at .016 (.05/3).
    f. The likelihood of dining at a fast-food restaurant differed for the type of wifi service offered, *Greenhouse-Geisser* adjusted $F(1.78, 16.00) = 20.53$, $p < .05$, partial $\eta^2 = .70$. Dependent-samples t tests revealed that people were more likely to eat at a restaurant if free wifi was offered ($M = 7.00$, $SD = 2.58$) than if the service was not free ($M = 3.80$, $SD = 2.30$), $t(9) = 4.95$, $p < .016$. People were also more likely to eat at a fast-food restaurant if free wifi was offered versus no wifi at all ($M = 3.40$, $SD = 1.96$), $t(9) = 5.25$, $p < .016$. There was not a significant difference in the likelihood of eating at a fast-food restaurant if there was pay-per-use wifi versus no wifi at all, $t(9) = .80$, $p > .016$.

(*Note*: If you prefer to use the sphericity assumed values, substitute the *Greenhouse-Geisser df* with 2 and 18 (the sphericity assumed *df*), and delete the phrase "*Greenhouse-Geisser* adjusted.")

Chapter 11—One-Between–One-Within ANOVA

1. a. H_0: $\mu_{\text{cognitive-behavioral}} = \mu_{\text{psychoanalytic}}$
        H_1: $\mu_{\text{cognitive-behavioral}} \neq \mu_{\text{psychoanalytic}}$
        H_0: $\mu_{\text{before program}} = \mu_{\text{week 8}} = \mu_{\text{week 16}}$
        H_1: At least one of the means is different from the others.
        H_0: There is not a time × therapy interaction.
        H_1: There is a time × therapy interaction.
    b. "Do well-being scores differ for those who receive psychoanalytic therapy versus cognitive-behavioral therapy?"
        "Do well-being scores differ over time?"
        "Do well-being scores change at different rates over time for the psychoanalytic and cognitive behavioral groups (that is, is there an interaction)?"
    c. Time ($p = .007$—*Greenhouse-Geisser*; $p = .002$—sphericity assumed) and time × therapy ($p < .001$—*Greenhouse-Geisser*; $p < .001$—sphericity assumed) are significant. Therapy is not ($p = .388$).
    d.

Test	Partial eta–square
Time	.29
Therapy	.04
Time × therapy	.49

Time × therapy has the largest effect.

    e. A one-between–one-within ANOVA was conducted on well-being with time (before, eight weeks, 16 weeks) as the within-subjects factor and type of therapy (cognitive-behavioral, psychoanalytic) as the between-subjects factor. There was a significant time effect on well-being, *Greenhouse-Geisser* adjusted $F(1.36, 24.44) = 7.46$, $p < .05$, partial $\eta^2 = .29$. There was not a significant therapy effect on well-being, $F(1, 18) = .78$, $p > .05$, partial $\eta^2 = .04$. There was a significant time × therapy interaction, *Greenhouse-Geisser* adjusted $F(1.36, 24.44) = 17.02$, $p < .05$, partial $\eta^2 = .49$. The interaction plot shows that there was little difference in well-being scores between the two therapy groups before the onset of therapy and at eight weeks; however, at 16 weeks, those who had cognitive behavioral therapy had considerably higher general well-being scores than those who had psychoanalytic therapy.
        (*Note*: If you prefer to use the sphericity assumed values, substitute the *Greenhouse-Geisser df* with 2 and 36 for time and time × therapy (the sphericity assumed *df*), and delete the phrase "*Greenhouse-Geisser* adjusted.")

2. The results of the simple effects analyses revealed that, at week 16, those who had cognitive behavioral therapy ($M = 24.00$, $SD = 3.71$) had significantly higher well-being scores than those who had psychoanalytic therapy ($M = 20.00$, $SD = 2.94$), $t(18) = 2.67$, $p < .016$. (The *p*-value for this test is approximately .0156, which can be found by double-clicking on the *Independent Samples Test* table and then double-clicking on the value .016.) There was not a significant difference in the well-being scores between the two therapies before the onset of therapy, $t(18) = -.54$, $p > .016$, or at 8 weeks, $t(18) = -.25$, $p > .016$.

3. a. H_0: $\mu_{\text{before mentored}} = \mu_{\text{4 weeks mentored}} = \mu_{\text{8 weeks mentored}}$
        H_1: At least one of the means is different from the others.
    b. "Do the stress levels of mentored teachers differ before beginning teaching, at four weeks, or at eight weeks?"

c. Yes, time is significant ($p = .001$—*Greenhouse-Geisser*; $p < .001$—sphericity assumed).

d. Stress levels at eight weeks were significantly lower than at four weeks and before. There was not a significant difference between before and four weeks.

e. Simple effects analyses were conducted to assess whether mentored teachers' stress scores differed over the three time occasions. The results of a one-way within subjects ANOVA showed that time was significant, *Greenhouse-Geisser* adjusted $F(1.17, 10.56) = 18.39, p < .05$, partial $\eta^2 = .67$. Follow-up dependent-samples t tests were conducted, with each test conducted at an alpha level of .016. The results indicated that mentored teachers reported significantly less stress at eight weeks compared to before the program began, $t(9) = 4.41, p < .016$, and at eight weeks compared to four weeks, $t(9) = 4.46, p < .016$. There was not a significant difference in stress scores between before the program began and at four weeks, $t(9) = 2.49, p > .016$. Means and standard deviations for the two groups at each level of time are reported in Figure B.1 below.

(*Note*: If you prefer to use the sphericity assumed values, substitute the Greenhouse-Geisser *df* with 2 and 18 (the sphericity assumed *df*), and delete the phrase "*Greenhouse-Geisser* adjusted.")

Time	Mentored	
	M	*SD*
Before	41.00	3.30
4 weeks	39.60	4.09
8 weeks	34.70	6.00

Figure B.1 Means and standard deviations for mentored teachers before the academic year began, at four weeks, and at eight weeks.

Chapter 12—Correlation

1. a. $H_0: \rho = 0$
      $H_1: \rho \neq 0$
   b. "Is there a relationship between the amount of time studying and the grade on the exam?"
   c. $r = .68$
   d. Yes ($p < .001$).
   e. The effect size is large ($r = .68$).
   f. There is a significant positive relationship between the amount of time studying and the grade on the exam, $r(23) = .68, p < .05$.

2. a. $H_0: \rho = 0$
      $H_1: \rho \neq 0$
   b. "Is there a relationship between marital satisfaction and empathic understanding?"
   c. $r = .56$
   d. Yes ($p = .004$).
   e. The effect size is large ($r = .56$).
   f. There is a significant positive relationship between marital satisfaction and empathic understanding, $r(23) = .56, p < .05$.

3. a. $H_0: \rho = 0$
      $H_1: \rho \neq 0$
   b. "Is there a relationship between the amount of time being read to as a three-year-old and scores on a second-grade English exam?"

c. $r = .52$

d.   Yes ($p = .003$).

e.   The effect size is large ($r = .52$).

f.   There is a significant positive relationship between the time being read to as a three-year-old and scores on a second-grade English exam, $r(28) = .52, p < .05$.

Chapter 13—Simple Regression

1. a. $H_0: \beta_{father} = 0$
         $H_1: \beta_{father} \neq 0$

    b.   "Is a father's level of optimism predictive of his son's optimism as a young adult?"

    c.   Yes ($p = .001$).

    d. $R^2 = .44$. This is a large effect.

    e. $\hat{Y}_{son} = 16.313 + .571(father)$

    f.   Fathers' optimism scores were a significant predictor of their sons' level of optimism, $\beta = .66, t(18) = 3.75, p < .05, R^2 = .44$.

2. a. $H_0: \beta_{math\ exam} = 0$
         $H_1: \beta_{math\ exam} \neq 0$

    b.   "Are the scores on a seventh-grade math entrance exam predictive of the end-of-the-year grade in mathematics?"

    c.   Yes ($p < .001$).

    d. $R^2 = .38$. This is a large effect.

    e. $\hat{Y}_{grade} = 47.92 + .506(mathexam)$

    f.   The entrance exam was a significant predictor of the final grade in seventh-grade mathematics, $\beta = .62, t(28) = 4.17, p < .05, R^2 = .38$.

3. a. $H_0: \beta_{agreeableness} = 0$
         $H_1: \beta_{agreeableness} \neq 0$

    b.   "Is an employee's level of agreeableness predictive of their supervisor's satisfaction with their work?"

    c.   No ($p = .093$).

    d. $R^2 = .12$. This is a medium effect in practice.

    e. $\hat{Y}_{satisfaction} = 5.332 + .097(agreeableness)$

    f.   Employees' level of agreeableness was not a significant predictor of their supervisor's satisfaction with their work, $\beta = .34, t(23) = 1.75, p > .05, R^2 = .12$.

Chapter 14—Multiple Regression

1. a. $H_0: \beta_{importance} = 0; H_0: \beta_{advance} = 0; H_0: \beta_{express} = 0$
         $H_1: \beta_{importance} \neq 0; H_1: \beta_{advance} \neq 0; H_1: \beta_{express} \neq 0$

    b. $H_0: R^2 = 0$
         $H_1: R^2 > 0$

    c.   Individual predictors:
         "Does the importance of one's job predict job satisfaction?"
         "Does the opportunity to advance in one's job predict job satisfaction?"
         "Does the ability to express ideas to one's boss predict job satisfaction?"
         All predictors simultaneously:
         "When taken together, does the importance of one's job, the opportunity to advance, and the ability to express ideas to one's boss predict job satisfaction?"

    d. $R^2 = .57$. Yes, the overall model is significant, $p < .001$.

    e.   Importance ($p = .001$) and express ($p = .018$) are significant. Advance ($p = .403$) is not significant.

    f. $R^2 = .57$. This is a large effect.

    g. $\hat{Y}_{job\ satisfaction} = -5.756 + 1.051(importance) + .205(advance) + 1.069(express)$.

h. A multiple regression was conducted predicting job satisfaction from the variables importance of one's job, the opportunity to advance, and the ability to express ideas to one's boss. Overall, the regression was significant, $F(3, 26) = 11.51$, $p < .05$, $R^2 = .57$. Of the predictors investigated, the importance of one's job was a significant predictor of job satisfaction, $\beta = .52$, $t(26) = 3.65$, $p < .05$, as was the ability to express ideas to one's boss, $\beta = .37$, $t(26) = 2.53$, $p < .05$. The opportunity to advance was not a significant predictor of job satisfaction, $\beta = .11$, $t(26) = .85$, $p > .05$.

2. a. H_0: $\beta_{forgiveness} = 0$; H_0: $\beta_{support} = 0$
   H_1: $\beta_{forgiveness} \neq 0$; H_1: $\beta_{support} \neq 0$
   b. H_0: $R^2 = 0$
   H_1: $R^2 > 0$
   c. Individual predictors:
   "Does forgiveness predict happiness?"
   "Does social support predict happiness?"
   All predictors simultaneously:
   "When taken together, do the variables forgiveness and social support predict happiness?"
   d. $R^2 = .46$. Yes, the overall model is significant, $p = .001$.
   e. Forgiveness ($p < .001$) is significant. Support ($p = .246$) is not.
   f. $R^2 = .46$. This is a large effect.
   g. $\hat{Y}_{happiness} = 5.798 + .399(forgiveness) + .299(support)$
   h. A multiple regression was conducted predicting happiness from the variables social support and forgiveness. Overall, the regression was significant, $F(2, 22) = 9.32$, $p < .05$, $R^2 = .46$. Of the predictors investigated, forgiveness was significant, $\beta = .66$, $t(22) = 4.22$, $p < .05$, while social support was not, $\beta = .19$, $t(22) = 1.19$, $p > .05$.

3. a. H_0: $\beta_{well-being} = 0$; H_0: $\beta_{meaning\ in\ life} = 0$
   H_1: $\beta_{well-being} \# 0$; H_1: $\beta_{meaning\ in\ life} \neq 0$
   b. H_0: $R^2 = 0$
   H_1: $R^2 > 0$
   c. Individual predictors:
   "Does well-being predict fear of death?"
   "Does meaning in life predict fear of death?"
   All predictors simultaneously:
   "When taken together, do the variables well-being and meaning in life predict fear of death?"
   d. $R^2 = .13$. Yes, the overall model is significant, $p < .05$.
   e. Meaning ($p = .010$) is significant. Well-being is not ($p = .176$).
   f. $R^2 = .13$. This is a medium effect.
   $\hat{Y}_{fear\ of\ death} = 36.434 + .290(wellbeing) - .349(meaning)$
   g. A multiple regression was conducted predicting fear of death from the variables well-being and meaning in life. Overall, the regression was significant, $F(2, 47) = 3.60$, $p < .05$, $R^2 = .13$. Of the predictors investigated, meaning in life was significant, $\beta = -.41$, $t(47) = -2.68$, $p < .05$, but well-being was not, $\beta = .21$, $t(47) = 1.38$, $p > .05$.

Chapter 15—Chi-Square Goodness of Fit Test

1. a. H_0: Eye size is not related to attractiveness (there is not a preference for one of the photos.)
   H_1: Eye size is related to attractiveness (there is a preference for one of the photos).
   b. "Is eye size related to attractiveness?"
   c. Yes ($p < .001$).
   d. There was a significant preference for the photos with larger eyes, $\chi^2(1, N = 80) = 20.0$, $p < .05$. Of the two types of photos, 75% of the participants rated the person

with larger eyes as more attractive, while 25% rated the person with the smaller eyes as more attractive.

2. a. H_0: There is not a difference in the perceived picture quality of plasma and LED televisions.

H_1: There is a difference in the perceived picture quality of plasma and LED televisions.

b. "Is there a difference in perceived picture quality of plasma and LED televisions?"

c. No ($p = .535$).

d. There is not a difference in perceived picture quality between plasma and LED televisions, $\chi^2(1, N = 65) = .39, p > .05$.

3. a. H_0: There is not a preference among the three coffees.

H_1: There is a preference among the three coffees.

b. "Is there a preference among the three coffees?"

c. Yes ($p = .002$).

d. There was a preference among the three coffees, $\chi^2(2, N = 150) = 12.16, p < .05$. Of the three price categories of coffee, 20% of the participants preferred the $3 brand, 41% preferred the $6 brand, and 39% preferred the $10 brand.

Chapter 16—Chi-Square Test of Independence

1. a. H_0: There is not a relationship between the type of feeding received as an infant and weight in first grade.

H_1: There is a relationship between the type of feeding received as an infant and weight in first grade.

b. "Is there a relationship between the type of feeding received as an infant and weight in first grade?"

c. Yes ($p = .022$).

d. Effect size $= -.13$ (or .13). This is a small effect.

e. There is a significant relationship between type of feeding received as an infant and whether or not a child is overweight in first grade, $\chi^2(1, N = 300) = 5.26$, $p < .05$, Cramer's $V = .13$. Those who were breastfed were overweight at a significantly lower rate (16% overweight) than those who were not breastfed (28% overweight).

2. a. H_0: There is not a relationship between gender and movie preference.

H_1: There is a relationship between gender and movie preference.

b. "Is there a relationship between gender and movie preference?"

c. Yes ($p < .001$).

d. Effect size $= -.40$ (or .40). This is a medium effect.

e. There is a significant relationship between gender and movie preference, $\chi^2(1, N = 160) = 26.02, p < .05$, Cramer's $V = .40$. Given the choice of an action film or drama, females preferred dramas (84% to 16%), while males preferred action films (54% to 46%).

3. a. H_0: There is not a relationship between exercise and heart attack rates among the elderly.

H_1: There is a relationship between exercise and heart attack rates among the elderly.

b. "Is there a relationship between exercise and heart attack rates among the elderly?"

c. Yes ($p = .029$).

d. Effect size $= -.11$ (or .11). This is a small effect.

e. There is a significant relationship between exercise and heart attack rates among the elderly, $\chi^2(1, N = 405) = 4.77, p < .05$, Cramer's $V = .11$. Those who did not exercise experienced a higher heart attack rate (13.7%) than those who exercised (6.7%). (*Note*: Even though the effect size is small using Cohen's guidelines, notice that the heart attack rate is twice as high (13.7/6.7 = 2.04) in the no exercise group, indicating that a small effect *can be* at times of great practical importance.)

References

American Psychological Association (2009). *Publication Manual of the American Psychological Association* (6th ed.). Washington, DC: Author.

Cohen, J. (1988). *Statistical Power Analysis for the Behavioral Sciences* (2nd ed.). Hillsdale, NJ: Lawrence Erlbaum Associates.

Cohen, J., Cohen, P., West, S. G., & Aiken, L. S. (2002). *Applied Multiple Regression/Correlation Analysis for the Behavioral Sciences* (3rd ed.). Mahwah, NJ: Lawrence Erlbaum Associates.

Howell, D. C. (2007). *Statistical Methods for Psychology* (6th ed.). Belmont, CA: Wadsworth.

Maxwell, S. E., & Delaney, H. D. (2004). *Designing Experiments and Analyzing Data: A Model Comparison Perspective* (2nd ed.). Mahwah, NJ: Lawrence Erlbaum Associates.

Stevens, J. P. (2002). *Applied Multivariate Statistics for the Social Sciences* (4th ed.). Mahwah, NJ: Lawrence Erlbaum Associates.

Tabachnick, B. G., & Fidell, L. S. (2007). *Using Multivariate Statistics* (5th ed.). Boston: Allyn and Bacon.

Index